Lecture Notes in Artificial Intelligence   10051

Subseries of Lecture Notes in Computer Science

More information about this series at http://www.springer.com/series/1244

Mohammad-Reza Namazi-Rad · Lin Padgham
Pascal Perez · Kai Nagel
Ana Bazzan (Eds.)

Agent Based Modelling of Urban Systems

First International Workshop, ABMUS 2016
Held in Conjunction with AAMAS
Singapore, Singapore, May 10, 2016
Revised, Selected, and Invited Papers

 Springer

Editors
Mohammad-Reza Namazi-Rad
University of Wollongong
Wollongong, NSW
Australia

Kai Nagel
Technische Universität Berlin
Berlin
Germany

Lin Padgham
RMIT University
Melbourne, VIC
Australia

Ana Bazzan
Universidade Federal do Rio Grande do Sul
Rio Grande do Sul
Brazil

Pascal Perez
University of Wollongong
Wollongong, NSW
Australia

ISSN 0302-9743   ISSN 1611-3349   (electronic)
Lecture Notes in Artificial Intelligence
ISBN 978-3-319-51956-2   ISBN 978-3-319-51957-9   (eBook)
DOI 10.1007/978-3-319-51957-9

Library of Congress Control Number: 2016962024

LNCS Sublibrary: SL7 – Artificial Intelligence

Printed on acid-free paper

This Springer imprint is published by Springer Nature
The registered company is Springer International Publishing AG
The registered company address is: Gewerbestrasse 11, 6330 Cham, Switzerland

Preface

The first international ABMUS (Agent Based Modelling of Urban Systems) workshop was held at the AAMAS (Autonomous Agents and Multi Agent Systems) conference in 2016, as a way of bringing together a group of researchers working in this growing area. The workshop had 16 paper submissions, with authors of 14 of these attending the workshop. Eight of the revised papers along with three invited papers appear in this collection. The workshop attracted about 25–30 participants and was run as four discussion sessions. The four broad topics were:

- Systems and frameworks
- Realistic vs. stylized environment/infrastructure
- Activities and behaviors
- Software support

These topics were selected based on important recurring aspects where it was deemed that discussion would be valuable. Three to five authors were assigned to each session and were asked to summarize their paper in no more than three to five minutes, with ten minutes dedicated to responding to specific questions on the discussion topic. Authors were expected to draw on their experience generally, as well as on the specific paper submitted. This was followed by approximately an hour of discussion by all participants.

The specific questions discussed in each session were as follows:

1. Systems and frameworks

    - What other platforms do you have experience of?
    - Why did you choose this platform?
    - What things did you find particularly useful with this platform?
    - Did this platform have some weaknesses with respect to your application?
    - How would you like to see this platform develop?

2. Realistic vs. stylized environment/infrastructure

    - What aspects of the environment did you need to model?
    - Was your modelling realistic or stylized (e.g., grid-based physical environment is stylized, road network is realistic)?
    - Did you use actual data for your simulation?
    - Was your agent population built using any actual data? If so what?
    - How much of the work in building the simulation was related to obtaining and incorporating data or realistic environment aspects?
    - What advantages do you think there are in using realistic vs. stylized representations?

3. Activities and behaviors

 - What agent activities or behaviors have you represented?
 - Are these activities/behaviors determined in advance, or do they depend on what happens in the simulation? Describe how they are determined.
 - How do the agent activities/behavior affect the environment in ways that affect other agents?
 - Do you have different "types" of agents, and if so what are they?
 - To what extent do agents of the same type end up behaving quite differently to each other, due to the simulation?

4. Software support — what general purpose support tools or additions or plug-ins beyond platforms, as discussed in session 1, will be useful in moving forward the field of ABMs for urban simulation?

 - How does your work support software re-use, or the ability of groups to leverage each other's work?
 - What software development principles are important if as a community we are to move this field forward?
 - What are some key components or support tools that could really make a difference for this field?

Participants were extremely engaged in discussion and the workshop was highly interactive. A couple of important themes that emerged were the need for greater sharing, re-use, and modularity in the software developed, as well as the importance of infrastructure supporting integration of complementary models within a domain. A noticeable trend was also the importance of detailed microsimulation data obtained from a variety of sources. In many cases far more effort was focused on this aspect of modelling the system than on agent behaviors. It would seem that for urban simulations to be trusted, this level of specific detail is important.

The papers collected here cover a range of topics relevant to modelling of urban systems.

Four papers are related to specific aspects of urban systems modelling: the paper by Stefano Picascia and Neil Yorke-Smith – "Towards an Agent-Based Simulation of Housing in Urban Beirut" – deals with patterns of degeneration and regeneration of housing stock in Beirut, in the presence of massive refugee migration, while the paper by Patrick Taillandier, Arnaud Banos, Alexis Drogoul, Benoit Gaudou, Nicolas Marilleau, and Chi Quang Truong – "Simulating Urban Growth with Raster and Vector Models: A Case Study for the City of Can Tho, Vietnam" – deals with representation of geographic space for applications studying urban growth. The paper by Nidhi Parikh, Madhav Marathe, and Samarth Swarup – "Integrating Behavior and Microsimulation Models" – is in the application domain of disaster management in an urban setting, with a focus primarily on integrating reasoned behaviors within the ABM using semi-Markov decision processes for each agent. This paper epitomizes the growing need to model more complex human decision-making than is often used in ABMs. The invited paper by Pascal Perez, Arnaud Banos, and Chris Pettit – "Agent-Based Modelling for Urban Planning: Current Limitrations and Future Trends" – outlines some challenges for the area of agent-based modelling for urban planning. A major focus is the need for modular systems comprising models of different aspects. This was also a conclusion of the workshop discussion. They also argue for the importance of theory-based models and models developed via participatory processes.

Four papers deal with aspects of traffic simulation: "Software Architecture for a Transparent and Versatile Traffic Simulator" by Michael Zilske and Kai Nagel describes a plug-in to MATSim to support integration of new components, while the one by Haitam Laarabi and Raffaele Bruno – "A Generic Software Framework for Carsharing Modelling Based on a Large Scale Multi-Agent Traffic Simulation Platform" – uses that framework, and describes an adaptation or extension of MATSim to support applications studying car sharing. "Mapping Bicycling Patterns with an Agent-Based Model, Census and Crowdsourced Data" by Simone Leao and Chris Pettit is an introductory exploration that is part of a longer-term study on bicycle transportation. The invited paper in this section – "Transportation in Agent-Based Modelling" – by Sarah Wise, Andrew Crooks and Michael Batty argues that transportation modelling is a critical aspect of urban systems modelling, even when it is not the main focus. The authors present different levels of complexity at which the transportation systems can be modelled and argue that it is important to ensure that the transportation model is at the appropriate level of granularity for the main focus of the urban system model. They also argue that direct agent–agent communication and interaction are important elements of ABM of urban systems and should, in fact, be part of the ABM specification for urban systems. They specifically look at the importance of transportation models in the different application areas of crime, disease spread, and land use.

The three remaining papers deal with some specific applications. The paper by Luca Crociani, Gregor Lämmel, and Giuseppe Vizzari – "Simulation Aided Crowd Management: A Multi-scale Model for an Urban Case Study" – also actually uses MATSim, although their focus is on pedestrian rather than vehicle movement, in an application exploring crowd management during a large event. "A National Heat Demand Model for Germany" by Esteban Munoz provides a detailed estimation of heat demand for the whole of Germany. This paper is an example of the use of detailed microsimulation data and infrastructure playing a more important role than agent behaviors. The invited paper from the Architecture and Town Planning Faculty at Technion in Israel, "How Smart Is the Smart City? Assessing the Impact of ICT on Cities" by Michal Gath Morad, Davide Schaumann, Einat Zinger, Pnina O. Plaut, and Yehuda E. Kalay, provides an interesting perspective on the important but unknown effects, side effects and after effects of incorporating ICT into "smart cities." Agent-based simulation can provide one of the tools to allow city planners to further explore these issues.

Other papers not included here covered an additional paper on pedestrian agents in an urban space, water and sanitation, public transport, microcars, and microsimulation as an approach distinct from ABM.

The paper by Patrick Taillandier, Arnaud Banos, Alexis Drogoul, Benoit Gaudou, Nicolas Marilleau, and Chi Quang Truong has been previously published in the AAMAS collection of the most innovative papers from the 2016 workshops [1], but is republished here with the permission of Springer. The paper by Luca Crociani, Gregor Lämmel, and Giuseppe Vizzari is a substantially extended version of the paper in the AAMAS collection of best papers from the 2016 workshops [2].

Overall, this collection provides a snapshot of some of the work in this growing area of agent-based urban simulation.

November 2016   Mohammad-Reza Namazi-Rad
                                                              Lin Padgham
                                                              Pascal Perez
                                                              Kai Nagel
                                                              Ana Bazzan

References

1. Simulating Urban Growth with Taster and Vector Models: A Case Study for the City of Can Tho, Vietnam, LNAI 10003, pp. 154–171. doi:10.1007/978-3-319-46840-2_10
2. Multi-Scale Simulation for Crowd Management: A Case Study in an Urban Scenario, LNAI 10002, pp. 147–162. doi:10.1007/978-3-319-46882-2_9

Organization

Organizing Committee

Mohammad-Reza Namazi-Rad	University of Wollongong, Australia
Lin Padgham	RMIT, Australia
Pascal Perez	University of Wollongong, Australia
Kai Nagel	TU Berlin, Germany
Ana L.C. Bazzan	Universidade Federal do Rio Grande do Sul, Brazil

Program Committee

Eric J. Miller	University of Toronto, Canada
Michael Batty	University College London, UK
Kay W. Axhausen	ETH Zürich, Switzerland
Peter Campbell	University of Wollongong, Australia
Jörg P. Müller	TU Clausthal, Germany
Eric Cornelis	Université de Namur, Belgium
Arnaud Banos	CNRS, France
Kouros Mohammadian	University of Illinois at Chicago, USA
Ram M. Pendyala	Georgia Institute of Technology, USA
Amal Kumarage	University of Moratuwa, Sri Lanka
Christopher J. Pettit	University of New South Wales, Australia
Robert Tanton	University of Canberra, Australia
Majid Sarvi	University of Melbourne, Australia
Stephane Galland	Université de Technologie de Belfort, France
Dhirendra Singh	RMIT University, Australia
Bilal Farooq	École Polytechnique de Montréal, Canada
Taha H. Rashidi	University of New South Wales, Australia
Michael North	Argonne National Laboratory, USA
Vadim Sokolov	Argonne National Laboratory, USA

Organization

Organizing Committee

Program Committee

Contents

Urban Systems Modelling

Towards an Agent-Based Simulation
of Housing in Urban Beirut

Stefano Picascia[1,2] and Neil Yorke-Smith[3(✉)]

[1] Centre for Policy Modelling, Manchester Metropolitan University, Manchester, UK
stefano@cfpm.org
[2] Laboratorio Dati Economici Storici Territoriali, University of Siena, Siena, Italy
[3] Olayan School of Business, American University of Beirut, Beirut, Lebanon
nysmith@aub.edu.lb

Abstract. Advances in agent-based modelling have led to theoretically-grounded spatial agent models of urban dynamics, capturing the dynamics of population, property prices, and regeneration. We leverage our extant agent-based model founded on the rent-gap theory, as a lens to study the effect of sizeable refugee migration in an abstracted model of a densely-populated Mediterranean city. Our exploratory work provides the foundation for calibration with real data, and offers a step towards a tool for policy makers asking what-if questions about the urban environment in the context of migration.

Keywords: Urban simulation · Rent-gap theory · Migration · Agent-based modelling · Lebanon · NetLogo

1 Introduction

The study of cities and their dynamics is a field where agent-based models (ABMs) have challenged econometric models [11]. Contemporary cities manifest themselves as complex and interconnected socio-technical systems. The literature uses ABMs to reproduce the evolution of the urban form [31], to model the urban dynamics typical of cities in the developed world, such as segregation (from [25] onwards) and gentrification [22], and to model dynamics typical of the megacities of the developing world, such as the emergence and evolution of informal settlements [8,20].

At the time of writing, rapid international migration of significant populations is generating profound implications for, not least, countries in Europe. Our motivation in this first paper is to develop an ABM to capture the existence of such migrant and refugee flows, and to explore the effect on urban dynamics.

Our previous work constructed a micro-level ABM, derived from the *rent-gap theory* (RGT) – an economic hypotheses on the dynamics of investment in housing – in an effort to model the economic mechanics of property investment along with their effects on the cultural and social diversity of urban areas. We examined the price dynamics triggered by different levels of capital flowing in a

© Springer International Publishing AG 2017
M.-R. Namazi-Rad et al. (Eds.): ABMUS 2016, LNAI 10051, pp. 3–20, 2017.
DOI: 10.1007/978-3-319-51957-9_1

city and the patterns of spatial inequality that may emerge [22], and we developed a model of housing regeneration, centred on the economic aspects and the mechanics of urban renewal, and applied it to a real-world regeneration programme in Manchester, UK, examining outcomes in property prices and social composition [21].

In this paper we extend our previous model and ground our work in the city of Beirut, Lebanon. This densely-populated Mediterranean city is the capital of a middle-income country which, according to official estimates [33], has experienced a refugee influx of 50% of its population in the last 3–4 years, determining huge pressure on the housing stock. Our model is particularly well suited to investigate the possible societal consequences of such pressure, since it was specifically designed to explore the interrelation of urban economic and cultural dynamics. We extend and adapt the ABM to the Beirut context, embedding ethnic and religious profiles, the tenure and price structure of residential areas across the city, immigration and emigration rates, and peculiar government policy regarding maintenance in Beirut's city centre. The outcome is an abstracted model of the city that simulates the residential mobility of agents – based on their ability to afford residential locations – along with changes in the price structure determined by investment in property. Such a model is useful to explore economic and social indicators under different plausible scenarios.

Results of our simulation model, implemented in NetLogo [34], indicate how sizeable migration into a city of low income populations impacts the number of slum locations, population density and over-population, prices, and income. Depending on the capital circulating in the economy and the rate of mobility, we find that excessive shock of refugees to the housing market can render neighbourhoods uninhabitable and in permanent disrepair, excluded from regeneration cycles, and hence cause both refugee and non-refugee populations to leave the city.

Section 2 provides the background of our work, including the rent-gap theory, and discusses related works. Section 3 describes our abstracted ABM of the city of Beirut. Section 4 reports our exploratory results from the model to date. Section 5 concludes the paper with a discussion of future directions.

2   Background and Related Work

Agent-based modelling and simulation is regarded as an ideal tool for understanding complex socio-technical systems like cities [18]. As surveyed by Huang et al. [13], the preferred approach in most residential mobility models is to centre on individual or household-level agents as the main actors and describe emerging patterns as purely bottom-up outcomes of the interaction of such agents. This approach poses a risk, in our view, of underestimating the broader economic processes that impact the urban form and constrain individual behaviour. A traditional line of research in human geography that has seen recent revival [12,28], views the socio-spatial phenomena that shape contemporary cities – suburban sprawl, income segregation, gentrification – as consequences of the varying influx of capital towards urban systems, rather than as strictly originating from individual-based residential choices.

Within this theoretic tradition the rent-gap theory, to which our model is inspired, is a supply-side approach to housing investment, noted in economics especially for its use in studying gentrification, i.e., "the process of renewal and rebuilding accompanying the influx of middle-class or affluent people into deteriorating areas that often displaces poorer residents" (Merriam-Webster). The rent gap is the difference between the actual (current) economic return from land, and the maximum potential return if the land were put to its "highest and best use" [27]. The rent gap is due to progressive decline in maintenance which properties undergo, together with changes in technologies which render dwellings obsolete. Restoration or rebuilding increases the economic return that a portion of land or a dwelling generates, bringing it to the maximum possible according to the theory. The locations with the highest difference between actual and potential economic return will be the ones more likely to attract investment capital and be put to best use. Although the RGT was proposed to explain a specific phenomenon, gentrification, in our view it can serve as a valid conceptualisation of general housing investment behaviour in capitalist economies, suitable for a broad exploration and not incompatible with other approaches, including standard economic theory [3].

Indeed, the literature holds a number of ABMs inspired by rent-gap theory in which the problem of identifying the highest and best use has been addressed by employing the notion of neighbourhood effect. We refer to Picascia et al. [22] for a survey. Prior to our work, Diappi and Bolchi's model [5,6] was the most complete implementation of the mechanics of the RGT, although it lacks any consideration of the demand side of the housing market and it does not consider migrant flows.

Besides models inspired by the RGT, the literature has a rich vein of ABMs that study aspects of residential mobility, either at the city level or at the national level. Among these, Ge [10] develops an agent-based spatial model of the US housing market, obtaining "sensible aggregated outcomes that capture important characteristics in the housing market." Zhang and Li [35] study the housing market in Beijing, China, with an ABM built on a model of buyer and seller search behaviours; we refer to their work for a wider survey of ABMs related to housing markets.

Among others disciplines, the sociology, urban design, and political economy literatures have considered the case of Beirut. The property market is described as "neo-liberal"; affordable housing is limited; public institutions are weak and regulations often not enforced [7,15,29].

We are not the first to recognize the relevance of agent-based modelling to approach the complexities and non-linearities of the socio-economic situation of Lebanon. Notably, Srour and Yorke-Smith [29,30] apply agent-based simulation to study import–export processes at the Port of Beirut. Their work does not address questions of urban dynamics that we do here, and their simulation features complex Belief-Desire-Intention (BDI) cognitive agents.

Our ABM is implemented in the well-known agent-based social simulation platform NetLogo [34]. The convenience of the relatively simple NetLogo platform is suitable for a model where agents have rule-based behaviours and no explicit deliberation. While we find that the execution speed of the NetLogo simulation slows as the number of agents increases, the scaling of the platform did not hinder the work we report in this paper. Kravari and Bassiliades [14] survey simulation platforms.

Relevant to urban ABMs with more complex agent behaviours, Singh and Padgham present a paradigm for integrating agent models (particularly, for instance, models in the BDI tradition) and simulation models (particularly, technical simulation engines or social simulation platforms) [26]. Demazeau et al. [9] argue that, as the agents become more complex, agent-oriented software engineering practices are relevant, and present a case study of a stylized urban dynamics model.

3   Abstract Model

We describe our agent-based model of an entire city, with multiple pre-defined districts. The entities represented in the simulation model are: (1) individual locations (residential properties), defined by their value, repair state, and population; (2) individual agents that represent households, characterised by an income, mobility propensity, and cultural configuration; and (3) economic forces, represented in the form of exogenous 'capital' level, aiming at profiting from redevelopment/restoration of residential locations. In the sequel we summarize the key points of the model, including the extensions over our earlier model; we refer to an earlier paper [22] for full details of the model variables and the emergent cultural 'allure' effect of neighbourhoods.

3.1   Locations: City Structure and Economic Dynamics

Following our earlier model formulation of [21,22] we represent the city as a 21×21 square grid of 441 residential locations[1] (Fig. 2, upper left) characterised by a value, V, a maintenance level, or repair state, r, and a population count, P. Locations are grouped into nine districts labelled by their compass coordinates: nw, n, ne, e, c [for centre], w, sw, s, se. In each district, locations closer to the centre of the district have greater allure for agents: the city is poli-centric.

Metropolitan Beirut is approximately square (Fig. 1), bounded by the sea to the north and west and by the Beirut River to the east. The Central Business District (CBD) is the top middle of the nine districts, i.e., 'n'. Other notable districts are Ras Beirut ('nw'), the cosmopolitan university district; Achrafieh ('e'), a high-end district; and poorer areas in the south-west. Upon model initialisation, r is randomly distributed in the range $[0, 1]$ and V is set at $V = r + 0.15$,

---

[1] Experiments show that larger abstract grid sizes yield the same observed dynamics, considering also that all the parameters are held proportional.

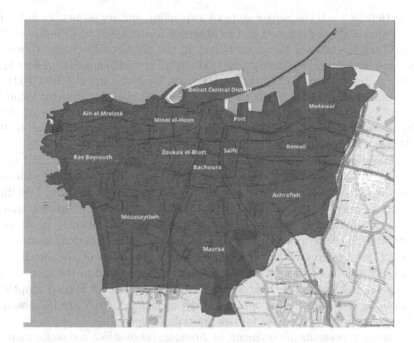

Fig. 1. The Beirut metropolitan area and its neighbourhoods.

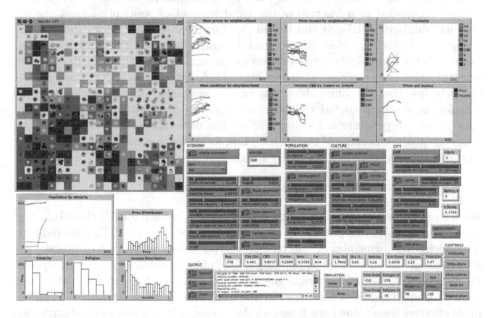

Fig. 2. Simulation interface in NetLogo [34]. City districts are seen upper left. Plots of price, income, condition are upper right. Plots of demographics are lower left. Parameter settings, outputs, and controls are centre and lower right.

assuming that at $t = 0$ the repair state of a dwelling and its monetary value are strongly correlated, as proposed in the abstract formulation of O'Sullivan [19]. Values and repair state for locations falling in the districts described above 'n', 'e', 'nw', and 'sw' are subsequently adjusted within specific ranges to reflect their subjective status relative to the rest of the city: locations in 'n' (the CBD) are well maintained and their median value is 60% above the city average; locations in 'nw' and 'e' are also well maintained and values 40% above city average; locations in 'sw' are in below average repair state and their median value is 40% below Beirut's average.

Locations can be occupied by zero or more residents, up to specified population limits. If the population exceeds the limit – or if the location's condition falls too low ($r \leq 0.15$) – then the location is deemed to be a slum. Dwellings progressively decay in their condition by a factor $d = 0.0012$ assuming that, if unmaintained, a location goes from 1 to 0 (becomes inhabitable) in 70 years (1 simulation step = 1 month). In order to match the theoretical assumption of a decline in property price over time, we set the value of the dwelling as decreasing by a depreciation factor of 0.02/year, as proposed in the formulation of Diappi and Bolchi [5]. We also assume that in case of prolonged emptiness of the dwelling (>6 steps) both decay and depreciation factors are increased by 20%. These factors also increase for over-populated locations.

The model represents investment in housing renovation/redevelopment as the fundamental economic force. The 'Capital' parameter, K, represents the maximum number of locations that can be redeveloped in the current economic climate, expressed as a fraction of the total number of residential locations of the city, similarly to Diappi and Bolchi [5]. The selection of the locations where investment lands is carried out deterministically, based on the value-gap of a location with the neighbouring properties, in accordance with the RGT. The relevant value gaps are determined in accordance with the *neighbourhood effect*, the principle that the amount of rent or the sale value attainable by a given location is always bounded by the characteristics and the desirability of the area where the property is located. We set the new value nV of a redeveloped property p at the average of the surrounding locations in a radius of 2, plus 15% (representing a premium for a newly-restored property):

$$nV_p = 1.15 * \text{avg}(V_{radius2}) \tag{1}$$

We also assume that if no locations surrounding p are inhabited, then $V_{radius2}$ is reduced by 35%; this parameter value is somewhat arbitrary. The mechanism implements the principles of the rent-gap hypotheses, but tries to mitigate its strong supply-side focus, by embedding a demand-side consideration in the price formation mechanism: i.e., should there be little demand for a location then the value of properties will reflect that. In our work on UK cities, we found (1) to be more effective than value gaps based on the average of the Moore neighbourhood or the district of p.

The value gap for location p will be $G_p = nV_p - (V_p + C)$, or 0 if $G_p < 0$. Here C is the cost of removing the present residents if the location is occupied.

The cost of removing a refugee (0.01) is lower than for a non-refugee (0.05), but there can be more refugees in a location (maximum population 6) than non-refugees (maximum 3). Once a location is selected for investment, its value is set at nV_p and its repair state is set at $r = 0.95$.

We also model government policy that mandates properties in the CBD to be maintained to a minimum standard and to have a lower maximum population than other districts, and imposes price controls to ensure a high rental value.

3.2   Agents: Residential Mobility and Cultural Exchange

Agents in the model represent individuals or households. Each agent is endowed with an income level, i, a mobility propensity, m, and a tuple that represents its cultural configuration, including ethnicity and religion. The agent's income level is strongly correlated with its ethnicity, reflecting the stratification of highly unequal Libanese society; incomes are normalised to the interval $[0, 1]$ and represent the highest price that the agent is able to pay for the right of residing in a property. Agents of most ethnicities, refuges excluded, are able to apply for credit that multiplies their purchasing power.

Agents of Lebanese or Arab nationalities (excluding refugees) are able to own property. If the property is owned, its condition depreciates more slowly. There can be at most one owner for each location, and owners have a reduced propensity to move compared to renters. Further, in contrast to renters, owners are not forced to leave their current residence if rental prices increase.

The agent's culture is modelled as a tuple of t multi-valued *traits*, inspired by Axelrod's classic ABM of cultural interaction [1] and originally applied to the urban context by Benenson [2]. The tuple represents an individual's 'memetic code' or 'cultural code'. Each cultural trait can assume v variations, giving rise to v^t possible individual combinations. The semantics of traits are emergent, with the exception of the first two traits which have reserved meaning. Namely, first, ethnicity may be one of five values: Lebanese, (Arab) refugee, affluent Arab non-refugee, professional non-Arab (e.g., from the west), and working class non-Arab (e.g., domestic servants from south-east Asia); ethnicity does not change. The second reserved trait models religion, which may be one of five values: Christian (various sects), Sunni Muslim, Shi'a Muslim, Druze, or other; religion has a small possibility of changing according to the process described next. Ethnicities are set according to 2010–12 estimates (the country has no official census since 1932) [4, 16]; religion of each ethnicity is set accordingly. Initial income is set according the estimated Gini coefficient of Lebanon and of non-Lebanese [32, 33].

In our model each of the non-reserved traits is susceptible to change under the influence of other agents. Cultural influence is localised: agents that have been neighbours for more than 6 consecutive steps are likely to interact and exchange traits, thus rendering the respective cultural tuples more similar. At the same time a cultural 'cognitive dissonance' effect is at work, implementing Portugali's concept of *spatial cognitive dissonance* [23, 24]. Similarity between two agents is defined as the proportion of traits they share.

Agents who spend more than six months surrounded by neighbours with few common traits increase their mobility propensity each subsequent time step. The mobility propensity attribute represents the probability that an agent will abandon the currently-occupied location in the subsequent time step. Mobility propensity is affected by the conditions of the currently occupied dwelling and the cognitive dissonance level. A special circumstance is when the price of the dwelling currently occupied exceeds the agent's income. This represents an excessive rent increase, unsustainable by the agent. The process of finding a new location is bounded by the agent's income: a new dwelling has to be affordable ($V \leq i * credit$), in relatively good condition (at least, not a slum), and as close as possible to the centre of the district which contains it. If no affordable and available location is to be found, the agent is forced to leave the city. The exception is refugees, who will consider moving to a location of poor condition or of high population, and only leave the city if even no slum is to be found.

4   Exploratory Results

Due to lack of access to GIS data and reliable property price indicators, for our current phase of work we have deliberately constructed an abstracted model of Beirut. To this end, property prices and agents' incomes are normalized to $[0, 1]$ scales. As noted earlier, each tick of the simulation corresponds to one month. We begin the simulation after the period of the Lebanese Civil War (approx. 1975–1990) and the following reconstruction, and prior to the influx of refugees from the Syrian Civil War (approx. 2011–). As described in Sect. 3, agent demographics are initially set proportional to estimated figures prior to the influx of Syrian refugees, which began in 2012–13.[2]

It is not among our research questions at this time to attempt to reproduce the historical evolution of population and property prices in Beirut after the Lebanese Civil War. There are many factors which make this difficult, not least the paucity of historical data about property prices (there are no published indices prior to 2016), multiple exogenous factors (including the 2006 conflict with Israel), legal changes which favoured redevelopment, legacy rental controls for pre-war tenants, debt-financed government reconstruction of the CBD, and extensive undocumented or illegal practices in Lebanon. While we do not validate our model in such a way yet, we have previously validated our earlier iterations of the ABM in the British cities of Manchester [21] and London [unpublished]. Although post-industrial Britain and contemporary Lebanon have obvious economic and societal differences, the underlying economic model, the RGT, is argued to be applicable in all housing markets in capitalist economies, as the fundamental processes described by the theory – profit-driven investment in house building – are not too dissimilar across different property markets. Our previous validation suggests that the model captures at least some of the dynamics involved in such process. More substantial differences between property markets are to be found in the distribution of wealth, income, and tenure,

---

[2] We do not consider other refugee populations, including those of Palestinian origin.

in government policy, in the amount of investment capital available in the economy. The model, despite its present decidedly abstract form, makes effort to account for these factors.

Our main research questions in the present work concern the effects of mass refugee inflow into Lebanon. With demographics of Lebanon being a delicate matter for sectarian and political reasons, estimates circa 2010 put the Lebanese population living in the country at around 4 million, plus approximately 0.5 million Palestine refugees from 1948 and later. By 2015, the UN recorded more than 1 million official refugees from Syria, whereas including undocumented refugees and those who have emigrated, e.g., to Europe, through Lebanon, the estimates are as high as 2 million, i.e., 50% of the Lebanese population. Profound consequences of such a large influx of population in a short (3–4 year) time period include social, economic, security, and political aspects. Our research questions focus on the first two aspects, as follows:

1. Can an abstracted model of Beirut housing be developed?
2. Can qualitative effects of the refugee influx to Beirut be seen?
3. What effects does a sudden large influx of low income people have on the economic housing cycle?
4. What public or Non-Governmental Organization (NGO) intervention actions might be effective?

We measure a number of output variables from the simulation, including location condition and prices, neighbourhood allure and cultural mix, population income and cultural traits, occupancy rates and mobility, and immigration and emigration counts. In particular, for the experiments reported below, we periodically recorded: (1) % of slum locations ($r \leq 0.15$), (2) % of well-maintained locations ($r > 0.5$), (3) % of over-populated locations ($P > 3$), (4) median price of all locations, (5) median income of all people, (6) the district with largest number of refugees, and (7) % of Lebanese, refugees, or another ethnicity.

We conducted three exploratory experiments directed towards our research questions. Simulation parameters were set as in our previous work [22], which in particular explored the effect of capital K and the type of rent gap computation; additional parameters settings are reported below.

4.1 Experiment 1: Impact of Refugee Influx

We simulate a refugee influx beginning at tick 90 and continuing until tick 180; the simulation runs until tick 600. The immigration rate for refugees, 0.15, is much higher than the rate for non-refugees, 0.02; the emigration rates are 0.012 and 0.019 respectively. The immigration and emigration rates reflect that after refugees arrive in Lebanon, many settle for an extended period of time before either obtaining access to a country of aslyum (e.g., Germany), returning to their own country (e.g., if the situation improves), or becoming de facto residents.

Figure 3 shows longitudinal views of the city districts under four settings: top, no refugees (i.e., refugee immigration rate is the same as other populations:

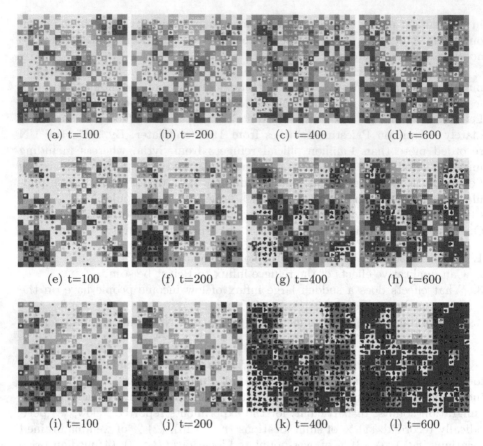

Fig. 3. City districts over time. Top row = no refugees, middle row = refugee influx between $t = 90$ and $t = 180$, bottom row = ongoing refugee influx from $t = 90$. Slum locations are dark blue, uninhabitable locations are dark purple. (Color figure online)

there is no influx); middle, refugee influx as described above; bottom, ongoing refugee influx, described below in the second experiment. Capital $K = 0.025$.

City districts are shaded according to their condition. The darker the shade of grey, the lower the condition of the location. Locations which have reached slum condition ($r \leq 0.15$) are coloured dark blue; locations which have become inhabitable ($r = 0$) are coloured dark purple.

Agents are depicted by colour, shape, and size. Colour denotes the income of the agent: darker green indicates highest quintile ($i \geq 0.8$), brighter green indicates above average ($0.8 > i \geq 0.5$), brighter purple indicates third quartile ($0.5 > i \geq 0.25$), and darker purple indicates bottom quartile ($i < 0.25$). Shape denotes the ethnicity of the agent: Lebanese are shown as filled circles, refugees as hollow circles, affluent Arab non-refugees as smiling faces, professional non-Arab as flat faces, and working class non-Arab as sad faces. Size denotes ownership: owners appear larger than non-owners.

Notice some decline and regeneration – the economic cycle – affecting different city districts in the no-refugees case (top row). For example, the CBD, the north district, starts with relatively high condition, has decayed to medium condition by $t = 400$, and has regenerated to a good condition by $t = 600$, stimulated by the price controls in that district.

Comparing the top two rows of Fig. 3, we see that the number of slum and uninhabitable locations is greater with the presence of refugees. Since refugees can have a higher population per location, the city's population is also greater, and since they are poorer, average income is lower. In the initially poor southwest district, refugees congregate at first. Later, as the economic cycle continues in different districts, we see refugees reside elsewhere. Their presence on one hand can be see as constraining regeneration, but on the other we see regeneration occurring in the south-west district around $t = 400$. In the CBD, from which refugees are excluded by government policy, condition and prices are more stable.

To explore further the impact of the refugee influx, we performed 100 iterations (with random seed) for various parameter settings, and computed output variables shown in Fig. 4. The top row of the figure shows the proportion of slum locations under no refugee (left) and refugee (right) conditions. In each graph, we examine four levels of capital K. At low levels of capital, the ability of owners to regenerate dwellings is limited, whereas at higher levels, they have greater ability. As expected, in both with- and without-refugee conditions, as K increases the proportion of slums decreases.

The middle row of Fig. 4 shows the proportion of slums without (blue leftmost columns) and with (red rightmost columns) refugees, at two levels of capital. As also seen in the top row of the figure, the presence of refugees and the proportion of slums are positively correlated at all levels of capital, albeit the level of capital is by far the main factor affecting the number of under-maintained locations. The impact of refugees on the number of slum areas can be traced back to the fact that refugees, unlike other persons, are willing to occupy nearly-derelict properties that would be empty otherwise. Their presence reduces the profitability of redevelopment in two ways: (1) when a location is occupied there is the resident removal cost C to be paid in order to redevelop it; and (2) since in the model the prices of non-empty locations decline more slowly than empty ones, price-gaps with higher priced neighbouring properties also widen more slowly. This last effect is more pronounced when a large contiguous area is under-maintained but occupied: there is less incentive for private capital to invest and regenerate the locations, so the area keeps declining gently for a longer time and we see more under-maintained properties for a longer period.

However, interestingly, as Fig. 4[a–d] shows, in the long run the impact of refugees on the amount of unmaintained locations is negligible. The normal economic cycle of investment is capable of absorbing the shock of the mass refugee influx that ends at tick 180, and by tick 600 the difference between refugee and non-refugee conditions is minimal. This is not the case when we test an ongoing refugee influx, in Experiment 2 below.

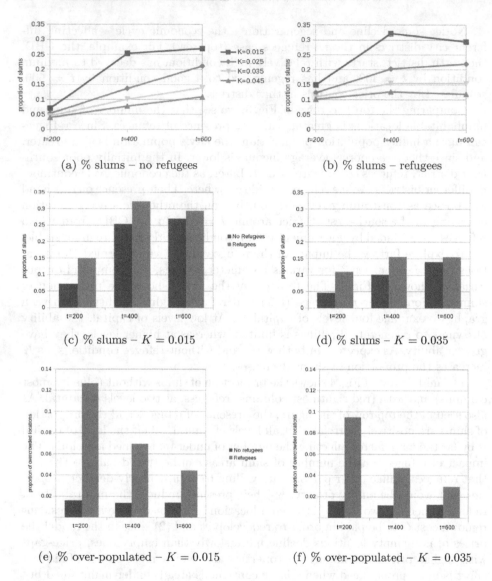

Fig. 4. Proportion of slums by level of capital in refugee and non-refugee conditions (top two rows); proportion of over-populated locations (bottom row).

The bottom row of Fig. 4 shows the proportion of over-populated locations, again at the two levels of capital. We observe that refugees have a higher impact on overcrowding (than on slums), as to be expected. The strong influx at $t = 90$ inevitably floods the available properties; overcrowding is seen to decline over time as refugee immigration ceases. By contrast, overcrowding is fairly stable and rare in the non-refugee condition, where only a small minority of the population (working class foreigners) will accept to live in an over-populated location.

However, the higher availability of capital does reduce the number of over-populated locations in the refugee condition. This is because with higher capital, more locations are redeveloped and gain in price, becoming unavailable for refugees. At the same time, the number of low maintenance areas – where only refugees concentrate – decreases.

It is worth commenting on an interesting effect seen for all levels of capital: the % of slums reaches a maximum and then levels off or declines (except $K = 0.025$, where the growth rate slows). Looking in detail, we see a correlation between the number of slums and the number of refugees. Median price and income follow the same pattern, but inverted, and see a fall and then some a recovery; for prices, the recovery has an extended time lag. The explanation for this phenomenon is that, especially at lower levels of capital, the number of refugees peaks and, after the influx has ceased, it begins to reduce towards a sometimes much lower stable level than its peak (Fig. 5, left). We see this as due to refugees leaving the city after the peak because they can find no inhabitable place where they can afford to reside (not even a slum with some space). In this case, the large, low income population exacerbates the effect of the low level of capital, in that only a limited set of districts are able to generate price-gaps wide enough to attract investment and participate in the economic cycles, while other districts fall in permanent disrepair.

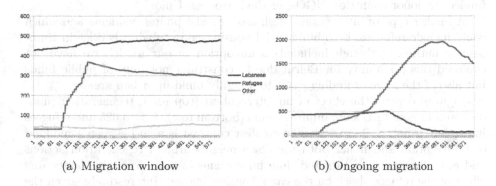

(a) Migration window   (b) Ongoing migration

Fig. 5. Evolution of city population by ethnicity. $K = 0.025$

4.2 Experiment 2: Impact of Ongoing Migration

When the flow of refugees is ongoing, the effects observed in Experiment 1 are further pronounced. The bottom row of Fig. 3 shows widespread highly popula-tion, slum, or even uninhabitable locations by $t = 400$; and by $t = 600$, about a third of the city is uninhabitable. Nonetheless, the economic cycle continues in some districts: observe the regeneration of the south-west between $t = 200$ and 400, and of parts of the south-east between $t = 400$ and 600. By the end of the simulation, the effect of the refugee exclusion and price controls in the CBD is a marked contrast to other districts.

Interestingly, the decline in location conditions and the spread of locations in permanent disrepair causes several effects. First, as one might expect, other districts become populated as highly as possible. Second, non-refugees leave the city despite falls in prices, as they can find no place of reasonable condition with space to which to move (Fig. 5, right). Third, refugees leave the city when they too can find no place, despite their willingness to accept poorer conditions and greater population density.

4.3 Experiment 3: Interventions

We consider two types of interventions in the housing market. First, as in our previous work, top-down government intervention to regenerate a location of poor condition. This periodic action (on average, every six months with our baseline parameter settings) seeks out one of the locations of lowest condition (it need not have decayed to slum condition), lifts its condition to $r = 0.95$ and also raises its price, and lifts similarly the condition of the surrounding locations. The second type of intervention targets locations that have reached slum condition. It makes specific, targeted, improvements to one such locations, to a condition $r = 0.5$, and it can occur on a monthly basis rather than bi-annually. While the first type of intervention has not occurred in Beirut, it could occur in principle given sufficient funds. In contrast, the second type has occurred in recent years, funded by donor countries, NGOs, or the European Union.

A further type of intervention, designed to assist poorer residents and which could include refugees, is to build social housing, akin to what is done in European countries. Although included as an option in our model, we have not explored this possibility for Beirut due to constraint not only of public funds but also of the issue of finding space in a highly build-up urban area.

Figure 6 depicts the effect of no intervention (top row), regeneration (middle), and targeted EU slum improvements (bottom row). $K = 0.025$ and refugees immigrate from $t = 90$ to 180. The greatest contrast is seen between some kind of intervention and none. Both top-down neighbourhood regeneration actions and more frequent and targeted slum improvements counteract the dampening effect of the refugee shock on the city's housing market. Interestingly, given the initial property values and conditions, the economic cycle is seen having the same approximate frequency in the initially-poor south-west district. If anything, the more frequent micro-interventions seen in the bottom row of the figure are better able to break out neighbourhood 'clusters' of poor condition dwellings. The suggestion opened for future study is that interventions can have value in sustaining the urban economy and population, mitigating the impact of the shock, and most importantly, improving the living condition of the poorest residents.

5   Summary and Future Work

Our motivation for this work comes from the sizeable contemporary transnational migrations affecting (at the time of writing) countries in Europe, especially, and its environs. Our aim is to use ABM to explore the effect of migrant

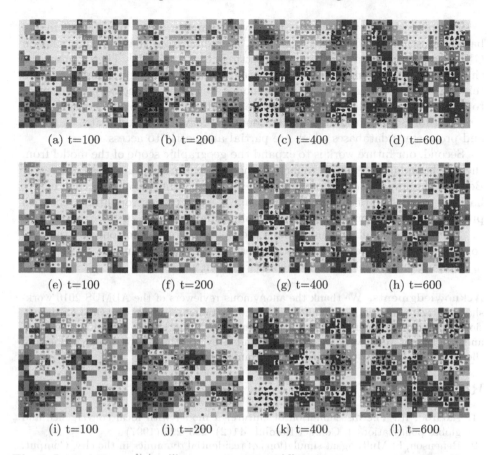

(a) t=100   (b) t=200   (c) t=400   (d) t=600

(e) t=100   (f) t=200   (g) t=400   (h) t=600

(i) t=100   (j) t=200   (k) t=400   (l) t=600

Fig. 6. Intervention policies. Top row = none, middle row = government regeneration, bottom row = EU slum improvements.

inflows on urban dynamics, and eventually to develop tools to aid policy makers with questions about the urban environment [17].

This paper presented a preliminary step towards such a longer-term goal, in the form of an abstracted simulation model of a Mediterranean city. Our model extends our earlier work by including designated cultural traits, property ownership (rather than a pure rental market), emigration, and refugees.

We found that refugees have impact on levels of slum locations, population density and over-population, prices, and income. Their presence appears to dampen the natural economic cycle, which continues nonetheless with waves of decay and regeneration, although with gentrification at a slower frequency after the shock of refugee influx. We observed an interesting effect depending on the capital in the economy and the rate of mobility, whereupon excessive shock of refugees – and in particular ongoing migration to the city – can render large parts of districts uninhabitable, causing both refugee and non-refugee populations to emigrate from the city.

The next step in this work is to move towards a more fine-grained model based on estimates of model parameters, including from the literature, and on GIS data following our work on urban settings in the UK [21]. There are several challenges in modelling Beirut using actual data. Reliable geo-referenced data relating to the variables relevant in the model are not easily accessible; and, prior to 2016, there is no official, published data about population or the housing stock – neither for Beirut nor indeed for the country – leaving only estimates by NGOs and proprietary databases which are partial and costly to access.

Second, our future work is to expand the geographic scope of the model from the city boundaries of Beirut to include the sub- and peri-urban areas of Greater Beirut. The importance of modelling the larger catchment area is that nearly half the population of Lebanon lives within the greater metropolitan area, with profound effects on property prices, mobility, and traffic [4,7].

Third, since significant migrations are being absorbed not only by regional countries such as Lebanon, but also by certain European countries, we see value in applying our model to cities in countries such as Germany.

Acknowledgments. We thank the anonymous reviewers of the ABMUS 2016 workshop for their constructive comments, and the participants at the workshop for discussions. We thank Joseph Bechara, Bruce Edmonds, Mona Fawaz, Alison Heppenstall, and Ali Termos. This work was partially funded by the University Research Board of the American University of Beirut under grant number 103183.

References

1. Axelrod, R.: The dissemination of culture: a model with local convergence and global polarization. J. Conflict Resolut. **41**(2), 203–226 (1997)
2. Benenson, I.: Multi-agent simulations of residential dynamics in the city. Comput. Environ. Urban Syst. **22**(1), 25–42 (1998)
3. Bourassa, S.: The rent gap debunked. Urban Stud. **30**(10), 1731–1744 (1993)
4. CIA World Factbook: Lebanon (2016). https://www.cia.gov/library/publications/the-world-factbook/geos/le.html
5. Diappi, L., Bolchi, P.: Gentrification waves in the inner-city of Milan: a multi agent/cellular automata model based on Smith's rent gap theory. In: Innovations in Design & Decision Support Systems in Architecture and Urban Planning, pp. 187–201. Springer, Berlin (2006)
6. Diappi, L., Bolchi, P.: Smith's rent gap theory and local real estate dynamics: a multi-agent model. Comput. Environ. Urban Syst. **32**(1), 6–18 (2008)
7. Fawaz, M., Sabah, M.: Charting a path: opening the path to affordable middle income housing. Executive Mag., 18 June 2015. http://www.executive-magazine.com/opinion/comment/charting-a-path
8. Feitosa, F.F., Le, Q.B., Vlek, P.L.: Multi-agent simulator for urban segregation (MASUS): a tool to explore alternatives for promoting inclusive cities. Comput. Environ. Urban Syst. **35**(2), 104–115 (2011)
9. Fuentes-Fernández, R., Galán, J.M., Hassan, S., López-Paredes, A., Pavón, J.: Application of model driven techniques for agent-based simulation. In: Demazeau, Y., Dignum, F., Corchado, J.M., Pérez, J.B. (eds.) Advances in Practical Applications of Agents and Multiagent Systems. AISC, vol. 70, pp. 81–90. Springer, Heidelberg (2010)

10. Ge, J.: Who creates housing bubbles? An agent-based study. In: Alam, S.J., Parunak, H.V.D. (eds.) MABS 2013. LNCS (LNAI), vol. 8235, pp. 143–150. Springer, Heidelberg (2014). doi:10.1007/978-3-642-54783-6_10
11. Giffinger, R., Seidl, R.: Micro-modelling of gentrification: a useful tool for planning? In: Modeling and Simulating Urban Processes, pp. 59–76. LIT Verlang (2013). Chap. 3
12. Harvey, D.: Rebel Cities: From the Right to the City to the Urban Revolution. Verso Books, London (2012)
13. Huang, Q., Parker, D.C., Filatova, T., Sun, S.: A review of urban residential choice models using agent-based modeling. Environ. Planning B Planning Des. 40, 1–29 (2014)
14. Kravari, K., Bassiliades, N.: A survey of agent platforms. J. Artif. Soc. Soc. Simul. 18(1), 11 (2015)
15. Krijnen, M., Fawaz, M.: Exception as the rule: high-end developments in Neoliberal Beirut. Built Environ. 36, 245–259 (2010)
16. Lebanese Information Center: The Lebanese demographic reality (2013). http://www.lstatic.org/PDF/demographenglish.pdf
17. Magee, L.: Simulating a 'Fierce Planet': a web-based agent platform and sustainability game. In: Proceedings of 2012 Spring Simulation Multiconference (SpringSim 2012) (2012)
18. North, M.J., Macal, C.M.: Managing Business Complexity: Discovering Strategic Solutions with Agent-based Modeling and Simulation. OUP, New York (2007)
19. O'Sullivan, D.: Toward micro-scale spatial modeling of gentrification. J. Geogr. Syst. 4(3), 251–274 (2002)
20. Patel, A., Crooks, A., Koizumi, N.: Slumulation: an agent-based modeling approach to slum formations. J. Artif. Soc. Soc. Simul. 15(4), 2 (2012)
21. Picascia, S.: A theory driven, spatially explicit agent-based simulation to model the economic and social implications of urban regeneration. In: Proceedings of the 11th Conference of the European Social Simulation Association (ESSA 2015) (2015)
22. Picascia, S., Edmonds, B., Heppenstall, A.: Agent based exploration of urban economic dynamics under the rent-gap hypotheses. In: Grimaldo, F., Norling, E. (eds.) MABS 2014. LNCS (LNAI), vol. 9002, pp. 213–227. Springer, Heidelberg (2015). doi:10.1007/978-3-319-14627-0_15
23. Portugali, J.: Toward a cognitive approach to urban dynamics. Environ. Planning B Planning Des. 31(4), 589–613 (2004)
24. Portugali, J.: Revisiting cognitive dissonance and memes-derived urban simulation models. In: Portugali, J. (ed.) Complexity, Cognition and the City. Understanding Complex Systems, pp. 315–334. Springer, Heidelberg (2011). doi:10.1007/978-3-642-19451-1_17
25. Schelling, T.C.: Dynamic models of segregation. J. Math. Sociol. 1(2), 143–186 (1971)
26. Singh, D., Padgham, L.: OpenSim: a framework for integrating agent-based models and simulation components. In: Proceedings of 21st European Conference on Artificial Intelligence (ECAI 2014), pp. 837–842 (2014)
27. Smith, N.: Toward a theory of gentrification a back to the city movement by capital, not people. J. Am. Plann. Assoc. 45(4), 538–548 (1979)
28. Smith, N.: The New Urban Frontier: Gentrification and the Revanchist City. Routledge, London (1996)
29. Srour, F.J., Yorke-Smith, N.: Towards agent-based simulation of maritime customs. In: Proceedings of 14th International Conference on Autonomous Agents and Multiagent Systems (AAMAS 2015), pp. 1637–1638 (2015)

30. Srour, F.J., Yorke-Smith, N.: Assessing maritime customs process re-engineering using agent-based simulation. In: Proceedings of 15th International Conference on Autonomous Agents and Multiagent Systems (AAMAS 2016), pp. 786–795 (2016)
31. Stanilov, K., Batty, M.: Exploring the historical determinants of urban growth patterns through cellular automata. Trans. GIS **15**(3), 253–271 (2011)
32. United Nations Development Programme: Poverty, growth and income distribution in Lebanon (2008). http://www.undp.org
33. United Nations High Commissioner for Refugees: 2015 UNHCR country operations profile - Lebanon (2015). http://www.unhcr.org/pages/49e486676.html
34. Wilensky, U.: NetLogo (1999). http://ccl.northwestern.edu/netlogo
35. Zhang, H., Li, Y.: Agent-based simulation of the search behavior in China's resale housing market: evidence from Beijing. J. Artif. Soc. Soc. Simul. **17**(1), 18 (2014)

Simulating Urban Growth with Raster and Vector Models: A Case Study for the City of Can Tho, Vietnam

Patrick Taillandier[1], Arnaud Banos[2], Alexis Drogoul[3], Benoit Gaudou[4(✉)],
Nicolas Marilleau[3], and Quang Chi Truong[3,5,6]

[1] UMR IDEES, University of Rouen, Mont-Saint-Aignan, France
patrick.taillandier@univ-rouen.fr
[2] UMR Géographie-cités, CNRS, Paris, France
arnaud.banos@parisgeo.cnrs.fr
[3] UMI 209 UMMISCO, IRD Bondy, Bondy, France
alexis.drogoul@gmail.com, nmarilleau@gmail.com
[4] IRIT, University of Toulouse 1 Capitole, Toulouse, France
benoit.gaudou@ut-capitole.fr
[5] CENRES & DREAM Team, Can Tho University, Can Tho, Vietnam
tcquang@ctu.edu.vn
[6] PDIMSC, University Pierre and Marie Curie/IRD, Paris, France

Abstract. Urban growth has been widely studied and many models (in particular Cellular Automata and Agent-Based Models) have been developed. Most of these models rely on two representations of the geographic space: raster and vector. Both representations have their own strengths and drawbacks. The raster models are simpler to implement and require less data, which explains their success and why most of urban growth models are based on this representation. However, they are not adapted to microscopic dynamics such as, for example, the construction of buildings. To reach such goal, a vector-based representation of space is mandatory. However, very few vector models exist, and none of them is easily adaptable to different case studies. In this paper, we propose to use a simple raster model and to adapt it to a vector representation of the geographic space and processes allowing studying urban growth at fine scale. Both models have been validated by a case study concerning the city of Can Tho, Vietnam.

Keywords: Agent-based simulation · Urban growth · Raster model · Vector model

This paper has already been published in: N. Osman and C. Sierra (Eds.): AAMAS 2016 WS, Visionary Papers, LNAI 10003, pp. 154–171, 2016.
DOI: 10.1007/978-3-319-46840-2_10

M.-R. Namazi-Rad et al. (Eds.): ABMUS 2016, LNAI 10051, pp. 21–38, 2017.
DOI: 10.1007/978-3-319-51957-9_2

1   Introduction

Being able to control urban growth has become a major challenge for our society. In this context, the possibilities offered by agent-based and cellular automata models to simulate this phenomena, and thus to evaluate possible outcomes of urban planning policies, are particularly interesting. These last years have seen the development of various urban growth models. If many of them are abstract models aiming at underlying the key factors behind the phenomena, only a few aim at reproducing observed urban growth. Concerning this second type of models, most of them are based on Cellular Automata, or at least on a raster representation of space. This representation, consisting in dividing the space in homogeneous (in terms of internal state) space units, has for advantage to require less data (or at least less precise data) and to be simpler to implement, in particular with the numerous platforms that exist today. However, this type of space representation does not allow simulations at fine scale. Moreover, as it was showed by [11] for segregation models, we state that using a vector (GIS) representation for urban growth models would allow to learn new knowledge.

In this paper, we propose to derive a vector model - a model at building scale - from a raster one and to use them to study the urban growth of the Can Tho city in Vietnam. Both models have been implemented using the GAMA platform. GAMA is an open-source modeling and simulation platform for building spatially explicit agent-based simulations ([1,14]). It integrates a complete and easy to learn modeling language and supports the definition of large-scale models (up to millions of agents). In addition, it allows a natural integration of GIS data (automatic agentification of data). At last, it integrates some built-in indicators such as the $Fuzzy - KappaSim$ [22] enabling to directly evaluate the simulation results.

This paper is organized as follow: Sect. 2 presents a state of the art of urban growth models. Section 3 is dedicated to the presentation of the case study of Can Tho. Section 4 presents the raster model developed and Sect. 5 the vector model. Section 6 proposes a discussion about the comparison of the two models. At last Sect. 7 concludes and proposes some perspectives.

2   State of the Art of Urban Growth Models

Modeling urban growth has been, since the seventies, one of the most documented domains in disciplines like geography [6,7,9], urbanism [16], or urban economy, and transportation [23,24] (see [2] for a comprehensive review), but also in disciplines not directly connected to urban systems but widely concerned with complex systems in general, such as physics [15,18]. However, despite this huge investment, it is still a challenging issue, especially when it comes to coupling processes and patterns at different geographic scales [25], which could require to use different representations of space.

Many of the first urban growth simulation models were based on a raster representation of space, in particular on square and hexagonal grids. Thus, the'90s

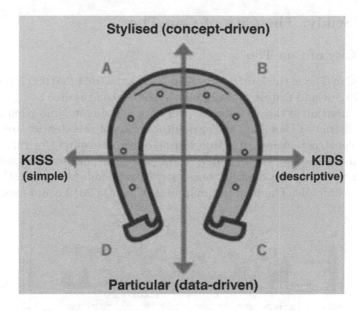

Fig. 1. "Horseshoe" reading template proposed by [5] to classify models in geography.

have seen the development of many Cellular Automata models such as the ones proposed in [6,10,26].

Even with the multiplication of GIS vector data, this representation of space is still dominant when modeling urban growth. In fact, many recent models still use it (see for instance [17,20,21]). These models cover a large part of the "stylized - particular" axis proposed by [5] to classify models (cf. Fig. 1). Indeed, some of these model are very stylized (e.g. [20]), others are based on a lot of local pieces of knowledge and are very specific to a case-study such as [3]. In the same way, for the second "axis" "KISS [4] - KIDS [12]", some models are very simple and integrate very few processes (e.g. [20]) while others, that use the possibilities offered by Agent-Based Modeling, integrate many factors (social, economic, human, etc.) (e.g. [3,17]).

Only very few research works have proposed a vector-based model, in particular at the building scale (explicit representation of building geometries). A notable work is [19] that proposes a general framework to build vector urban growth models. This framework is based on the hierarchical decomposition of space in districts, blocks and geographical objects (roads, buildings, etc.). It provides modelers some built-in measures and indicators to help them to define their own dynamics. However, the use of the framework requires a lot of work to adapt it to a given case-study and requires to write Java code.

Our work aims at filling the lack of simple to use and easily adaptable vector models. In particular, we propose a KISS stylized vector-based model, adapted from a raster model, that can be easily implemented for different case-studies.

The Sects. 4 and 5 present respectively the raster model and the vector model.

3   Case Study: The City of Can Tho

3.1   The City of Can Tho

The city of Can Tho is the fourth-largest in Vietnam with 1 200 000 inhabitants and is the largest and fastest growing city in the Mekong Delta.

The urbanization of this city shows a very fast growing in Ninh Kieu district, the central district of Can Tho, the agricultural area of this district are quickly replaced by construction area. An Binh ward is only one example for this process. The chart in Fig. 2 shows the rice area of this ward has sharply decreased more than 150 ha while the residential zones, street, economic and education area have increased rapidly. The land-use map in 2005 and in 2010 could explain this shifting (Fig. 3).

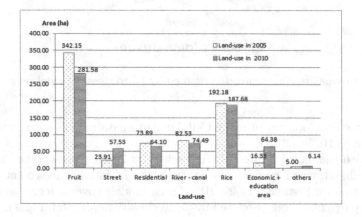

Fig. 2. Evolution of the Land Use between 2005 and 2010 in the An Binh ward. (Source: Generated from the Land Use maps of An Binh ward in 2005 and in 2010)

As many similar cities in developing countries, it has to face a number of economic, social and ecological challenges linked to this fast growth, such as the colonization of rural and wild-land spaces (and thus the preservation of ecosystems), the social impact (increase of spatial segregation of social groups, spatial fragmentation of labor markets, increase of traffic jams...). But due to its location in the Mekong Delta, it has also to face some specific challenges related to sea level rise (climate change), such as flooding by high tides from the river and canal system in rain season.

It is important to notice that Can Tho being located in the Mekong Delta, it is surrounded by rivers. Inhabitants are located not only along streets but along rivers as they use them for transportation. As a consequence, we have taken into account the importance of rivers in the micro-level vector model. In this model they have the same role as roads.

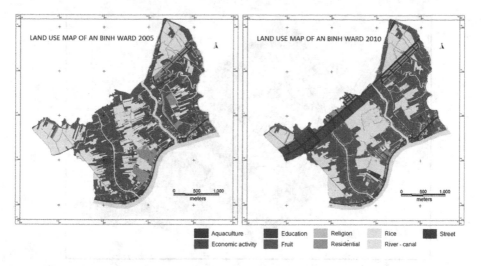

Fig. 3. Map of the Land Use evolution between 2005 and 2010 in the An Binh
ward. (Source: Department of Environmental and Natural resources of Can Tho City,
Vietnam)

3.2   The 2020 Local Urban Masterplan of Can Tho City

The Can Tho urban spread is mainly driven by a plan (the last one has been
drawn until 2020 and is presented in Fig. 4). It determines which roads should
be built or enlarged. It defines also area that will be dedicated to activity or
residential buildings. This plan is used to decide investments that will be made
in the city in terms of infrastructures.

The interest of models such as the ones presented in the following is (could be)
to give some insights to decision-makers about the impacts and efficiency of their
plans. It can in particular often be observed in Vietnam a significant difference
between plans and actual results, with the consequence of a waste of resources
due to the construction of infrastructures that are not adapted or efficient.

3.3   Description of Data

A comprehensive dataset on the evolution of the city shape has been gathered
and built by researchers and practitioners.

The dataset contains data at the city level and more precise data for one of
the city wards (An Binh ward). This is a ward of the center district (Ninh Kieu)
where the urbanisation is very fast:

-   Raster map (asc files) of Can Tho in 1999 and 2014 (resolution: 200×200 m).
    Three possible values for each cell have been defined: urban, non urban and
    river,
-   Shapefile of roads of Can Tho in 2010,
-   Shapefile of rivers (and canals) of Can Tho in 2010,

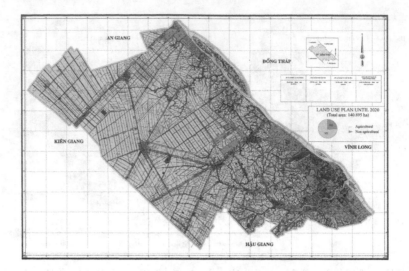

Fig. 4. Plan for Can Tho city in 2020. Red roads will be enlarged and built. Pink and red polygons are planned to become residential buildings. (Color figure online)

- Shapefile of the district boundaries of Can Tho,
- Vector land use maps (shapefiles) of An Binh ward (Ninh Kieu district) in 2005 and 2010. One type of land use is defined per vector object: river, road, non urban, rice, perennial tree, aquaculture, economic activity, education, religion, residential[1].

   Figure 5 shows the dataset. The picture displaying vector data merges shapefiles of roads, rivers and buildings.

4   Raster Model

4.1   Model Description

As stated in Sect. 2, there are many raster agent-based models. As our goal is to simulate urban growth with minimum local knowledge, we chose to develop a KISS stylized raster model that requires a small amount of data. Our model was strongly inspired by the model proposed by [20]. This model proposes two dynamics: the construction of buildings and the construction of roads. The road construction dynamics is not adapted to our application context as its goal is more to study the emergence of classic city patterns than to reproduce real city evolutions. We made then the choice not to integrate the road network construction dynamics, and to consider the construction of roads as part of the input scenario.

---

[1] We only use the urban-related entities from land use map in the following models.

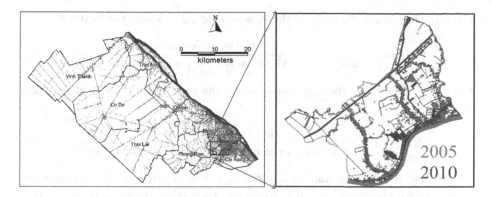

Fig. 5. Raster data (left) of Can Tho city and vector data (right) of An Binh ward, Ninh Kieu district. (Source: Department of Environmental and Natural resources of Can Tho City, Vietnam)

As an illustration we use the Can Tho city raster map, aiming at simulating urban growth over 15 years from 1999 to 2014 (with a simulation step duration of 1 year).

In this model, the main agents are `cells` that represent a homogeneous area of space. A cell agent has two attributes:

- `is_built`: is the cell built or not (Boolean value),
- `constructability`: level of constructability of the cell (float value between 0 and 1): 0 means that it is not interesting at all to build on this cell (i.e. to switch the variable `is_built` to true), 1 that it is very interesting.

We have introduced an additional agent, `city center`, in order to locate the center of the city, i.e. the place that concentrates the administrative activity. In the Can Tho city, we have located it following expert recommendations. In addition this type of agent gives us more flexibility if we want to apply our model on other cities and in particular in polycentric cities.

4.2 Model Dynamics

The general process of the model is based on two steps:

- each cell computes its level of constructability,
- the `nb_build_units` cells with the highest level of constructability are built (which induces that the attribute `is_built` is set to true).

The number of cells built at each simulation step, `nb_build_units`, is one of the parameters of the simulation.

The level of constructability of a cell depends on 3 criteria:

- CR_1: the density of construction in the neighborhood (the highest, the better):

$$CR_1 = \frac{\text{nb of built cells in the neighborhood}}{\text{nb of cells in the neighborhood}} \tag{1}$$

- CR_2: the euclidean distance to the closest road (the closer, the better):

$$CR_2 = 1 - \frac{\text{dist to the closest road}}{\text{max dist to the closest road (among all the cells)}} \qquad (2)$$

- CR_3: the distance to the city center using the road network (the closer, the better):

$$CR_3 = 1 - \frac{\text{dist to the city center}}{\text{max dist to the city center (among all the cells)}} \qquad (3)$$

Note that the original model integrated a fourth criteria: the distance to activity. As we chose to minimize the local knowledge required to make the model works, we do not integrate this criteria in our model.

The level of constructability is the weighted average of these 3 criteria:

$$constructability = w_1 * CR_1 + w_2 * CR_2 + w_3 * CR_3 \qquad (4)$$

The three weights (w_1, w_2 and w_3) are parameters of the model.

4.3   Results

Figure 6 illustrates the results of the simulation after 15 steps. It highlights the impact of the three weights and thus of the three processes included in the urban growth model: to this purpose we run experiments with 2 of the 3 weight parameters at 0 and the last one at 1. This gives three different kinds of cities. If only the density criterion is used, the city tends to expand its city center in a homogeneous way. If only the distance to road criterion is used, the construction of buildings reflects the road network. At last, if only the distance to city center criterion is used, the city tends to expand its center following the road network.

4.4   Model Calibration

Finally we looked at the combination of parameters that provides the best simulation results, i.e. results that minimize the error compared to real data. In order to compute the error between two raster images (in our case the real and simulated results) it is easy to simply compare pixel by pixel (cell by cell in our case) the two images; the error is the rate of different pixels. But we consider that this error computation is too strict in our case. In particular because of the random factor in the selection of the cells that will be built among the one with the best constructability, we cannot get exact results. So, instead of this strict comparison between maps, we adopt a fuzzy approach and use the $Fuzzy - KappaSim$ similarity indicator [22]. It does not compute the similarity of cells two by two, but computes the similarity of a cell (in simulated data) with the corresponding cell in the real data and its neighborhood. If the real and simulated cells are different, but there is a similar cell on the neighbourhood, the similarity will be greater than 0.

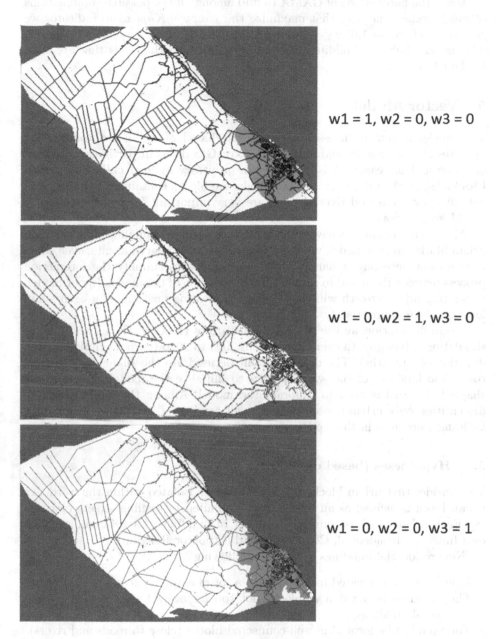

w1 = 1, w2 = 0, w3 = 0

w1 = 0, w2 = 1, w3 = 0

w1 = 0, w2 = 0, w3 = 1

Fig. 6. Results of the raster model in three particular cases: (top) with only the density criterion ($w_1 = 1$, $w_2 = 0$ and $w_3 = 0$); (center) with only the distance to road criterion ($w_1 = 0$, $w_2 = 1$ and $w_3 = 0$); (bottom) with only the distance to city center criterion ($w_1 = 0$, $w_2 = 0$ and $w_3 = 1$). Orange cells represent built cells.

Using the batch mode of GAMA to find among all the possible combinations of weight values the ones that maximize the $fuzzy - KappaSim$ indicator we get: $w_1 = 0.5$, $w_2 = 1.0$, $w_3 = 1.0$ and a result of $fuzzy - KappaSim = 0.497$. This means that new buildings have to be built along the roads that are close to the city center.

5   Vector Model

This model is similar in essence to the one based on cellular automata but operates at a finer scale and only uses vector GIS data. In particular, the unit of space and of reasoning is no more the arbitrary defined **cells** but **urban blocks** [8]. In the urban area, urban blocks are blocks containing buildings and delimited by roads and rivers (which are very important for transportation in the Mekong Delta).

Many types of entities have to be taken into account: buildings, roads, rivers, urban blocks. In this model, we chose to represent all them as agents, even when they do not have any dynamic. This choice helps to simplify the interaction process between them and to simplify the description of the model. In our model, simulating urban growth will thus consist in creating new building agents and locating them appropriately.

As an illustration we use the An Binh ward of the Can Tho city, aiming at simulating urban growth over 5 years from 2005 to 2010 (with a simulation step duration of 6 months). The data that will be used are the shapefiles of rivers, roads and land-use of the ward in 2005 to initialize the model. The land-use shapefile in 2010 is used to calibrate the model. Among the land-use shapefile entities, only urban-related ones (i.e. all residential, religion and economic buildings) are used in the model.

5.1   Hypotheses (based on [20])

We consider that urban blocks (cf. Fig. 7) can be isolated within the ward. An urban block is defined as an urban space delimited by cycling streets or rivers [8]. Each urban block is composed of a set of buildings. Each building has its own function (Residential, Commercial, Education or Religion).

New residential buildings are created following 3 rules:

- They tend to be created in blocks with a lot of empty space.
- They tend to be located in blocks not too far away from "services" (non-residential buildings).
- They tend to be located in well-connected blocks (close to roads and rivers).

5.2   Model Description

In this model and due to the capacities of the modeling and simulation platform chosen (GAMA, version 1.6.1) in terms of agentification of GIS data, the model

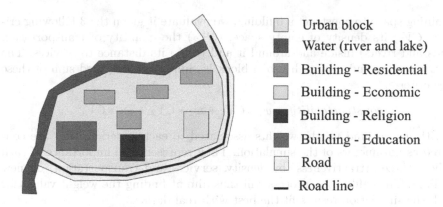

Fig. 7. Illustration of an urban block

contains agents representing **rivers**, **roads** and **buildings**. These agents are created directly from Can Tho GIS data. They are all characterized by their **shape** and **location**. In addition buildings have a **type** attribute taken its value among residential, commercial, religion and education. The last three types of buildings are considered as services.

Finally the model also contains **urban_blocks** agents. They are created at the initialization of the model from the existing data. In addition to its **shape** and **location** attributes, it contains also the attributes:

- **buildings** (resp. **roads** and **rivers**): it contains the set of building (resp. road and river) agents included in this urban block,
- **constructability**: this numerical attribute contains the constructability value of the urban block.

5.3 Model Dynamics

The dynamics of the model follows a 2-step process, repeated at every simulation step:

1. The constructability of each urban block is computed,
2. The **nb_build_units** urban blocks with the highest constructability create **nb_new_buildings** buildings inside them.

Both steps base their computations on the intensive use of geometrical operations (computation of distances (using road network), intersections, extrusions, etc.). **nb_build_units** and **nb_new_buildings** are two parameters of the simulation.

Step 1 - Evaluation of Urban Blocks Constructability. The aim of this first step is to give a mark to each urban block in order to rank them and determine which ones should be constructed first. So for each urban block with enough remaining space to construct a building, we evaluate it given the 3 following criteria: (CV_1) its density of empty space, (CV_2) the quantity of transportation (roads and rivers) inside and around it and (CV_3) its distance to services. The constructability index of each urban block is simply the weighted sum of these three criteria:

$$constructability = w_1 * CV_1 + w_2 * CV_2 + w_3 * CV_3$$

with w_1, w_2 and w_3 the weights associated to each criterion; they are considered as parameters of the simulation. They represent the importance of each of these three attractiveness (by density, services and transportation) on new buildings. The calibration process will thus aim at finding the weight values for which the simulation results fit the best with real data.

For each urban block, at each simulation step, the three criteria are computed as follows:

– CV_1 is the density of free space, i.e. the rate of free space in the urban block:

$$CV_1 = \frac{\text{area of free space}}{\text{area of the urban block}}$$

– CV_2 is the total area of transportation (roads and rivers) inside and around (at a distance of $1\,\text{m}$) the urban block compared to the area of the urban block:

$$CV_2 = \frac{\text{area of roads \& rivers within a 1 m distance from the urban block}}{\text{area of the urban block}}$$

– CV_3 is the distance of the urban block to services. We consider here as services the educational, religious and commercial buildings. CV_3 thus depends on the distance to the closest educational building ($d_{educational\_building}$), religious building ($d_{religious\_building}$) and commercial building ($d_{commercial\_building}$). It is normalized by the maximum possible distance in the environment ($max\_distance$):

$$CV_3 = 1 - \frac{d_{educational\_building} + d_{religious\_building} + d_{commercial\_building}}{3 * max\_distance}$$

Step 2 - Selection of the nb_build_units urban blocks with the highest constructability and creation of nb_new_buildings buildings inside each. Once each urban block has computed its own constructability, the nb_build_units urban blocks with the higher constructability are chosen and nb_new_buildings new buildings are created on them.

To simplify the model, we chose not to create new building shapes. When creating a new building we simply copy the shape of an already existing building. We consider it is a good compromise between the creation of very simple rectangular buildings and of buildings with a random (and thus perhaps not realistic) shape.

In each chosen urban block, a new building is created following the 4 steps (cf. Fig. 8):

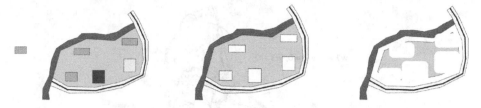

Fig. 8. Steps of the selection of possible locations for a new building. The remaining pink geometry in the right picture represents these possible locations. (Color figure online)

1. Choose an existing building in the block or in a neighboring one if none is available,
2. Extrude the shape of its buildings from the block geometry,
3. Erode the resulting shape by the maximum dimension of the chosen building,
4. If the resulting geometry is not empty, choose a random location inside it, create a building at this location (with the shape of the chosen building) and proceed similarly for the next building.

5.4   Results

The Fig. 9 shows preliminary results by considering separately the impact of each criterion. It highlights the impact of the three weights and thus of the three processes included in the urban growth model: to this purpose we run experiments with 2 of the 3 weight parameters at 0 and the last one at 1.

As expected, we get three very different locations for new buildings. If only the density criterion is used, new buildings are created in the empty urban blocks. If only the transportation criterion is used, new buildings are created in area with lot of roads and rivers around. Finally if only the activity criterion is used, new buildings are concentrated in the city center (and a few to another block with several activities).

5.5   Calibration and Validation of the Models on Can Tho Data

The calibration will be the minimization of the distance (i.e. the error) between the simulation results and the data. Contrarily to the raster model where it is easy to compute the error cell by cell, in the vector model we cannot use this grid discretization. As a consequence, the error is computed as the rate of new real buildings that are not intersected (with a given buffer) by buildings obtained by simulation, weighted by their area. As an example in the Fig. 10, the error between real data and simulated data (in 2010) is 0.5. This way of computing error is very close in essence to the fuzzy indicator used in the raster model.

After calibration, the best weights we get are: $w_1 = 0.2$, $w_2 = 1.0$ and $w_3 = 0.0$. The lowest error we get is $error = 0.288$. This means that most of new

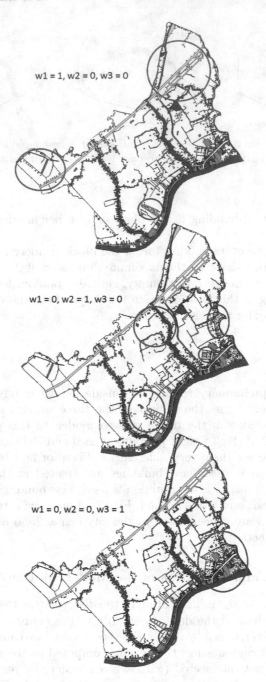

Fig. 9. Results of the vector model in three particular cases: (top) with only the density criterion ($w_1 = 1$, $w_2 = 0$ and $w_3 = 0$); (center) with only the quantity of transportation criterion ($w_1 = 0$, $w_2 = 1$ and $w_3 = 0$); (bottom) with only the distance to services criterion ($w_1 = 0$, $w_2 = 0$ and $w_3 = 1$). Red circles highlight the location of new buildings. Education buildings are in green, religion ones in violet, commercial in orange and residential in gray. (Color figure online)

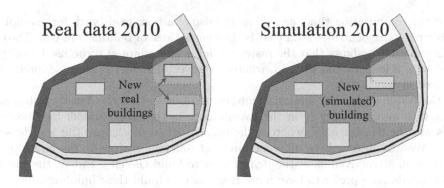

Fig. 10. Computation of the distance between real and simulated data. In this case the distance is 0.5.

buildings are in urban blocks with a high density of free space and surrounded by many roads and rivers. This also shows that in the best combination the third criteria (related to the distance to services) does not seem to have an impact.

6   Comparison and Discussion

The two models are based on the same general process: at each simulation step, the choice of a certain number of cells/blocks to build/densify. However, the difference in space representation has a deep impact on the questions the model can answer.

The raster model has for major advantage to require less data: only landsat data and a shapefile of roads were used in our case study. In addition, the time consumption of the model can be easily controlled through the resolution of the grid. These advantages make it particularly interesting for application context when the data are scare (which was typically the case for the city of Can Tho) and when the city is composed of many buildings.

The vector model requires not only to have a shapefile of roads, but also a shapefile of buildings (eventually with the function of each building). This model allows to simulate with details where buildings are going to be built. It allows as well to precise the function of each new building.

Concerning the comparison of the computational cost of the two models, we carried out an experiment in which we ran the previously presented models for 50 simulation steps on respectively the complete city of Can Tho for the raster model (335×222 cells with a size of $200\,\text{m} \times 200\,\text{m}$) and the An Binh ward (1037 buildings and 93 urban blocks) for the vector model. The experiment was carried out on an old Macbook computer (early 2011). The average step duration without considering the initialization stage (computation of the distances to roads and to city centers) for the raster model was 1.9 s and 2.4 s for the vector one. These results show that the computation cost is acceptable for both models. Of course, running the vector on the complete city of Can Tho will have increased a lot the computation time, as well as the use of a finer grid (with for example cells with a size of 20 m × 20 m that is the average size of buildings in Can Tho). This experiment shows that the raster model is well adapted to be used as city level with a low granularity grid, whereas the vector model is more adapted to be used at ward level.

Concerning this scale level, it is interesting to note that the density criterion is used in an opposite way in the two models: in the raster model the chosen cells are the densest ones, whereas the chosen urban blocks are the less dense ones. We can observe here different forces at different scales. At the city level, there is an attractiveness of the denser area to build the city. But at the ward level, inhabitants prefer to have more free space to build their buildings.

The two models are complementary. An interesting work could be to couple these models in order to be able to use the raster model for the parts of the city where we do not need precise details on building construction, and the vector model for the other parts. Such hybrid model could have for benefits to require less data and be less time consuming than the use of the vector model on the complete city.

7   Conclusion

In this paper, we have presented two complementary KISS urban growth models: a model based on a raster representation at city-scale and a vector one at ward-scale. As discussed in Sect. 6, the two models have their own advantages and drawbacks. The raster model requires less data and can be less time-consuming if the resolution of the grid is not too high. It is well-adapted to simulate urban growth at city scale. In contrary, the vector model allows studying the urban growth at fine scale and simulating the construction of buildings - and thus to answer new questions. This model is well-adapted to simulate the urban growth at district-scale.

Both models have their advantages and drawbacks. They also make sense at different scales: fine scales for the vector-based model, more global ones for the raster-based one. However, coupling these two models within an integrated multi-scale approach is definitely a challenge the research team seeks to address in the next future.

In order to validate the genericity of our two models (and the hybrid one), we plan to test them on other cities.

We plan as well to improve the vector model by adding new criteria in the choice of the urban blocks to densify. In particular, we could add the criterion proposed by [20] concerning the accessibility of the urban blocks toward different activities. Another possible improvement could consist in using a more robust multi-criteria decision-making method to sort the cells/urban blocks. A possibility could be to use the Choquet integral to compute the constructability [13] that allows to take into account the redundancy and synergy between criteria.

Acknowledgements. This work was part of and supported by the Tam Dao Summer School in Social Sciences (JTD) – http://www.tamdaoconf.com/.

References

1. GAMA website (2015). http://gama-platform.org
2. Acheampong, R.A., Silva, E.: Land use-transport interaction modeling: a review of the literature and future research directions. J. Transp. Land Use **8**(3), 1–28 (2015)
3. Arsanjani, J.J., Helbich, M., de Noronha Vaz, E.: Spatiotemporal simulation of urban growth patterns using agent-based modeling: the case of Tehran. Cities **32**, 33–42 (2013)
4. Axelrod, R.M.: The Complexity of Cooperation: Agent-Based Models of Competition and Collaboration. Princeton University Press, Princeton (1997)
5. Banos, A., Sanders, L.: Modéliser et simuler les systèmes spatiaux en géographie. Modéliser et Simuler-Epistémologies et Pratiques des Modèles et des Simulations Ebook des éditions Matériologiques **1**, 833–863 (2013)
6. Batty, M., Xie, Y., Sun, Z.: Modeling urban dynamics through GIS-based cellular automata. Comput. Environ. Urban Syst. **23**(3), 205–233 (1999)
7. Benenson, I.: Multi-agent simulations of residential dynamics in the city. Comput. Environ. Urban Syst. **22**(1), 25–42 (1998)
8. Boffet, A., Coquerel, C.: Urban classification for generalisation orchestration. In: 19th International Symposium of Photogrammetry and Remote Sensing (ISPRS 2000), Amsterdam (Netherlands), pp. 16–23, July 2000
9. Caruso, G., Vuidel, G., Cavailhès, J., Frankhauser, P., Peeters, D., Thomas, I.: Morphological similarities between DBM and a microeconomic model of sprawl. J. Geogr. Syst. **13**(1), 31–48 (2011)
10. Clarke, K., Hoppen, S., Gaydos, L.: A self-modifying cellular automaton model of historical. Environ. Plann. B **24**, 247–261 (1997)
11. Crooks, A.T.: Constructing and implementing an agent-based model of residential segregation through vector GIS. Int. J. Geogr. Inf. Sci. **24**(5), 661–675 (2010)
12. Edmonds, B., Moss, S.: From KISS to KIDS in Multi-Agent and Multi-Agent Based Simulation. LNCS, vol. 3415. Springer, Heidelberg (2005). pp. 130–144
13. Grabisch, M., Labreuche, C.: A decade of application of the Choquet and Sugeno integrals in multi-criteria decision aid. Ann. Oper. Res. **175**(1), 247–286 (2010)
14. Grignard, A., Taillandier, P., Gaudou, B., Vo, D.A., Huynh, N.Q., Drogoul, A.: GAMA 1.6: advancing the art of complex agent-based modeling and simulation. In: Boella, G., Elkind, E., Savarimuthu, B.T.R., Dignum, F., Purvis, M.K. (eds.) PRIMA 2013. LNCS (LNAI), vol. 8291, pp. 117–131. Springer, Heidelberg (2013). doi:10.1007/978-3-642-44927-7_9
15. Haken, H., Portugali, J.: The face of the city is its information. J. Environ. Psychol. **23**(4), 385–408 (2003)
16. Hillier, B., Leaman, A., Stansall, P., Bedford, M.: Space syntax. Environ. Plann. B Plann. Des. **3**(2), 147–185 (1976)
17. Liu, Y., Feng, Y.: A logistic based cellular automata model for continuous urban growth simulation: a case study of the Gold Coast City, Australia. In: Heppenstall, A.J., Crooks, A.T., See, L.M., Batty, M. (eds.) Agent-Based Models of Geographical Systems, pp. 643–662. Springer, Heidelberg (2012)
18. Louf, R., Barthelemy, M.: Modeling the polycentric transition of cities. Phys. Rev. Lett. **111**(19), 198702 (2013)
19. Perret, J., Curie, F., Gaffuri, J., Ruas, A.: A Multi-agent system for the simulation of urban dynamics. In: 10th European Conference on Complex Systems (ECCS 2010), Lisbon, Portugal (2010)

20. Raimbault, J., Banos, A., Doursat, R.: A hybrid network/grid model of urban morphogenesis and optimization. In: Aziz-Alaoui, M.A., Bertelle, C., Liu, X.Z., Olivier, D. (eds.) Proceedings of the 4th International Conference on Complex Systems and Applications (ICCSA 2014), pp. 51–60, June 2014
21. Torrens, P.M.: Simulating sprawl. Ann. Assoc. Am. Geogr. **96**(2), 248–275 (2006)
22. van Vliet, J., Hagen-Zanker, A., Hurkens, J., van Delden, H.: A fuzzy set approach to assess the predictive accuracy of land use simulations. Ecol. Model. **261**, 32–42 (2013)
23. Waddell, P.: Urbansim: modeling urban development for land use, transportation, and environmental planning. J. Am. Plann. Assoc. **68**(3), 297–314 (2002)
24. Wegener, M.: Overview of land-use transport models. Handb. Transp. Geogr. Spat. Syst. **5**, 127–146 (2004)
25. White, R.: Modeling multi-scale processes in a cellular automata framework. In: Portugali, J. (ed.) Complex Artificial Environments, pp. 165–177. Springer, Heidelberg (2006)
26. White, R., Engelen, G.: Cellular automata and fractal urban form: a cellular modelling approach to the evolution of urban land-use patterns. Environ. Plann. A **25**(8), 1175–1199 (1993)

Integrating Behavior and Microsimulation Models

Nidhi Parikh[✉], Madhav Marathe, and Samarth Swarup

Network Dynamics and Simulation Science Lab,
Biocomplexity Institute of Virginia Tech, Virginia Tech, Blacksburg, VA, USA
{nidhip,mmarathe,swarup}@vbi.vt.edu

Abstract. Microsimulations focus on modeling routine activities of individuals and have been used for modeling and planning urban systems like transportation, energy demand, and epidemiology. On the other hand, planning for emergency situations (e.g., disasters) needs to account for human behavior which is not routine or pre-planned but depends upon the current situation like the amount of physical damage or safety of family. Here, we focus on modeling the aftermath of a hypothetical detonation of an improvised nuclear device in Washington DC. We review various behavior models from the literature and provide motivation for our model which is conceptually based on the formalism of decentralized semi-Markov decision processes with communication, using the framework of options. We describe our approach for integrating behavior and microsimulation models where the behavior model specifies context-dependent behaviors (like looking for family members, sheltering, evacuation, and search and rescue) and the synthetic population provides information about demographics and infrastructures. We present results from a number of simulation runs.

Keywords: Behavior models · Disaster modeling · Microsimulations

1 Introduction

Microsimulation is used to extrapolate the large-scale consequences of individual interactions. For instance, if we wish to approximate the traffic conditions on all the roads all the time, we have to model individual daily activity patterns and individual vehicles on the road, as was demonstrated by the TRANSIMS project [5]. In this case, data about individual activity schedules was used to create a model of the travel patterns of every individual in the population and the consequent interactions between vehicles on the roads determined the traffic conditions. Activities here refer to events such as going to work, going to school, going shopping, and so on.

In many microsimulation scenarios, we wish to model behaviors which are distinct from activities. For example, during a flu epidemic, a behavior which might be manifested by some agents would be to avoid crowded places. This behavior would modify the agent's activity patterns, but isn't itself an activity

© Springer International Publishing AG 2017
M.-R. Namazi-Rad et al. (Eds.): ABMUS 2016, LNAI 10051, pp. 39–59, 2017.
DOI: 10.1007/978-3-319-51957-9_3

in the sense of having a set location and time. It could be endogenously triggered in the simulation, perhaps if the agent perceives that a certain fraction of the people he comes into contact with during normal daily activities are sick. In this case, the alternate activity patterns triggered by the behavior of avoiding crowded places can be "canned" in the sense of being pre-defined, or they can be dynamically chosen.

The latter, arguably, results in more realistic simulations for scenarios such as the aftermath of a disaster, where people don't follow typical daily activity patterns, but engage in a range of dynamically determined behaviors, depending on multiple factors such as their health state, whether they are with their family members, environmental conditions, and more. For such scenarios, we need to integrate a behavioral model with a microsimulation model in order to endow agents with the capability to respond to changing conditions.

There have been a host of behavioral models and modeling techniques that have been developed in various contexts over the years. Here we survey a number of candidates with the goal of developing a behavioral model for disaster microsimulations. The main criteria are generality and scalability—the modeling framework needs to be able to represent a wide range of behaviors and scale to simulations of hundreds of thousands or millions of agents.

Our key philosophical position is that individual-level models can be phenomenological, which means we don't need to model the internal state and reasoning process of the agents, so long as their observed behavior is a good match for data. This is valid so long as what we are concerned with are the population-scale outcomes, and not sub-individual level causes for these outcomes.

In what follows, we survey a number of behavioral models and modeling techniques before describing our choice which is based on the options framework for (decentralized) semi-MDPs [37]. We describe how we have implemented a behavioral model for a large-scale simulation of the aftermath of a hypothetical improvised nuclear detonation in Washington DC [29], and present results from several simulations.

2   The Scenario: Modeling the Aftermath of a Disaster

The scenario that we model is hypothetical detonation of a 10kT improvised nuclear device at the corner of 16th and K street NW in Washington DC on a weekday morning. It results in large numbers of mortalities and casualties, and also significant infrastructural damage. The fallout cloud generated by the explosion is expected to spread mainly eastward and east-by-northeastward. We call the area that is studied the detailed study area (DSA; Fig. 1). It is the area under thermal effect polygon (circle) and widest boundary of fallout cloud bounded by DC region county boundaries (which includes DC plus surrounding counties from neighboring states Virginia and Maryland).

Our simulation is designed around a synthetic information (or microsimulation) framework [25]. It uses a detailed, realistic representation of the population of the region including their demographics, locations, and daily activity routines

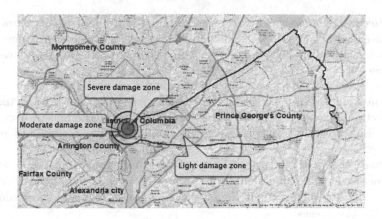

Fig. 1. The detailed study area (DSA). The severe damage zone extends from ground zero to 0.6 miles. The moderate damage zone is an annular region from 0.6 to 1 mile from ground zero. The light damage zone is the area further than 1 mile from ground zero [9].

and four infrastructures: the power system, the transportation network [1], the cell phone communication system [10], and the healthcare system [24].

Once such a disaster occurs, it is expected that people will abandon their normal daily activities and engage in a range of behaviors such as looking for their family members, sheltering, seeking healthcare, and more. These behaviors are driven by limited knowledge of the situation in combination with certain drives, such as the drive to reconstitute households, assist others in need, shelter or evacuate, and tend to personal injuries and sickness [9,31]. In the next section, we discuss the suitability of several different behavior modeling approaches for this problem. Following that, in Sect. 4, we describe the simulation in more detail and results from multiple simulation runs.

3 Behavior Models

Here we review various behavior models from the areas of health behavior, cognitive architecture, and reinforcement learning and discuss their suitability and limitations for modeling our disaster scenario.

3.1 Health Behavior Models

These models provide understanding of individual health behavior as well as directions for further research and interventions.

The Health Belief Model: The Health Belief Model (HBM) was developed to understand the failure of people to accept disease preventives or screening tests for early detection of asymptomatic diseases [33]. Basic constructs of the HBM are as follows:

1. *Perceived susceptibility:* This refers to an individual's perception of how likely they are to contract a disease. The model suggests that people are more likely to engage in healthy behaviors if they think they are susceptible to developing the disease.
2. *Perceived severity:* It refers to an individual's perception of seriousness of the consequences of contracting the disease. An individual is more likely to take action if he believes that developing the disease has serious physical (e.g., pain, disability, death) or social (e.g., effect on family life, social relationships), consequences.
3. *Perceived benefits:* While acceptance of personal susceptibility and severity to a disease leads to an action, it does not specify which action. This depends upon individual belief about the effectiveness of various actions available in reducing the disease.
4. *Perceived barriers:* While an individual may believe that a given action would reduce the threat of the disease, the action might be unpleasant, expensive or painful. Such perceived barriers act as an impediment to engaging in recommended behavior.
5. *Cue to action:* It refers to a cue or a trigger that is necessary to prompt an individual to take an action. The cue could be internal (e.g., symptoms) or external (e.g., mass media communications).
6. *Self-efficacy:* It refers to an individual's confidence in his ability to successfully perform the recommended behavior.

Recently, the HBM has been used in agent-based simulations to model individual decision making process for adopting preventive behaviors like wearing face mask for SARS epidemic in Hong Kong [15] and adopting vaccination and social distancing interventions for seasonal influenza epidemic [20].

Though widely used in studying and modeling health behaviors, HBM has many limitations: It does not account for habitual behaviors or social influence, and assumes that everyone has the same access to information. The latter two aspects are very important for modeling human behavior in the aftermath of an improvised nuclear detonation because people may not be aware of what has happened and their perception of the event would depend largely upon the physical damage that they could observe. Also, in emergency situations, people are not just concerned about themselves but also about the safety of their family and injured people around them.

Theory of Reasoned Action (TRA): This is a theory that was developed to predict volitional behavior and to understand psychological factors that influence them [16]. As the name suggests, it assumes that people are rational beings and they take an action after considering its implications. It postulates that the intention to perform a behavior is strongly related to the actual performance of that behavior. An individual's intention is a function of two factors: behavioral attitude and subjective norms.

Behavioral attitude is determined by salient beliefs towards the behavior. Each belief represents individual's perception (or perceived probability) that the behavior leads to some outcome. Behavioral attitude is determined by evaluation of each outcome and the strength of the associated belief.

Subjective norms refers to individual's perception of social pressure to perform or not perform the behavior. It is determined by normative beliefs, individual's beliefs that specific group of individuals would think that he should or should not perform the behavior and by his motivation to comply with it.

Theory of Planned Behavior: Theory of reasoned action assumes that behavioral intention is immediate determinant of actual behavior. However, there are many factors (e.g., personal deficiencies, external obstacles) that can obstruct the actual performance of behavior, despite the intention. To account for non-volitional factors, theory of reasoned action was extended to include perceived behavioral control (originated from the concept of self-efficacy), which is known as the theory of planned behavior (TPB) [2]. Perceived behavioral control is determined by individual's beliefs about the presence of factors that may facilitate or impede performance of the behavior (known as control beliefs) and perceived power of these factors. It affects both, actual behavior (to account for non-volitional factors) and behavioral intention (as motivational implication).

Theory of planned behavior has recently also been used in agent-based models to predict diffusion of innovations [35] and adoption of solar plant [32].

While TRA and TPB account for behavioral attitude and social influence, they do not take into account factors like environmental influence and alternative behaviors. People often have a choice among behaviors e.g., to shelter or to evacuate. These decisions can depend on factors like availability of transportation and communication, which are affected by a disaster. TRA and TPB do not offer a clear operationalizable framework for implementing an individual decision-making model that takes into account these types of factors. A more general and operationalizable framework for behavior modeling is the belief-desire-intention model.

3.2   Belief-Desire-Intention Model

The Belief-Desire-Intention (BDI) model of practical reasoning was developed to explain future directed intentions and plans. In the BDI model [17], agents are viewed as having certain mental attitudes: belief, desire, and intention.

Belief refers to what agent believes about the world. It may be obtained from sensing the world or computed from internal inference. Beliefs are important because agents act in a dynamic world and they only have a local view of the world so past needs to be remembered. Agents are also resource bounded and so they need to cache important information rather than recomputing it. Beliefs need not necessarily be true, they are just the agent's perception of the world.

Desire refers to goals or desired end states. An agent may have multiple desires, which may conflict with each other.

Intentions are built on the notion of commitment. It refers to both, agent's commitment to desires and commitment to plans selected to achieve these goals.

Once the agent commits to a goal or a plan, it does not drop the commitment easily. Commitment is important because agents act in a dynamic environment (the world might have changed making the current plan ineffective) and agents are resource bounded (they can not replan at every change). An agent arrives at a commitment after reasoning and then the commitment constrains further reasoning. Intentions cannot conflict with each other; they must be consistent.

Finally, a BDI system also consists of a set of plans, known as plan library. Each plan consists of precondition, termination condition, and plan body which can be abstract or concrete set of actions. A plan is activated when its preconditions match current beliefs and intention. Actions in the plan can lead to further commitment and create intention hierarchy. Most primitive intention and associated plan leads to primitive actions. Termination conditions represent commitment strategies, i.e., conditions for reconsidering intentions.

BDI has been used in a number of domains including traffic modeling [28,34] and evacuation [36]. It has been used for simulations with tens of thousands of agents. Our scenario consists of about 730,000 people in Washington DC, which would require an order of magnitude increase in scaling. BDI also models individual agents in greater detail that is necessary for our purposes, since we are mainly concerned with population-level consequences of individual behavioral interactions, but not necessarily with the details of the reasoning mechanism by which individuals make choices. Thus we adopt a simpler behavioral representation, which nevertheless has plans with preconditions and termination conditions. This is discussed in Sect. 3.4 below.

3.3 Cognitive Architectures

Another stream of research in computational cognitive science has focused on the development of cognitive architectures for individual intelligent agents, such as Soar [22] and ACT-R [3]. See [14] for recent survey of cognitive architectures. The key aspect of intelligent agents is their ability to perform variety of task using a large body of knowledge acquired through experience, in a dynamic environment. As the knowledge acquired can change over time, cognitive architecture refers to the underlying infrastructure for intelligent agents that remains fixed over tasks. It includes memory for storage of knowledge, representation of elements in memory, and processing units that support acquisition and use of knowledge. Broadly, these approaches are focused on detailed modeling of individual cognition, which makes them unsuitable for integrating with microsimulation models of large populations because they cannot scale to simulations of millions of agents.

3.4 Reinforcement Learning-Based Models

Reinforcement learning focuses on learning goal-oriented behavior by trial-and-error-based interacting with an uncertain environment. An agent in this formalism has explicit goals which are specified in terms of reward. At each time step, the agent receives some representation of environment's state and takes an action. As a result of this action, it receives some reward and finds itself into a new environmental state and the process continues. The agent takes actions to maximize the reward (and in turn achieve its goals).

Many practical systems include actions that may be temporally extended. Such systems could be modeled as semi-Markov decision processes (SMDP). An SMDP is defined as (S, A, P, R, τ) where S, A, P, and R are defined as in MDP and τ is duration function where $\tau(s, a)$ is duration of taking action a in state s. Algorithms (policy iteration, value iteration, TD methods, and Q-learning) used for MDP can be extended to solve SMDP [11].

An SMDP assumes temporally-extended actions to be indivisible. Sutton et al. [37] proposed a framework of options where these temporally extended actions (called options) are comprised of low-level actions. Options in this framework are policies (over low-level actions) with initiation condition (states where given option is available) and termination condition (for each state, probability that the option terminates in given state). Conceptually, this makes them close to the BDI model. Planning corresponds to learning policies over options and methods for solving SMDPs (e.g., value iteration, Q-learning) can be used to learn an optimal policy.

Many multi-agent problems can be formulated as a decentralized Markov decision processes (dec-MDP). In this framework, each agent has a local view of the system and exchanging information among them constantly is impossible as it may incur some cost. In this system, none of the agents can fully observe the system state but the performance of the system depends upon some global reward. Even though the state transition and observations may be independent for each agent, the global problem can not be decomposed into separate individual problems. As different local behaviors can lead to different global reward, agent need to exchange information.

We choose this reinforcement learning framework to model behavior because it is simple, intuitive, and easy to implement. We do not do any optimization (learn optimal policy for agents) because our goal is to study the effects of natural human behavioral instincts and its interactions with various infrastructural system, in case of a disaster. Also, it would not be possible to control people's behavior in such a situation. However, many problems in planning for such events can be formulated as optimization problems in terms of some resources and a reinforcement learning based model could be useful in the future to solve such problems. An MDP-based framework (without optimization) has also been used for many large-scale agent-based simulations consisting of millions of agents [30].

Our multi-agent simulation requires modeling behaviors like looking for family members, evacuation, and seeking healthcare which take variable amount of time. Further they depend upon infrastructure (e.g., availability of cellular communication system and transport system). This makes dec-SMDP with communication with the framework of options suitable for our simulation as it can scale to a large number of agents and also facilitates modeling interaction of behavior (modeled as options) with infrastructural systems (modeled as low-level actions).

This is a phenomenological modeling approach, where the descriptions of the behaviors are drawn from surveys (both prospective and retrospective) and qualitative descriptions of behaviors in past disasters. We prefer this approach because it is grounded in data at the level at which data are available, without having to make assumptions about the cognitive processes that lead to these behaviors. The goal of our multiagent simulation is to evaluate the effects of various individual behaviors on the population-level outcomes, such as numbers of mortalities and casualties. It is not to model the decision-making processes of individuals in a disaster context, about which there is surprisingly little information available. In the literature, models of decision-making in disasters generally focus on decision-making by responders, emergency managers, policy-makers, and so on.

More broadly, the phenomenological approach can be understood as a *level of understanding* in the sense of Marr [26]. His basic argument is that a complex system can be understood at multiple levels, and these explanations are largely independent of each other. Thus, an explanation at the population and behavioral level can rigorously exist without explicitly relying on a lower level description such as a cognitive or neural description.

Next we describe our implementation of the behavioral model and how it integrates with the microsimulation.

4   Agent Design and Behavior

The scenario affects all people present in the DSA at the time of detonation, including area residents, tourist, business travelers, and dorm students. The health and behavior of an agent depend upon its demographics and location at the time of the blast. This information is obtained from the synthetic population as described next.

4.1   The Synthetic Population

A synthetic population is a detailed, high fidelity, agent-based representation of a population of a region including their demographics (e.g., age, income) and daily activity routine (e.g., type of activity, start time, duration, and location of activity) [18,25]. It has been used for modeling and planning for many applications like epidemiology [30] and transportation [19]. It is created by combining data from multiple sources (Table 1).

We use a synthetic population of the Washington DC metro area which has been extended to include transients and dorm students. The process of generating resident [25], transient [30], and dorm student [29] populations is briefly outlined below:

Base Population (Residents): The population is generated in several steps. *Generating Synthetic Population:* In this step, demographic distributions and sample household data from the American Community Survey (ACS) are combined using iterative proportional fitting algorithm [8] to create synthetic

Table 1. Datasets used for population generation.

Used for	Data source
Base US population	American Community Survey
	National Center for Education Stat.
	National Household Travel Survey
	Navteq
	Dun & Bradstreet
Transient population (additional)	Destination DC
	Smithsonian visit counts
Dorm students (additional)	CityTownInfo
	District of Columbia public access
	Online Data Catalog

individuals (along with demographics) grouped into households. The generated population matches marginal demographic distributions from ACS at census block group level and also preserves the anonymity of individuals.

Locating Households: Each synthetic household is then assigned a home location using street data from Navteq and housing structure data from the ACS.

Assigning Activities: Each synthetic individual is assigned a schedule of activities (i.e., home, work, school, shop) to perform during the day. Activity templates are created using the National Household and Travel Survey (NHTS) and data from the National Center for Education Statistics (NCES). Each synthetic household is mapped to a survey household based in its demographic and synthetic individuals are assigned corresponding activities.

Locating Activities: An appropriate activity location (building) is assigned for each activity of an individual. This is done using the gravity model and SIC (Standard Industrial Classification) codes from Dun & Bradstreet (D&B) data.

Transient Population: According to Destination DC [1], there are about 50000 visitors (55% of which are tourists and the rest are business travelers) visiting Washington DC every day. It also provides marginal demographic distributions which are used in conjunction with some rules about the party structure to generate transients along with their demographics, grouped into parties. Each party is assigned a hotel using D&B data. All individuals in a party are assumed to travel together and assigned the same set of activities to perform during a day like staying in a hotel, visiting tourist destinations (or work activities, for business travelers), going to restaurants, and night life activities. Activity locations have been assigned using data from D&B. Activity assignment is also calibrated to match the visit counts at Smithsonian Institution locations.

Dorm students: Synthetic population of dorm students is created for major colleges in the DSA. Data about the number of dorm students in each college and

---

[1] http://washington.org.

college boundary are obtained from CityTownInfo[2] and the District of Columbia public access online Data Catalog[3] respectively. For simplicity, students are assigned only two types of activities, staying in the dorm and school activities located at any of the locations within their college campus.

Apart from demographics and location, agents are defined by many other state variables like health (modeled on 0 to 7 continuum with 0 being dead and 7 being in full health), behavior (as described in next paragraphs), knowledge about healthstates of family members (which gets updated whenever it makes a successful call to a family member or meets him in person), mobility, if agent is out of area, if agent has received emergency broadcast, time of the last call, if last call was successful, etc.

We also model "follow the leader" behavior, i.e., whenever family members encounter each other, they stay together from there on. One of them becomes a leader and others follow him. This kind of behavior is well-documented in disaster literature [13]. Similarly, whenever a person is rescued by someone, he travels with him until he reaches hospital or meets his family on the way.

Our behavior model is conceptually based on the formalism of decentralized semi-Markov decision process with communication (dec-SMDP-com) using the framework of options, as described earlier. We model six behaviors: household reconstitution, evacuation, shelter-seeking, healthcare-seeking, panic, and aid & assist. These high level behaviors are modeled as options which are policies in terms of low-level actions: call, text or move. Whom to call or where to move depends upon the current behavior, e.g., in the household reconstitution option, an agent tries to call or move towards its family member while in healthcare-seeking option, an agent tries to call 911 or move towards nearest hospital. Initiation conditions for options are the factors that affect human behavior, e.g., time elapsed from the time of blast, if an agent is injured, if family is safe, etc. For simplicity, these behaviors are organized in a decision tree (Fig. 2). More details about the behavior model can be found in [29].

4.2   Integrating the Behavior and Microsimulation Models

The simulation is implemented using a database-driven computational architecture [6]. The state of the simulation is maintained in a database table for each iteration (time step). The sequence of operation of modules and data flow are shown in Fig. 3. At each iteration, once the physical environment has been updated, the behavior model chooses an option and action for each agent. Then various infrastructure modules determine the extent to which these actions are successful.

The behavior update is done in three steps: first the agent checks to see if the current option terminates. If so, the agent chooses a new option using the decision tree in Fig. 2. Third, the agent chooses an action based on its current option.

---

[2] http://www.citytowninfo.com/.
[3] http://data.dc.gov.

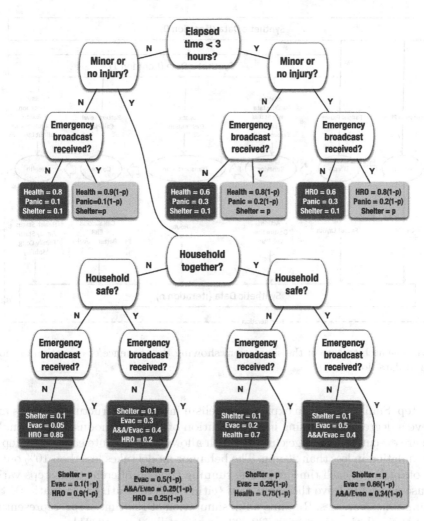

Fig. 2. Decision tree for behavior option selection.

As mentioned earlier, actions involve moving towards some location (or staying at the current location) and attempting to contact someone (by calling or texting). The success of these actions is determined by other modules in the simulation: the routing module determines how far the agent is able to get towards its destination and the cell phone infrastructure module determines the success of calling/texting attempts. These modules take into account the damage to the infrastructure as well as congestion.

In order to achieve scaling, we exploit parallelism in the simulation wherever possible. Behavioral decisions of the agents depend only on other agents at the same location and outcomes of communication attempts at the previous time step. Thus we can parallelize the simulation of the agents at different locations in each

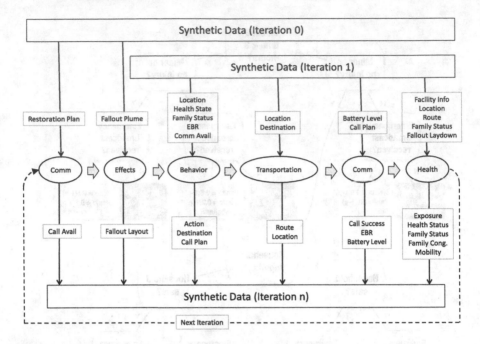

Fig. 3. The architecture of the simulation, showing the sequence of operation of modules and data flow.

time step. Similarly, we can exploit parallelism in the infrastructure modules and achieve a degree of pipelining in the execution of different modules. The simulations are executed on a large cluster, which allows us to execute each time step of the simulation in less than 20 min. The behavior model takes less than 10% out of this total time at each time step. The running time of different time steps varies because as agents leave the simulation (either due to death or evacuation), the running time decreases. Running a full simulation of 100 time steps, representing 2 days of simulation time, with 730,833 agents, still takes over 24 h.

Next we present results from four input scenarios, with 5 replicates for each, which represent over 20 days of computation time.

4.3   Experiments and Results

The primary goal in any emergency situation is to save life, so we evaluate the effect of two factors on health.

The first factor is the probability of sheltering on receiving an emergency broadcast. We choose this factor because it is the recommended strategy in the event of a nuclear explosion to minimize radiation exposure. We assume that authorities would send out emergency broadcasts (EBR) on cell phones, providing information about the event and advising people to shelter. However, prospective surveys [23] suggest that people may not comply with such a directive due to the concern for family members. Hence, we try two values of this factor, 0.1 for the worst case scenario, and 0.9 for the best case scenario.

The second factor is communication as survey [23] suggests that if people can communicate with their family members and establish the safety of their families, they would shelter when being asked to do so. The blast is expected to destroy cell towers near ground zero. Thus, the first case for this factor is a "no communication scenario" where the region that loses mobile phone coverage does not regain it for the period of simulation. The second case is the "partial communication scenario" where cell towers are destroyed in a 0.6 mile radius due to the blast but communication is restored for the 0.6 to 1 mile annular region with 50% capacity within 3 h. This is done by bringing in cells-on-wheels (COWS). Outside the 1 mile radius, communication is available for both cases. These two factors, each with two values, result in a four cell experiment as shown in Table 2.

Table 2. Experiment design.

Cell	P(Shelter|EBR)	Communication restored
1	0.1	No restoration
2	0.1	Partial restoration
3	0.9	No restoration
4	0.9	Partial restoration

Each cell (or experiment) consists of five replicates. We run 100 iterations for each replicate, where first 6 iterations represent 10 min intervals and the rest simulate 30 min intervals, which results in a total simulated time of 2 days. Since radiation levels vary sharply in the first hour, smaller time intervals are simulated for the first hour.

Figure 4 shows differences in numbers of people with low health (moderately injured or worse) between different cells. The difference between cells 3 and 1 is almost zero. This suggests that without restoring communication, increasing the probability of sheltering does not help [25].

Differences between cells 2 and 1 show benefits of restoring communication, even if people do not follow the recommended strategy, sheltering in place. We have shown in our previous work [29] that the communication affects behavior in multiple ways. As people are able to receive emergency broadcast and make successful 911 calls, the number of people panicking reduces. This makes people switch to other behaviors early on in cell 2. Also, as people are able to communicate and establish safety of family members, they are more likely to aid & assist others which has a positive impact on health.

As expected, cell 4 has the best outcomes across all cells because both communication is restored partially and people also comply with the recommended action of sheltering on receiving EBR.

Surprisingly, restoring communication with low probability of sheltering (cell 2) is better than the scenario where people follow the current recommended strategy of sheltering in place (cell 3) (Fig. 4). Figure 5 shows differences in number of people with each behavior between cells 2 and 3. Initially cell 2 is worse off because a large number of people are doing household reconstitution, seeking healthcare, and evacuating, which make them go outside and exposed to more radiation. While in cell 3 more people are sheltering. But later on, cell 2 has better outcomes because even though a large number of people are evacuating, many turn to aiding & assisting others as they are able to communicate and establish safety of family members in cell 2. There are about 2100–2450 people engaged in aid & assist behavior after 20 iterations (about 8 h) which has a direct effect on saving life. While in cell 3, more people turned to household reconstitution behavior and hence were exposed to radiation.

In order to gain further insight into the spatio-temporal patterns of behaviors across cells 2 and 3, we use tensor decomposition. A tensor is a multidimensional or n-way array, for example, a vector is a first-order tensor, a matrix is a second-order tensor, and tensors of order three or higher are called higher-order tensors. Tensor decomposition methods like CANDECOMP (canonical decomposition), also known as PARAFAC (parallel factorization) decomposition, and Tucker decomposition can be considered as a higher-order generalizations of the matrix singular value decomposition (SVD) and principal components analysis (PCA) techniques. Here we use PARAFAC decomposition because it has a unique solution which makes it easier to compare results for two different cells. It factorizes

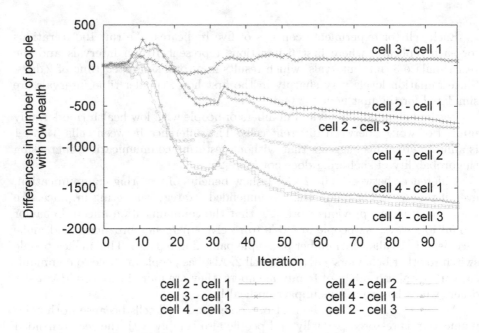

Fig. 4. Differences in numbers of people with low health

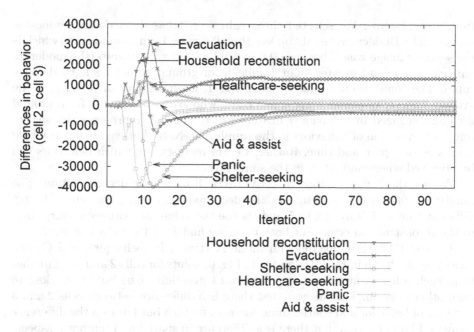

Fig. 5. Differences in behavior between cells 2 and 3

a tensor into a sum of rank-one tensors, for example, for a third-order tensor $\mathcal{X} \in \mathbb{R}^{I \times J \times K}$,

$$\mathcal{X} \approx \sum_{r=1}^{R} \mathbf{a}_r \circ \mathbf{b}_r \circ \mathbf{c}_r \qquad (1)$$

where R is a positive integer and $\mathbf{a}_r \in \mathbb{R}^I$, $\mathbf{b}_r \in \mathbb{R}^J$, and $\mathbf{c}_r \in \mathbb{R}^K$, and $\circ$ represents the vector outer product. Each element of $\mathcal{X}$ can be calculated as

$$x_{ijk} \approx \sum_{r=1}^{R} a_{ir} \times b_{jr} \times c_{kr}, \qquad (2)$$

where $1 \leq i \leq I$, $1 \leq j \leq J$, and $1 \leq k \leq K$. Vectors $\mathbf{a}_r$s are column-wise arranged into a matrix $\mathbf{A}$ and similarly vectors $\mathbf{b}_r$s and $\mathbf{c}_r$s into matrices $\mathbf{B}$ and $\mathbf{C}$, respectively. Matrices $\mathbf{A}$, $\mathbf{B}$, and $\mathbf{C}$ are known as the factors or loadings. PARAFAC decomposition has been used for clustering [27], classification [7], and network discovery [12]. Details about PARAFAC and other tensor decompositions can be found in [21].

We compute the spatio-temporal decomposition of behaviors for cells 2 and 3. For each cell, we create an order-three tensor. Here, the first dimension represents temporal scale, i.e., iterations in the simulation, where the first 6 iterations represent 10 min each and the rest represent 30 min of time interval each, with 99 iterations (about 48 h) in total. The second dimension represents 6 behaviors as mentioned earlier. The third dimension represents spatial components (distance from ground zero). We selected three values of it based on damage zones as suggested by Buddemeier et al. [9]: less than 0.6 miles from ground zero (which is the severe damage zone), between 0.6 to 1 mile from ground zero (the moderate damage zone), and greater than 1 mile from ground zero (the light damage zone). The zones are also illustrated in Fig. 1. Each element of $\mathcal{X}$, x_{ijk}, is the average number of people (across five runs) who are at distance k from ground zero and engaged in behavior j in iteration i. Thus, $\mathcal{X}$ represents the spatio-temporal evolution of behaviors in the simulation. Note that we are not tracking agents across space and time. Rather, we are representing which behaviors can be observed where and when in the simulation.

We use the N-way toolbox for MATLAB [4] for tensor decomposition. The number of factors, R, to retain in the decomposition is a parameter. We try different values of R from 2 to 5 and choose the value that causes a sharp drop in the reconstruction error. For both cells, we find $R = 3$ gives a low error.

Plots of PARAFAC loadings for mode $\mathbf{A}$ (time), $\mathbf{B}$ (behavior), and $\mathbf{C}$ (distance) are as shown in Figs. 6, 7 and 8. In Fig. 6, points for cells 2 and 3 are further from each other in first few hours (about 14 iterations, 5 h) but come close to each other later on. This suggest that there is a difference between cells 2 and 3 in terms of behavior and spatial dimensions in first 5 h but later on the difference reduces. Figure 7 shows that there is a difference in spatial and temporal aspects of evacuation and sheltering behaviors and to a smaller extent for household constitution behavior between cells 2 and 3. On the other hand, spatial and temporal aspects are similar for healthcare-seeking, panic, and aid & assist behaviors.

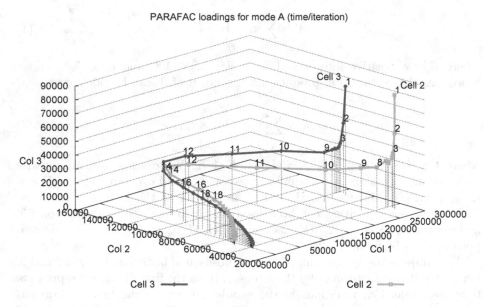

Fig. 6. PARAFAC loadings for mode $\mathbf{A}$ (time/iteration), for cells 2 and 3. Here, labels on points show iteration numbers.

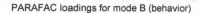

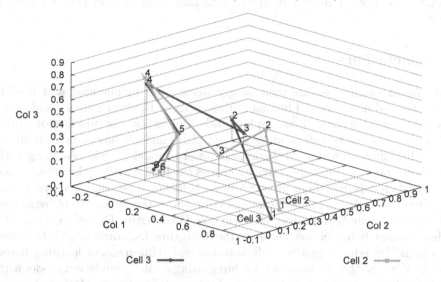

Fig. 7. PARAFAC loadings for mode **B** (Behaviors), for cells 2 and 3. Here, labels on points show behaviors as follows: 1-Household reconstitution, 2-Evacuation, 3-Shelter-seeking, 4-Healthcare-seeking, 5-Panic, 6-Aid & assist.

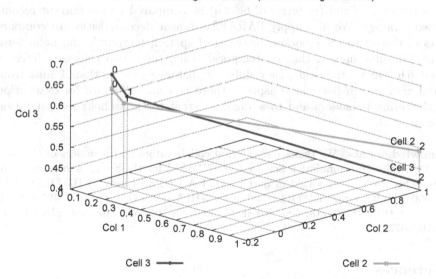

Fig. 8. PARAFAC loadings for mode **C** (distance from ground zero), for cells 2 and 3. Here, labels on points show distance as follows: 0-less than 0.6 mile, 1-between 0.6 and 1 mile, 2-greater than 1 mile.

Finally, Fig. 8 shows that temporal and behavioral aspects are similar near ground zero (upto 1 mile) but different further from ground zero for cells 2 and 3.

5   Conclusion

Agent-based simulations are increasingly being used in planning and modeling for natural disasters and human initiated crises. Designing such simulations requires knowledge about demographics and geographical distributions of a population of a region as well as modeling natural human behavior in such situations. Microsimulations or synthetic populations model individuals along with their demographics and daily activity routines (including activity location) while behavioral models explain or predict human behavior based on the current context. Here, we focus on modeling human behavior in the aftermath of hypothetical improvised nuclear device detonation in Washington DC metro area. We review various behavior models from the literature including health behavior models, BDI model, cognitive architectures, and reinforcement learning based models. We describe our approach for integrating a microsimulation model with our behavior model which is based on the formalism of semi-Markov decision process with communication, using the framework of options. We model six behaviors: household reconstitution, evacuation, sheltering, panic, healthcare-seeking, and aid & assist. Finally, we present experiments evaluating the effects of sheltering (which is the recommended strategy) and infrastructural intervention (restoring communication partially). Surprisingly, infrastructure based intervention is more beneficial (in terms of health) as compared to the current recommended strategy. We also apply PARAFAC tensor decomposition to compare effects of these two interventions in terms of spatial, temporal, and behavioral aspects. Results suggest that on temporal scale, these two cells are different in first 5 h. On spatial scale, they differ at distance greater than 1 mile from ground zero and in behavioral aspects, there is some difference for evacuation and sheltering behaviors and to a smaller extent for household reconstitution behavior.

Acknowledgments. We thank our external collaborators and members of the Network Dynamics and Simulation Science Lab (NDSSL) for their suggestions and comments. This work is supported in part by DTRA CNIMS Contract HDTRA1-11-D-0016-0001, DTRA Grant HDTRA1-11-1-0016, NIH MIDAS Grant 5U01GM070694-11, NIH Grant 1R01GM109718, NSF NetSE Grant CNS-1011769, and NSF SDCI Grant OCI-1032677.

References

1. Adiga, A., Mortveit, H.S., Wu, S.: Route stability in large-scale transportation systems. In: The Workshop on Multiagent Interaction Networks (MAIN), Held in Conjunction with AAMAS 2013, pp. 3–8, St. Paul, MN, USA, 7 May 2013

2. Ajzen, I.: From intentions to actions: a theory of planned behavior. In: Kuhl, J., Beckmann, J. (eds.) Action Control, pp. 11–39. Springer, Heidelberg (1985). doi:10.1007/978-3-642-69746-3_2

3. Anderson, J.R., Bothell, D., Byrne, M.D., Douglass, S., Lebiere, C., Qin, Y.: An integrated theory of the mind. Psychol. Rev. **111**(4), 1036–1060 (2004)

4. Andersson, C.A., Bro, R.: The N-way toolbox for MATLAB. Chemometr. Intell. Lab. Syst. **52**(1), 1–4 (2000)

5. Barrett, C., Beckman, R., Berkbigler, K., Bisset, K., Bush, B., Campbell, K., Eubank, S., Henson, K., Hurford, J., Kubicek, D., Marathe, M., Romero, P., Smith, J., Smith, L., Speckman, P., Stretz, P., Thayer, G., Eeckhout, E., Williams, M.D.: TRANSIMS: Transportation analysis and simulation system. Technical report LA-UR-00-1725, Los Alamos National Laboratory (2001)

6. Barrett, C., Bisset, K., Chandan, S., Chen, J., Chungbaek, Y., Eubank, S., Evrenosoğlu, Y., Lewis, B., Lum, K., Marathe, A., Marathe, M., Mortveit, H., Parikh, N., Phadke, A., Reed, J., Rivers, C., Saha, S., Stretz, P., Swarup, S., Thorp, J., Vullikanti, A., Xie, D.: Planning, response in the aftermath of a large crisis: an agent-based informatics framework. In: Pasupathy, R., Kim, S.-H., Tolk, A., Hill, R., Kuhl, M.E. (eds.) Proceedings of the 2013 Winter Simulation Conference, pp. 1515–1526 (2013)

7. Bauckhage, C.: Robust tensor classifiers for color object recognition. In: Kamel, M., Campilho, A. (eds.) ICIAR 2007. LNCS, vol. 4633, pp. 352–363. Springer, Heidelberg (2007). doi:10.1007/978-3-540-74260-9_32

8. Beckman, R.J., Baggerly, K.A., McKay, M.D.: Creating synthetic baseline populations. Transp. Res. Part A Policy Pract. **30**(6), 415–429 (1996)

9. Buddemeier, B.R., Valentine, J.E., Millage, K.K., Brandt, L.D., Region, N.C.: Key response planning factors for the aftermath of nuclear terrorism. Technical report LLNL-TR-512111, Lawrence Livermore National Lab, November 2011

10. Chandan, S., Saha, S., Barrett, C., Eubank, S., Marathe, A., Marathe, M., Swarup, S., Vullikanti, A.K.S.: Modeling the interaction between emergency communications and behavior in the aftermath of a disaster. In: Greenberg, A.M., Kennedy, W.G., Bos, N.D. (eds.) SBP 2013. LNCS, vol. 7812, pp. 476–485. Springer, Heidelberg (2013). doi:10.1007/978-3-642-37210-0_52

11. Das, T.K., Gosavi, A., Mahadevan, S., Marchalleck, N.: Solving semi-Markov decision problems using average reward reinforcement learning. Manag. Sci. **45**, 560–574 (1999)

12. Davidson, I., Gilpin, S., Carmichael, O., Walker, P.: Network discovery via constrained tensor analysis of fMRI data. In: Proceedings of the 19th ACM SIGKDD International Conference on Knowledge Discovery and Data Mining, KDD 2013, pp. 194–202. ACM, New York (2013)

13. Drabek, T.E., Boggs, K.S.: Families in disaster: reactions and relatives. J. Marriage Fam. **30**, 443–451 (1968)

14. Duch, W., Oentaryo, R.J., Pasquier, M.: Cognitive architectures: where do we go from here? In: Proceedings of the 2008 Conference on Artificial General Intelligence 2008: Proceedings of the First AGI Conference, pp. 122–136. IOS Press, Amsterdam (2008)

15. Durham, D.P., Casman, E.A.: Incorporating individual health-protective decisions into disease transmission models: a mathematical framework. J. R. Soc. Interface **9**(68), 562–570 (2012)

16. Fishbein, M., Ajzen, I.: Belief, Attitude, Intention and Behavior: An Introduction to Theory and Research. Addison-Wesley, Reading (1975)

17. Georgeff, M., Pell, B., Pollack, M., Tambe, M., Wooldridge, M.: The belief-desire-intention model of agency. In: Proceedings of Intelligent Agents V. Agent Theories, Architectures, Languages: 5th International Workshop, ATAL 1998, Paris, France, July 1998, p. 630 (2000)

18. Huynh, N., Namazi-Rad, M.-R., Perez, P., Berryman, M.J., Chen, Q.: Generating a synthetic population in support of agent-based modeling of transportation in Sydney. In: 20th International Congress on Modelling and Simulation (MODSIM 2013), pp. 1357–1363 (2013)

19. Huynh, N.N., Cao, V., Denagamage, R.W., Berryman, M., Perez, P.: An agent based model for the simulation of road traffic and transport demand in a Sydney metropolitan area. In: Proceedings of the Eighth International Workshop on Agents in Traffic and Transportation, pp. 1–7, May 2014

20. Karimi, E., Schmitt, K., Akgunduz, A.: Effect of individual protective behaviors on influenza transmission: an agent-based model. Health Care Manag. Sci. **18**(3), 318–333 (2015)

21. Kolda, T.G., Bader, B.W.: Tensor decompositions and applications. SIAM Rev. **51**(3), 455–500 (2009)

22. Laird, J.E.: Extending the Soar cognitive architecture. In: Proceedings of the 2008 Conference on Artificial General Intelligence 2008: Proceedings of the First AGI Conference, pp. 224–235. IOS Press, Amsterdam (2008)

23. Lasker, R.D., Hunter, N.D., Francis, S.E.: With the Public's Knowledge, We Can Make Sheltering in Place Possible. New York Academy of Medicine, New York (2007)

24. Lewis, B., Swarup, S., Bisset, K., Eubank, S., Marathe, M., Barrett, C.: A simulation environment for the dynamic evaluation of disaster preparedness policies. J. Public Health Manag. Pract. **19**, S42–S48 (2013)

25. Marathe, M., Mortveit, H., Parikh, N., Swarup, S.: Prescriptive analytics using synthetic information. In: Hsu, W.H. (ed) Emerging Trends in Predictive Analytics: Risk Management and Decision Making, pp. 1–19. IGI Global (2014)

26. Marr, D.: Vision: A Computational Approach. Freeman & Co., San Francisco (1982)

27. Mirzal, A., Furukawa, M.: Node-context network clustering using PARAFAC tensor decomposition. In: International Conference on Information & Communication Technology and Systems Discover the World's Resea, pp. 283–288 (2010)

28. Padgham, L., Nagel, K., Singh, D., Chen, Q.: Integrating BDI agents into a MAT-Sim simulation. In: Proceedings of the 21st European Conference on Artificial Intelligence, pp. 681–686, August 2014

29. Parikh, N., Swarup, S., Stretz, P.E., Rivers, C.M., Lewis, B.L., Marathe, M.V., Eubank, S.G., Barrett, C.L., Lum, K., Chungbaek, Y.: Modeling human behavior in the aftermath of a hypothetical improvised nuclear detonation. In: Proceedings of the International Conference on Autonomous Agents and Multiagent Systems (AAMAS), Saint Paul, MN, USA, pp. 949–956, May 2013

30. Parikh, N., Youssef, M., Swarup, S., Eubank, S.: Modeling the effect of transient populations on epidemics in Washington DC. Scientific Reports, 3: Art 3152, November 2013

31. Perry, R.W., Lindell, M.K.: Understanding citizen response to disasters with implications for terrorism. J. Contingencies Crisis Manag. **11**(2), 49–60 (2003)

32. Robinson, S.A., Stringer, M., Rai, V., Tondon, A.: GIS-integrated agent-based model of residential solar PV diffusion. In: 32nd USAEE/IAEE North American Conference, pp. 28–31 (2013)

33. Rosenstock, I.M.: Historical origins of the health belief model. Health Educ. Monogr. **2**(4), 328–335 (1974)
34. Rossetti, R.J., Bordini, R.H., Bazzan, A.L., Bampi, S., Liu, R., Vliet, D.V.: Using BDI agents to improve driver modelling in a commuter scenario. Transp. Res. Part C Emerg. Technol. **10**(5–6), 373–398 (2002)
35. Schwarz, N., Ernst, A.: Agent-based modeling of the diffusion of environmental innovations an empirical approach. Technol. Forecast. Soc. Chang. **76**(4), 497–511 (2009). Evolutionary Methodologies for Analyzing Environmental Innovations and the Implications for Environmental Policy
36. Shendarkar, A., Vasudevan, K., Lee, S., Son, Y.-J.: Crowd simulation for emergency response using BDI agents based on immersive virtual reality. Simul. Model. Pract. Theory **16**(9), 1415–1429 (2008)
37. Sutton, R., Precup, D., Singh, S.: Between MDPs and semi-MDPs: a framework for temporal abstraction in reinforcement learning. Artif. Intell. **112**(1–2), 181–211 (1999)

Agent-Based Modelling for Urban Planning Current Limitations and Future Trends

Pascal Perez[1](✉), Arnaud Banos[2], and Chris Pettit[3]

[1] SMART Infrastructure Facility, University of Wollongong, Wollongong, Australia
pascal@uow.edu.au
[2] UMR Géographie-cités, CNRS, Paris, France
arnaud.banos@parisgeo.cnrs.fr
[3] City Futures Research Centre, University of New South Wales,
Kensington, Australia
c.pettit@unsw.edu.au

Abstract. With the global population expected to increase form 7.3 billion in 2015 to 9.5 billion by 2050 [41], smart city planning is becoming increasingly important. This is further exasperated by the fact that an increasing number of people are relocating to cities as we live in a highly urbanised world. Cities are evolving in complex and multi-dimensional ways that can no longer be limited to land use and transport development. In increasingly important that cities planning embraces a more holistic, participatory and iterative approach that balances productivity, livability and sustainability outcomes. A new generation of bottom up, highly granular, highly dynamic and spatially explicit models have emerged to support evidence-based and adaptive urban planning. Agent-based modelling, in particular, has emerged as a dominant paradigm to create massive simulations backed by ever-increasing computing power. In this paper we point at current limitations of pure bottom-up approaches to urban modelling and argue for more flexible frameworks mixing other modelling paradigms, particularly participatory planning approaches. Then, we explore four modelling challenges and propose future trends for agent-based modelling of urban systems to better support planning decisions.

Keywords: Agent-based modelling · Key challenges · Urban modelling · Urban planning

1 Introduction

Over the last 50 years, urban planning has drastically evolved from a traditional top-down and linear process of survey-analysis-plan to a more integrated and inclusive approach whereby cities are considered as systems of increasingly

A. Banos—While joining SMART Infrastructure Facility as a Visiting Professorial Fellow for three months (july-august-september 2016), Arnaud Banos benefited from the International Mobility Support Program (edition 2016) - InSHS-CNRS.

M.-R. Namazi-Rad et al. (Eds.): ABMUS 2016, LNAI 10051, pp. 60–69, 2017.
DOI: 10.1007/978-3-319-51957-9_4

interconnected parts (Chadwick, 1971, cited in [15] p. 3). This evolution coincides with the transformation of modern cities into evermore complex organisms in which social, material and information flows grow always faster while relying on infrastructure systems characterised by stronger inertia. Samuel Arbesman describes this clumsy though functional patching as an urban 'kludge' [1]. In this context, comprehensive monitoring of cities to better inform planning has led to the broad appeal of so-called 'smart cities'. However, a fully comprehensive monitoring of cities has proved to be unrealistic to date, leading Couch ([15], p. 4) to suggest an alternate strategy inspired by Etzione whereby a mixed-scanning approach allows for a light touch routine monitoring able to detect abnormalities justifying more detailed urban investigations.

Since the early 50s, urban planners have increasingly relied on models to better understand and predict the consequences of urban policies on land use, transport and people's wellbeing. Batty [6] suggests that successive urban modelling paradigms can hardly be dissociated from their object (city), purpose (planning) and inputs (data) ; thus, this "intersecting time line" implies that urban models are strongly history-contingent and context-dependent metaphors (Fig. 1). For example, centralised urban planning backed by strong market drivers characterised the 60s and partly explained the reliance on static macro-economic models. In contrast, current best practice urban planning is driven by bottom up participatory approaches and thus bottom up CA and thus bottom up agent based modelling provide a suitable support modelling paradigm.

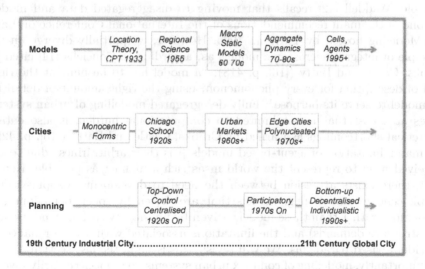

Fig. 1. Intersecting models, cities and planning time lines, reproduced from [6]

2   Current Limitations in Urban Modelling

This evolution suffers from various imperfections, as these timelines are loosely synchronized the intensity of synchronisation depending on theoretical advances in planning and modelling, as well as technological ones in urbanism and computing. This issue was first identified by Lee in his famous requiem [25] and analysed by Michael Batty [5] twenty years ago: the major reasons for lack of practical applications, in our view, are the volatility of the problem context that planning addresses and our inability to develop tools sufficiently robust to withstand such shifts in viewpoint ([5], p. 7). Despite significant computing advances this was still an issue of concern until recently as cities are getting more complex at a rate faster than we can develop theories for their understanding [8]. The current period might bring a tighter synchronization as it is largely admitted that: (1) cities can and should be interpreted as complex adaptive systems ([7,10]), (2) urban planning should evolve towards a more bottom-up and decentralized process ([15,33]) and (3) urban models may not be seen anymore as predictive black boxes but rather as mediating objects accompanying knowledge building and sharing in an ever changing complex environment ([7,29]).

Unsurprisingly, these three characteristics converge with the fundamental properties of agent-based modelling. In this context, several authors like Rasouli and Timmermans ([35], p. 19) call for a shift towards more integral microscopic models of choice behavior, allowing more integral policy performance assessments. Such an emphasis on desegregation is by no means a recent one; for example, Waddell [42] recalls that moving to disaggregated data and models was one of the main recommendations of the International Conference on Land Use Modeling hosted by TMIP in 1995. However, we partially diverge on the principle of integral microscopic models as, according to Couclelis [14] cited by Crooks, Castle and Batty ([16], p. 418), "a model has to be built at the right level of description for every phenomenon, using the right amount of detail for the model to serve its purpose". Fully desegregated modelling of urban systems comes at a cost that is not limited to computational burden, it also entails theoretical shortcomings as warned by Crooks, Castle and Batty ([16], p. 429): one major limitation of agent-based models [] is their arbitrariness due to the perceived need to represent the world in as rich a manner as possible. Henceforth, there exists a tension between the need to develop more sophisticated 'people-centric' models (e.g. models that are driven by social behaviour and interactions rather than those models driven by physicality such as land use and infrastructure demands) and the limitations associated with a pure reliance on individual-based paradigms. We will revisit this issue in the last section.

Importantly, modelling of complex urban systems does not necessarily involve developing complex models - a complex model being different from a model of a complex system. Following Axelrod [3], we argue that the complexity of a model - especially of agent-based ones - might reside in its simulation outputs, not in its hypotheses and structure. More to the point, Simon [37] emphasized how exploring a complex system can be done with simple models. In an urban modelling context, [21] concludes that unraveling complexity requires complex

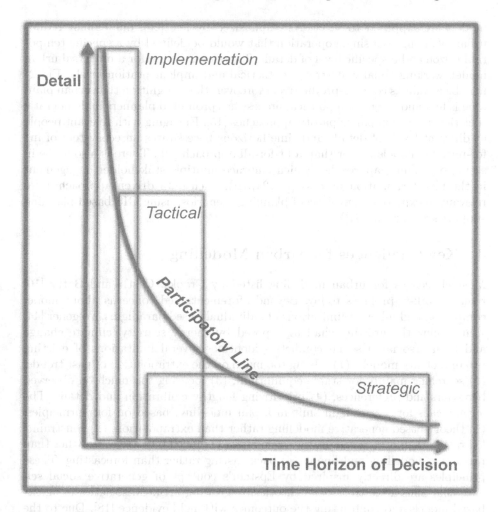

Fig. 2. Trade-offs among strategic, tactical and implementation planning and the necessity to include participation at every stage of the process (adapted from [26], p. 38)

and sophisticated analysis. If such analysis is supported by models, then the modeling system is bound to be complex (although it may be composed of simpler and more readily understandable sector components) ([21], p. 33).

Brömmelstroet and Pelzer [11] warn against the temptation of developing too complicated models as progress in computational power and availability of more data on higher levels of detail has allowed models to move into a higher level of detail, both in their structure (e.g., agent-based, CA) as well as in their geographical scale. Yet these models are much less operational for policy purposes than the previous generation of land-use-transport models, and are largely pedagogic in emphasis and often intent ([11], p. 383). This somehow counter-intuitive statement needs to be evaluated in the context of urban planning processes these models are supposed to serve. As emphasized by Lee [26], one cannot reduce urban planning to a single operation that would be defined by a specific temporal horizon and a specific level of details. Therefore, aiming for a universal urban model, working equally at strategic, tactical and implementation levels (Fig. 2) may be as vain as counter-productive. Moreover, the recognition that urban planning is first and foremost a political process has prompted planners in democratic societies to develop participatory approaches [15]. Engaging with relevant people at different levels of details and time horizons necessitates an ecosystem of fit-for-purpose models rather than a fit-for-all approach [29]. There is also a rise in scenario planning approaches which embrace multiple stakeholder engagement in the plan formulation process ([23,24,32]). Such data driven approaches are relevant to explore an envelope of planning scenarios, using GIS based planning support systems ([30,31]).

3   Key Challenges for Urban Modelling

Most challenges for urban modelling listed by Crooks, Castle and Batty [16] remain work-in-progress today. Beyond aforementioned concerns about model complexity and inherent limitations of individual-based paradigms, Wegener [44] - envisaging the growing challenges posed by energy scarcity, climate change and their associated social conflicts - identifies several limitations of existing urban mobility models: (1) relying too much on the extrapolation of past trends, (2) searching mainly for stable equilibrium, (3) focusing too much on observed behaviors and preferences, (4) prioritizing lengthy calibration and details. The author calls for a paradigm shift in urban modeling, based on four principles: (1) theory-based generative modelling rather than extrapolation, (2) constraint-led rather than preference-driven modelling, (3) plausibility analysis rather than predictive modelling and finally (4) back-casting rather than forecasting. These principles are directly inspired by Epstein's concept of generative social science that aims at testing social theories by growing artificial societies in agent-based models and confronting the outcomes with field evidence [18]. Due to the complexity of urban systems and the fragmented nature of evidence, the proposed paradigm shift can only operate in a multi-disciplinary environment which embraces a what if? exploratory scenario planning approach which is driven by the best available data, models combined with expert and citizen opinions.

These challenges can also be addressed according to core features of urban planning. Modern urban planning is characterized by (1) the complexity of urban processes and their responses to policies, (2) the multi-dimensional nature of urban planning's focus and outcomes, (3) the necessity to deliver plausible futures for cities and (4) the increasing demand for participative policy-making in democratic societies [16].

3.1   Addressing the Complexity of Urban Processes

Following Harris [21] and Crooks, Castle and Batty [16], we don't see any advantage in building massive and highly detailed agent-based models of urban systems for the only reason that modern computing allows it. Arbitrary heuristics and intractable feedback loops will always limit the analytical power of these cybernetic juggernauts. We suggest instead developing modular architectures that can host complementary modelling paradigms in different and fit-for-purpose modules. Each module would allow for proper and replicable theory testing and should reduce path dependencies and lock-in effects. For example, a well-designed modular architecture would allow for continuous traffic modelling [20] to co-exist with traffic micro-simulation [4] or agent-based transport demand modelling [22]. Although the need for hybrid traffic models has been long identified [12], there is still a need for operational models to be developed (see [39]). Hybridization can affect both lateral interactions between various classes of agents and hierarchically nested architectures. Melbourne-Thomas et al. [28] provide an example of a simulation model coupling within a cellular automaton a differential equation-based model of fish-coral-algae dynamics and an agent-based model of coastal development and fishing activities along the Yucatan peninsula (Mexico). This approach allowed for the integration and validation of phase transitions in the ecological model and for the creation of an empirical model of human activities based on historical records and social surveys. Pumain and Sanders [34] provide a comparison of various hierarchical architectures in the context of interconnected cities.

As long as the theoretical integrity and tractability of each module is preserved, these agent-based architectures can be massively distributed on high performance computing (HPC) clusters. Connectivity and interoperability between modules can efficiently be dealt with hierarchical formalisms like DEVS [45]. However, regardless of their architecture and constituting modules, validation of such modelling frameworks will always require mixed methods approaches, involving direct observations, model-to-model comparison and expert judgment [27].

3.2   Addressing the Multi-dimensional Nature of Urban Growth

As urban growth has long been recognised as a multi-dimensional process [15], these various dimensions apply not only to planning outcomes, but also to the processes influencing or being affected by policy decisions. While some integrated models already take into account some of these dimensions like land use, transport and residential mobility ([4,22]), none of them to date are able to preserve the integrity of embedded social entities. Ideally, these models should be able to link individual behaviours across various dimensions of urban life (switch on the light, turn on the tap, drive the car,) in order to take into account essential trade-offs and synergies.

Within a modular and incremental architecture ([13]), ontology-based synthetic populations could feed into various conceptual modules describing relevant urban components. At the implementation level shuttle models would encapsulate simplified or limited combinations of the modules in order to engage with specific stakeholders on a given set of issues. Following Perez ([29], p. 156), these shuttle models, to be consistent with the global conceptual model, would need to respect the integrity of a common ontological architecture. Each interactive model could use a subset of ontological components or simplified versions of some of them as long as their local solution space doesn't violate the boundaries of the overall solution space generated by the core model.

3.3 Addressing the Need to Deliver Plausible Futures for Urban Systems

Trend-based forecasting models aren't suitable for exploring the evolution of complex urban systems as they are characterised by (1) strong path dependency [2] and (2) endogenous and sometimes spontaneous changes [38]. Therefore data-driven extrapolations have to be replaced by theory-driven generative approaches [18], favouring back-casting reconstruction of past urban dynamics in order to validate endogenous assumptions and detect path dependencies before moving into forecasting mode [36]. In this context, data assimilation methods, guiding simulated urban forecasts, will play an increasingly important role [43]. The use of evolving synthetic populations rather than demographic trend-based projections is also becoming an alternative approach to develop more plausible futures [22]. Finally, when it comes to individual and collective behaviours, we need to move from traditional preference-based utility functions to alternative approaches focusing on response and adaptation to constraints in order to develop more robust and more plausible constraint-based scenarios [19].

3.4 Addressing the Need for Participation in Urban Planning

The political nature of urban planning has first forced authorities in democratic societies to communicate with communities through public consultations and exhibitions [15]. Then, some twenty years ago, they have taken advantage of advances in information technology to properly engage with communities through participation. Three approaches are particularly suited to coupling with urban modelling. First, Virtual Reality (VR) technology allows for 3D visualisation of actual and hypothetical urban spaces that can be assessed by various groups of stakeholders [40]. Participatory Planning Support Systems (PPSS), such as What if? can be used to discuss and select various planning scenarios ([24,30]). Finally, serious gaming and Role Playing Games (RPG) have proven highly successful in creating consensus around specific planning options in contexts like infrastructure renewal [17] or peri-urbanisation [9]. The development of these games can be easily associated with the concept of shuttle model proposed by Perez [29] whereby each game aims at exploring specific aspects or issues of a broader urban model with relevant participants in order to provide them with deeper insights and/or eliciting new knowledge to enrich or validate the core model.

4   Conclusions

Understanding the dynamic of urban systems, in an era of ever growing complexity, is more than ever of crucial importance. Increased collaborations between scientific research and urban planning are needed. Moreover, pushing towards more individual-based and people-centric approaches should not dismiss the importance of (1) multi-scale both spatial and temporal protocols, and (2) coupling whenever needed theories, concepts, formalisms and technologies. Urban modelling for urban planning needs to move away from massively distributed individual-based models in order to concentrate on more modular approaches mixing various modelling paradigms. The latter have proven their efficiency in testing theories dealing with the complexity of urban systems and the multidimensional nature of urban growth, in order to build and explore plausible trajectories of urban systems.

All the above cannot improve outcomes from urban planning without taking into account its political nature. In democratic societies, participation has become a vade mecum of urban planning. However, we argue that more needs to be done in order to involve stakeholders in the modelling process itself. Participatory modelling may therefore help bridging the gap between public expectations and policy makers.

This is an ambitious agenda that will need the multiplication of mediating forums between modellers and planners (such as the Centre for Urban Science and Progress in New York, the Advanced Urban Modelling Conference in Cambridge or the UrbanGrowth NSW University Roundtable in Australia). We hope that the Agent-Based Modelling for Urban Systems (ABMUS) community will become one of these international forums. Such a bottom up modelling approach lends itself to being incorporated in What if? scenario planning support system methodologies and offer great potential in assisting city planning endeavours as we plan for a global population fast approaching 10 billion.

References

1. Arbesman, S.: Overcomplicated: Technology at the Limits of Comprehension. Current, New-York (2016). 244 p
2. Arthur, B.: Urban systems and historical path dependence. In: Ausubel, J., Herman, R. (eds.) Cities and Their Vital Systems: Infrastructure Past, Present and Future, pp. 85–97. National Academy of Engineering, Washington DC (1988)
3. Axelrod, R.: The Complexity of Cooperation: Agent-Based Models of Competition and Collaboration. Princeton Studies in Complexity. Princeton University Press, NJ (1997). 232 p
4. Balmer, M., Axhausen, K., Nagel, K.: Agent-based demand-modeling framework for large-scale microsimulations. Transp. Res. Rec. J. Transp. Res. Board **1985**, 125–134 (2004)
5. Batty, M.: A chronicle of scientific planning: the Anglo-American modeling experience. J. Am. Plann. Assoc. **60**(1), 7–16 (1994)
6. Batty, M.: Fifty Years of urban modeling: macro-statics to micro-dynamics. In: Albeverio, S., Andrey, D., Giordano, P., Vancheri, A. (eds.) The Dynamics of Complex Urban Systems An Interdisciplinary Approach, pp. 1–20. Physica-Verlag, Heidelberg (2008)
7. Batty, M.: The New Science of Cities. MIT Press, US (2013)

8. Batty, M.: Can it happen again? planning support, Lee's requiem and the rise of the smart cities movement. Environ. Plann. B Plann. Des. **41**, 388–391 (2014)

9. Becu, N., Frascaria-Lacoste, N., Latune, J.: Experiential learning based on the newdistrict asymmetric simulation game: results of a dozen gameplay sessions. In: Hybrid Simulation and Gaming in the Networked Society: The 46th ISAGA Annual Conference 2015 (2016). www.hal-01253024

10. Bretagnolle, A., Daude, E., Pumain, D.: From theory to modelling: urban systems as complex systems. Cybergeo Eur. J. Geogr. (2006). http://cybergeo.revues.org/2420. Accessed 19 Sep 16

11. Brommelstroet, M., Pelzer, P.: Forty years after Lee's requiem: are we beyond the seven sins? Environ. Plann. B Plann. Des. **41**, 381–391 (2014)

12. Casas, J., Perarnau, J., Torday, A.: The need to combine different traffic modelling levels for effectively tackling large scale projects adding a hybrid meso/micro approach. Procedia Soc. Behav. Sci. **20**, 251–262 (2011)

13. Cottineau, C., Chapron, P., Reuillon, R.: Growing models from the bottom up. An evaluation-based incremental modelling method (EBIMM) applied to the simulation of systems of cities. J. Artif. Soc. Soc. Simul. **18**(4), 9 (2015)

14. Couclelis, H.: Modelling frameworks, paradigms, and approaches. In: Clarke, K.C., Parks, B.E., Crane, M.P. (eds.) Geographic Information Systems and Environmental Modelling. Prentice Hall, London (2002)

15. Couch, C.: Urban Planning: An Introduction. Palgrave Macmillan, London (2016). 344 p

16. Crooks, A., Castle, C., Batty, M.: Key challenges in agent-based modelling for geo-spatial simulation. Comput. Environ. Urban Syst. **32**(6), 417–430 (2008)

17. Dray, A., Perez, P., Jones, N., Le Page, C., D'Aquino, P., White, I., Auatabu, T.: The AtollGame experience: from knowledge engineering to a computer-assisted role playing game. J. Artif. Soc. Soc. Simul. **9**, 1 (2006)

18. Epstein, J.M.: Generative Social Science: Studies in Agent-Based Computational Modeling. Princeton University Press, Princeton (2007). 350 p

19. Fosset, P., Banos, A., Beck, E., Chardonnel, S., Lang, C., Marilleau, N., Thévenin, T.: Exploring intra-urban accessibility and impacts of pollution policies with an agent-based simulation platform: GaMiroD. Systems **4**, 5 (2016)

20. Geroliminis, N., Sun, J.: Properties of a well-defined macroscopic fundamental diagram for urban traffic. Transp. Res. Part B **45**, 605–617 (2011)

21. Harris, B.: The real issues concerning Lee's requiem. J. Am. Plann. Assoc. **60**(1), 31–34 (1994)

22. Huynh, N., Perez, P., Berryman, M., Barthelemy, J.: Simulating Transport and land use interdependencies for strategic urban planning - an agent based modelling approach. Systems **3**(4), 177–210 (2015)

23. Klosterman, R.E.: The what if? collaborative planning support system. Environ. Plann. B Plann. Des. **26**(3), 393–408 (1999)

24. Klosterman, R.E., Pettit, C.J.: An update on planning support systems. Environ. Plann. B Plann. Des. **32**(4), 477–484 (2005)

25. Lee Jr., D.B.: Requiem for large-scale models. J. Am. Inst. Plann. **39**(3), 163–178 (1973)

26. Lee Jr., D.B.: Retrospective on large-scale urban models. J. Am. Plann. Assoc. **60**(1), 35–40 (1994)

27. Macal, C.M., North, M.J.: Tutorial on agent-based modelling and simulation. J. Simul. **4**(3), 151–162 (2010)

28. Melbourne-Thomas, J., Johnson, C.R., Perez, P., Eustache, J., Fulton, E.A., Cleland, D.: Coupling biophysical and socioeconomic models for coral reef systems in Quintana Roo, Mexican Caribbean. Ecol. Soc. **16**(3), 23 (2011)
29. Perez, P.: Science to inform and Models to engage. In: Finnigan, J., Raupack, M. (eds.) Negotiating Our Future: Living scenarios for Australia to 2050, vol. 2, pp. 147–160. Australian Academy of Science, Canberra (2013)
30. Pettit, C.J., Klosterman, R.E., Delaney, P., Whitehead, A.L., Kujala, H., Bromage, A., NinoRuiz, M.: The online what if? planning support system: a land suitability application in Western Australia. Appl. Spat. Anal. Policy **8**(2), 93–112 (2015)
31. Pettit, C.: Use of a collaborative GIS-based planning support system to assist in formulating a sustainable development scenario for Hervey Bay, Australia. Environ. Plann. B Plann. Des. **32**(4), 523–545 (2005)
32. Pettit, C., Pullar, D.: A way forward for land use planning to achieve policy goals using spatial modeling scenarios. Environ. Plann. B Plann. Des. **31**, 213–233 (2004)
33. Pumain, D., Sanders, L., Bretagnolle, A., Glisse, B., Mathian, H.: The future of urban systems. In: Lane, D., Pumain, D., Van der Leeuw, S., West, G. (eds.) Complexity perspectives on innovation and social change ISCOM. Methods Series, pp. 331–359. Springer, Berlin (2009)
34. Pumain, D., Sanders, L.: Theoretical principles in interurban simulation models: a comparison. Environ. Plann. A **45**, 2243–2260 (2013)
35. Rasouli, S., Timmermans, H.: Uncertainty in predicted sequences of activity travel episodes: measurement and analysis. Transp. Res. Rec. J. Transp. Res. Board **2382**, 46–53 (2013)
36. Sanders, L., Pumain, D., Mathian, H., Guerin-Pace, F., Bura, S.: SIMPOP: a multi-agent system for the study of urbanism. Environ. Plann. B **24**, 287–305 (1997)
37. Simon, H.: The architecture of complexity. Proc. Am. Philos. Soc. **106**, 467–482 (1962)
38. Sole, R., Manrubia, S.C., Luque, B., Delgado, J., Bascompte, J.: Phase transitions and complex systems: simple, non-linear models capture complex systems at the edge of chaos. Complexity **1**(4), 13–25 (1996)
39. Taplin, J., Taylor, M., Biermann, S.: Transport Modelling Review: Independent Review. Planning and Transport Research Centre (PATREC), Curtin University, Perth (2014). 124 p
40. Trubka, R., Glackin, S., Lade, O., Pettit, C.J.: A web-based 3D visualisation and assessment system for urban precinct scenario modelling. ISPRS J. Photogrammetry Remote Sens. **117**, 175–186 (2016)
41. United Nations. Population Division. World Population Prospects: The 2015 Revision: Highlights. UN (2015)
42. Waddell, P.: UrbanSim: modeling urban development for land use, transportation, and environmental planning. J. Am. Plann. Assoc. **68**(3), 297–314 (2002)
43. Ward, J.A., Evans, A.J., Malleson, N.S.: Dynamic calibration of agent based models using data assimilation. R. Soc. Open Sci. **3**(4), 150703 (2014)
44. Wegener, M.: The future of mobility in cities: challenges for urban modelling. Transp. Policy **29**, 275–282 (2013)
45. Zeigler, B.P.: Discrete event system specification framework for self-improving healthcare service systems. IEEE Syst. J. **99**, 1–12 (2016)

Traffic Simulation in Urban Modelling

Software Architecture for a Transparent and Versatile Traffic Simulation

Michael Zilske[✉] and Kai Nagel

Verkehrssystemplanung und Verkehrstelematik, Technische Universität Berlin,
Berlin, Germany
michael.zilske@tu-berlin.de

Abstract. MATSim is a traffic simulation software package which can
be customized and extended in the Java programming language using a
set of interfaces. It recently acquired a plug-in system which was implemented using framework-assisted dependency injection, a pattern more
typically used in enterprise rather than research software. We describe
the extension points and the implementation of the plug-in system. The
architecture makes it easier and safer to combine independently developed components to complex simulation models, compared to many ad-
hoc solutions often found in research software.

Keywords: Traffic simulation · Software architecture · Dependency
injection

1 Transparent and Versatile Simulation Software

Since its inception, the MATSim project[1] [7] has aimed at being a transparent
and versatile research tool. Versatility means that the tool can be used for novel
research questions which are not on the mind of its inventors. Transparency
means that researchers who publish results obtained with the help of the tool
can and will phrase the steps which they undertook in a way which makes them
easy to reproduce [4], as in "We used revision r of the software with settings S on
input I, and obtained the following results." Anyone with access to the data and
software will then be able to re-run the original experiment, and anyone with
sufficient knowledge of the software and the domain will be able to re-evaluate
the original findings.

Translated to software engineering terms, the demand for versatility requires
the software to be extensible. There are certainly research problems which are
novel, yet can be phrased as reductions to MATSim runs, without the need to
modify the tool or indeed write any code beyond generating input and trans-
forming output. Many applications of MATSim, however, are not of this type,
but require extending the functionality of the software.

Any software product can be extended in functionality as long as the source
code is available. Also, when the modified source code and the input data are in

---

[1] also see http://matsim.org.

© Springer International Publishing AG 2017
M.-R. Namazi-Rad et al. (Eds.): ABMUS 2016, LNAI 10051, pp. 73–87, 2017.
DOI: 10.1007/978-3-319-51957-9_5

a public repository, under version control, any research citing a revision number is, in principle, reproducible. However, the further the custom version diverges from the main line, the less likely it is that another community member or a research advisor will be able to confidently interpret the results using previous knowledge of the software, because it is not clear which parts of the behavior of the software system have changed under global modifications.

Extending software in a transparent way means, rather than modifying code in place, to use interfaces which the software provides as hooks for extensions. In that case, the extended system consists of a previously published revision of the original software, together with custom code implementing the extension interfaces, as well as custom code wiring custom and standard components together. A full plug-in system removes the need for the last step: Extensions are only declared, not imperatively created and connected. Their instantiation is managed by the framework, which can now keep a model of which extensions are active in a particular configuration, since that concern is removed from user code.

In this paper, we discuss the architecture of MATSim and its plug-in system as it relates to the goals of versatility and transparency. Section 2 briefly introduces MATSim just as much as is needed to explain what it means to extend it. In Sect. 3, its *extension points* are identified, which are interfaces against which a user can implement new functionality. Section 4 describes the implementation of the extension mechanism itself, using the Guice software framework for dependency injection. In Sect. 5, we conclude with some remarks about possible future developments on the software side of the MATSim project.

2   Controller

MATSim is an iterative simulation. A simulation run begins with constructing an initial person-based travel demand model, which is done in user code prior to calling the simulation itself. The simulation progresses in a loop, which relaxes the demand with respect to a utility function. When a termination criterion is satisfied, the loop terminates, and control is returned to the client, where analysis code can be run.

A class called Controller[2] implements the simulation loop as depicted in Fig. 1, starting after the initial demand generation and ending before analysis:

Preparation initializes the agent population read from an input file to a state where it can be executed by the physical simulation. This includes registering activity locations with network links and finding initial routes.

PhysicalSimulation[3] executes the travel demand of the agent population on the capacity-constrained transport network. It produces a timeline of the simulation outcome, represented by a stream of Events.

---

[2] Wrongly spelled Controler in MATSim.
[3] Called Mobsim (= mobility simulation) in MATSim.

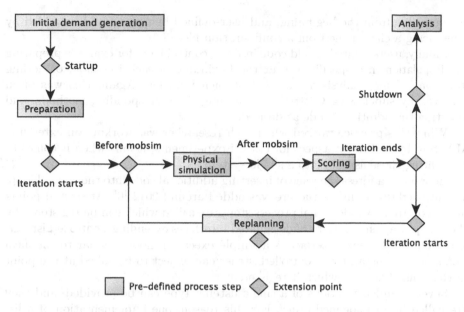

Fig. 1. The extensible MATSim simulation loop. (Adapted from [7].)

Scoring observes the Events stream, calculates for each agent a score for its
   outcome, and stores it in the agent memory.
Replanning lets each agent mutate its planned travel behavior.

Each iteration consists of three pre-defined process steps, PhysicalSimulation,
Scoring, and Replanning, while Preparation is a pre-processing step. The simulation loop with its process steps has been in place since the beginning of the
MATSim project, first by sequentially calling stand-alone scripts, later by calling
the process steps from an early version of Controller [11].

3   Extension Points

The implementations of these process steps can be switched by the user. The
standard implementations shipped with MATSim are almost completely independent components, sharing state only through two simple mutable data containers, Population and Network, and the Events stream. This makes them easily
replaceable. Historically, the way to achieve this was to subclass the Controler
instance and override the methods that were calling these process steps.

   Often, rather than replacing the entire PhysicalSimulation or Replanning stage,
a user wants to extend or modify the behavior of their standard implementations.
The general way of doing this was to subclass or copy the standard implementation class. Additionally, the user would once more subclass Controller and replace
the *construction* of the standard implementation instance, in order to decorate
it with the new behavior. Only the Replanning implementation was designed

as extensible from the beginning, and user-defined behavior could be added by referencing a class name from a configuration file.

Finally, users wanted to add code into the control loop, for example preparing the Population in a specific way at the beginning of each iteration, or adding iteration-specific analysis at the end of each iteration. Again, this was often achieved by subclassing Controller, overriding the corresponding methods, and inserting the additional code as desired.

While this practice worked when each researcher was working on extending MATSim by a different aspect for one-off experiments, it fails when it comes to integrating those aspects into a single system.

In order to address the issue of inserting additional code into the control loop, a ControllerListener infrastructure was added around 2012 [6]: At several points in the control flow, additional process steps are called which can be registered by the user as implementations of designated interfaces extending ControllerListener. The ControllerListener interface is a simple execution hook, similar to the Java Runnable. An instance of ControllerListener can expect to be called at the point in the control flow for which it registered.

Several implementations of a single listener type can be provided, and they are called in an undefined order. For this reason, one implementation of a listener type cannot assume a computation specified in another implementation of the same listener type to have been carried out. For ControllerListener implementations which register for the points at the Scoring or the Replanning step (cf. Fig. 1), the contract is that these listeners are conceptually executed concurrently to the corresponding process step.

It also became possible to replace some of the implementations of the predefined process steps by changing factory properties on the Controller instance. Additionally, it became possible to replace some of the objects which are used by specific process steps, such as the routing algorithm, which is used during Replanning, or the current link traversal time estimate and generalized cost function, TravelTime and TravelDisutility, which are in turn used by the routing algorithm.

The rest of this section describes the standard process steps from Sect. 2 in sufficient detail to motivate their extension points. In Sect. 4, we describe the implementation of a component or plug-in system, where the user does not write and maintain component construction code, but describes components, and declares the extension points they implement, in recombinable modules.

3.1   Physical Simulation and Events

The PhysicalSimulation concurrently simulates travel plans in a capacity-constrained traffic system. Given a fixed traffic infrastructure, it is a function of a set of plans to a set of outcomes. As a software component, its dependencies are the scenario data containers, Population and Network, and it produces a stream of Events, describing the outcome. A custom implementation of a PhysicalSimulation need not be written in the Java programming language: The framework includes a helper class to call an arbitrary executable which is then expected to write its event stream into a file [1, 15].

The traffic flow simulation moves the agents around in the virtual world according to their plans and within the bounds of the simulated reality. It documents their moves by producing a stream of Events [14]. Examples of such events are:

- An agent finishes an activity
- An agent starts a trip
- A vehicle enters a road segment
- A vehicle leaves a road segment
- An agent boards a public transport vehicle
- An agent arrives at a location
- An agent starts an activity

Each event has a timestamp, a type, and additional attributes required to describe the action like a vehicle identifier, a link identifier, an activity type or other data. In theory, it should be possible to replay the traffic flow simulation just by the information stored in the events. While a plan describes an agent's intentions, the stream of events describes how the simulated day actually was.

As the events are so basic, the number of events generated by a traffic flow simulation can easily reach a million or more, with large simulations even generating more than a billion events. But as the events describe all the details from the execution of the plans, it is possible to extract mostly any kind of aggregated data one is interested in. Practically all analyses of MATSim simulations make use of events to calculate some data. Examples of such analyses are the average duration of an activity, average trip duration or distance, mode shares per time window, number of passengers in specific transit lines and many more.

The scoring of the executed plans makes use of events to find out how much time agents spent at activities or for traveling. MATSim extensions can observe the traffic flow simulation by interpreting the stream of Events.

3.2 Scoring

The parameters of the standard MATSim scoring function are configurable. The code which maps a stream of traffic flow simulation Events to a score for each agent is placed behind a ScoringFunctionFactory interface and replaceable. Within the factory method, users can build a custom utility formulation which can be different for each synthetic person. There are building blocks for common terms like the utility of performing an activity, or the disutility of travelling. Custom terms can be added. For instance, a module which simulates weather conditions might calculate penalties for pedestrians walking in heavy rain. A modeler who wishes to compose a scoring function from the standard MATSim utility and the rain penalty can re-use the former and add the latter.

3.3 Replanning

Replanning in MATSim is specified by defining a weighted set of strategies. In each iteration, each agent draws a strategy from this set and executes it.

The strategy specifies how the agent changes its behavior. Most generally, it is an operation on the plan memory of an agent: It adds and/or removes plans, and it marks one of these plans as selected.

Strategies are implementations of the PlanStrategy interface. The two most common cases are:

– Pick one plan from memory according to a specified choice algorithm, and mark it as selected.
– Pick one plan from memory at random, copy it, mutate it in some specific aspect, add the mutated plan to the plan memory, and mark this new plan as selected.

The framework provides a helper class which can be used to implement both of these strategy templates. The helper class delegates to an implementation of PlanSelector, which selects a plan from memory, and to zero, one or more implementations of PlanStrategyModule, which mutate a copy of the selected plan.

The maximum size of the plan memory per agent is a configurable parameter of MATSim. Independent of what the selected PlanStrategy does, the framework will remove plans in excess of the maximum from the plan memory. The algorithm by which this is done is another implementation of PlanSelector and can be configured.

The most commonly used strategies shipped with MATSim are:

– Select from the existing plans at random, weighted by their current score.
– Mutate a random existing plan by re-routing all trips.
– Mutate a random existing plan by randomly shifting all activity end times backwards or forwards.
– Mutate a random existing plan by changing the mode of transport of one or more trips and then re-routing them with the new mode.

Routes are computed based on the previous iteration's traffic conditions, measured by analyzing the Events stream. Using the same pattern, a custom PlanStrategy can use any data which can be computed from the physical simulation outcome.

3.4 Travel Time, Disutility and Routing

Re-routing as a building block of many replanning strategies is a complex operation by itself. It can even be recursive: For example, finding a public transport route may consist of selecting access and egress stations as sub-destinations, finding a scheduled connection between them, and finding pedestrian routes between the activity locations and the stations. With the TripRouter service, the framework includes high-level support for assembling complex modes of transport from building blocks provided by other modules or the core.

The TripRouter provides methods to generate trips between locations, given a mode, a departure time, and an identifier of the travelling person [2]. It is used in the replanning stage of the simulation loop to modify the behavior of the simulated agents by replanning their trips. A trip is a sequence of plan elements representing a movement. It typically consists of a single leg, or of a sequence of legs with *stage activities* in between. For instance, public transport trips contain stage activities which represent changes of vehicles in public transport trips.

The behavior of the TripRouter is assembled from RoutingModule instances, one of which is associated with each mode. A RoutingModule defines the way a trip is computed, and declares the stage activities it generates.

The association between main modes and RoutingModule instances is configurable, and a user can provide custom RoutingModule implementations. This is required for use-cases which require custom routing logic, for instance if a new complex mode of transport is to be evaluated.

The standard behavior is that there are two RoutingModule implementations: For *network routing*, and for *teleportation*. By network mode, we refer to a mode whose trips are represented by paths through the network. By teleportation, we mean that travel times are determined based on a non-network property of the origin-destination relation, such as the bee-line distance. Even though no network route is calculated, this concern is implemented by a RoutingModule, because it determines the characteristics of a trip, given origin, destination and mode.

The network router, but not the teleportation router, makes use of two further interfaces: First, TravelDisutility, which answers queries about the time-dependent traversal cost of each edge. And second, TravelTime, which returns the time-dependent traversal time for each edge. This is used by the least-cost path algorithm to advance the time as paths are expanded.

The standard implementation of TravelTime answers queries from an in-memory map from $(link, time)$ to *duration*, which is initialized with free-flow traversal times as determined by the road category. After each iteration, it is updated with measured travel times, which are obtained by observing the Events stream.

The standard implementation of TravelDisutility evaluates a linear function of the link length and the travel time, the coefficients of which are configuration settings.

4   Dependency Injection

We now have identified several interfaces as extension points to modify the standard behavior of the simulation. In Fig. 2, we show them in a class diagram in the context of the components whose behavior they modify. Notice their different multiplicities. There is a single ScoringFunctionFactory, since it can be written to create a different function object for each agent, in case heterogeneous scoring over agents is desired. Because of the way the replanning works, there is a single PlanSelector for plans removal, but there can be an arbitrary number of weighted PlanStrategy instances. There is one RoutingModule for each defined mode of transport, and there is one TravelTime and one TravelDisutility for each mode which is routed on the network.

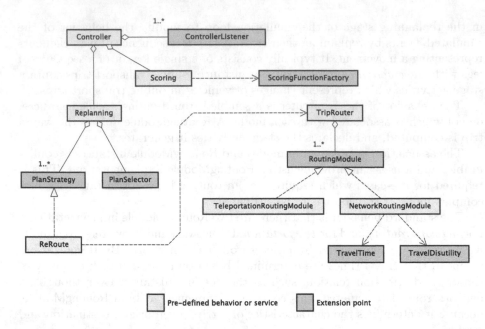

Fig. 2. Extension points in the context of the components whose behavior they modify.

The problem is now to provide a facility by which a user can create a Controller instance whose functionality is extended by custom implementations of one or more of these interfaces, with the additional requirement that such extensions be combineable.

At first glance, this could be done by making the Controller a JavaBean-like class with settable properties. Taking into account the different multiplicities, and the fact that some of the extension points are indexed by mode of transport, this could be usable like this:

```
Controller controller = new Controller();
controller.setScoringFunctionFactory(new RainScoringFunctionFactory());
controller.addTravelTime("bike", new BikeTravelTime());
```

Modularity could be realized by passing the Controller instance to several methods, where each method would correspond to a module, and would modify the properties of the Controller to register the extensions this module provides.

The main problem with this approach is this: The no-argument constructors of the user-provided classes in the above example are an idealization. Typically, these classes will have dependencies of their own, and some of these will be services provided by MATSim. For instance, a user-defined ScoringFunctionFactory may want to use the TripRouter to judge a chosen alternative relative to others. To make this possible, TripRouter would have to be a gettable property on Controller. However, a TripRouter internally consists of RoutingModule instances, which in turn are settable properties on the same level. Hence, the TripRouter is only constructable and gettable as soon as all desired RoutingModule instances are set, and there is no easy way to enforce this, except asking the user to sort their usage of getters and setters and checking internally that no setter of A is ever called after something which depends on A has been constructed.

4.1   Manual Dependency Injection

The fully-general, elementary solution to this problem is to require the entire object graph to be constructed bottom up, creating the most basic objects and services first and passing them to higher-level objects by their constructors. This forces the user, on a programming language level, to create the objects in the correct order, producing code like the following:

```
BikeTravelTime bikeTravelTime = new BikeTravelTime();
TripRouter tripRouter = new TripRouter(bikeTravelTime);
RainScoringFunctionFactory rainScoringFunctionFactory =
   new RainScoringFunctionFactory(tripRouter);
Controller controller =
   new Controller(rainScoringFunctionFactory, tripRouter);
```

With this, the property of modularity is lost. There is no general way of factoring parts of code like the above into independent methods with a common signature. Every such script by every user would have to contain the constructor calls for every required object. Moreover, this approach breaches encapsulation: While TripRouter is meant as a service interface, to be consumed by user code rather than implemented, its instantiation has now been moved to user code, exposing the implementation class.

4.2   Framework-Assisted Dependency Injection

An established solution to these problems in enterprise software is framework-assisted dependency injection [3], where dependencies within a set of managed objects are resolved by a software framework. This enables a user-side simplicity and modularity similar to the inital example, even when the user-provided classes have additional dependencies, while achieving the safety and generality of the explicit approach where all dependencies are passed by constructor.

Guice [5] is a dependency injection framework developed by Google.[4] Its core concepts are *binding* an interface type to an implementation, and *injecting* managed instances of bound types, sometimes called components, with other components. Bindings are defined within *modules*, which are Java classes. An advantage to earlier frameworks like Spring [8], which defined its bindings in XML files, is that module definitions are automatically included in refactoring tools provided by popular IDEs, and no additional tooling is needed. Also, since bindings are Java statements, it is easy to transform the general language

---

[4] The current release version, 4.0, was used for this implementation.

provided by Guice to declare bindings into a more domain-specific language, specifically for binding extensions to our designated extension points.

An example for a module which extends two extension points by adding two bindings, one for a custom ScoringFunctionFactory, and one for a custom TravelTime, is the following:

```
bindScoringFunctionFactory().to(RainScoringFunctionFactory.class);
addTravelTimeBinding("bike").to(BikeTravelTime.class);
```

Note that these two statements do not share any variables, so they can be decomposed into two modules. In particular, bindings do not have to occur in any particular order. In contrast to the example in Sect. 4.1, the TripRouter instance does not have to be constructed before RainScoringFunctionFactory is bound, and its constructor does not even have to be visible.

Once an interface type is bound, it can be injected into instances which are managed by the framework, in particular of classes on the right-hand side of bind statements. Since such instances are created by the framework, their classes must have an injectable constructor, which is one taking either no arguments or only arguments of other bound types. When the framework creates an instance, its dependencies have already been created and can be passed to the constructor (injected).

For example, the main implementation class of the Scoring stage includes an annotated field definition by which it declares a dependency to the possibly user-defined ScoringFunctionFactory component, which it then uses to create ScoringFunction instances for simulated entities:

```
class ScoringFunctionsForPopulation implements PlansScoring {
  final ScoringFunctionFactory sff;
  @Inject
  ScoringFunctionsForPopulation(ScoringFunctionFactory sff) {
    this.sff = sff;
  }
  public void scorePlans() {
    for (Person person : persons) {
      ScoringFunction sf = sff.createScoringFunction(person);
      // ...
    }
  }
}
```

At startup time, the framework detects the dependency by inspecting the constructor annotated with @Inject. It finds the corresponding binding and passes the appropriate instance when the constructor is called. As with regular initializations made in constructors, the instance method scorePlans() can expect a fully initialized instance.

Since modules are Java code, binding statements can be made conditional upon configuration parameters. In MATSim, a user-extensible data structure with system-wide configuration parameters is read from a file and made available at startup time. At that point, a set of modules shipped with MATSim, together with user-provided modules, is evaluated by the framework to construct the object graph, which is afterwards immutable for the simulation run.

A slightly simplified version of the object graph of the standard configuration of MATSim is shown in Fig. 3. Every dashed line corresponds to a binding. The dashed boxes are bound interfaces appearing on the left-hand side of bind statements, and the solid boxes are implementation types appearing on the right-hand side of bind statements. Each injection produces a solid edge in the graph.

For cases where it is not possible to leave the creation of instances to the framework, for example when an instance needs to be built programmatically in multiple steps, a similar construct can be used to specify a custom Provider (denoted by double arrows in Fig. 3), a functional interface which is called by the framework and is expected to return an instance. Orthogonally, another construct exists for binding a single concrete instance of the type or the Provider, when it is already available at configuration time.

Since the creation of components is managed by the framework, their dependency graph is inspectable at run-time. In contrast to the hand-drawn class diagram of Fig. 2, the object diagram can be plotted and saved to the output directory of a simulation run. It conserves and visualizes the structure as determined by the set of modules and the configuration. The (slightly simplified) example of Fig. 3 shows a standard configuration of MATSim, but the graph will track configuration changes and custom modules introduced by users of the framework.

5   Discussion and Future Work

We believe that being able to automatically generate visualizations of the configuration of a simulation run like in Fig. 3 is an important step for transparency. Before, user code plugged into MATSim would typically contain statements such as

controller.setXFactory(xFactory);

Since such a statement could be inserted multiple times, time-consuming code inspection was necessary to find out in which sequence they were called, and if the factory may already have been used before being replaced by another one. This could lead to obscure bugs, especially when different collaborators would work on different aspects of the simulation. The approach described in Sect. 4 completely solves this, by (1) prohibiting that an component managed by the dependency injection framework can be switched after it has been used for the first time, and (2) by automatically logging the full dependency graph with each run.

Framework-assisted dependency injection is a pattern more typically used in enterprise rather than research software. We are tracking other developments in the Java world which may be put to use for system-level simulation development. In particular, the process step summarized under physical simulation is a complex, extensible piece of software by itself. A close-up view would identify another set of extension points on that layer. This is also where interaction

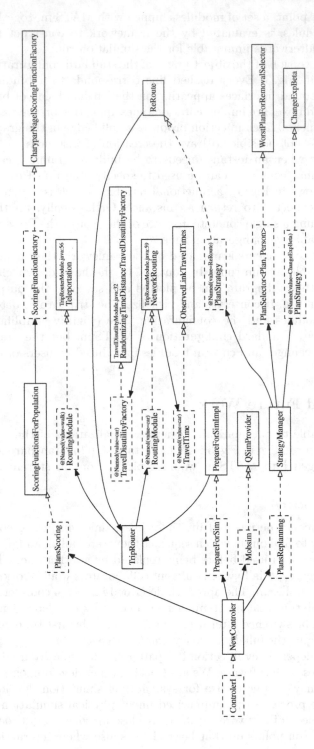

Fig. 3. The run-time object graph for a typical MATSim instance. The included classes implement the simulation logic. The graph is created at startup time, determined by a set of system and user-defined modules and their configuration. It is immutable for the duration of a simulation run. Since it is framework-managed, the graph can be plotted and saved automatically with the simulation output. This is the graph resulting from the MATSim standard configuration. Experimental extension points not mentioned in the text, as well as trivial or technical components such as proxies, were manually excluded.

between agents takes place. MATSim does not use any framework for agent-based microsimulations, but implements all its aspects, including concurrency, directly in Java.

The stream of microsimulation **Events** described in this paper is implemented as a simple event publisher, where interested parties can subscribe and register a call-back function, which is called every time an event of a specific type occurs. When seen as a virtue, this pattern is sometimes called reactive programming, and its main use cases are GUI applications and real-time stream processing, but also event-driven parts of simulations: It is a natural programming style for describing how the state of one object, such as the cell of a spreadsheet or the current estimate of the average speed on a link, is supposed to change over time in reaction to other observable processes, such as other cells of the spreadsheet or vehicles entering and leaving the link. To support this style, there are frameworks, such as [13], which provide syntax similar to the Java 8 Stream interface, but for events emitted by asynchronous, pushing producers. In this framework, event streams are first-class objects which can be transformed and combined with functional operators such as filter, map and fold. For instance, if one only wanted to react to every fifth event, one would traditionally implement a state machine in the event handler, which counts to five and only reacts every fifth time. With framework-assisted reactive programming, one would transform the original event stream into one which only emits every fifth event, and subscribe to it with the same syntax as used for the original one. This sometimes leads to more concise code with less explicit state.

However, sometimes the call-back oriented or reactive programming style is chosen not because it is the most expressive style for the problem, but out of technical neccessity. Consider the behavior-driven part of simulations: For agents, the inversion of control flow is unnatural, and they will always have to implement state machines based on the values of their properties. Rather than writing:

```java
int state = 0;
public void determineNextAction() {
    if (state
    else if (state
    else if (state
    ++state;
}
```

one would prefer to write

```java
public void act() {
  while (true) {
    travelTo("A");
    travelTo("B");
    travelTo("C");
  }
}
```

Note that in the first example, travelTo would return immediately, and calling a second travelTo action in the same function call would be possible though meaningless. In the second example, behavior is coded like a script for the simulated entity, and the state is captured in the program flow. The travelTo function call blocks until the simulation time has progressed to the point where the agent arrives at its destination.

However, in the Java programming language, this programming style would only be possible if every simulated entity would run in its own thread, which generally is not an option because threads have a high performance overhead, which is why simulations in Java generally use the reactive style for agents.

The interest in light-weight alternatives to threads has most recently been re-popularized by their presence in the Go programming language, but in contrast to other and much older programming languages such as Scheme, Java does not have first-class continuations, which are the missing bit to implement a non-reactive agent framework natively in Java. The Continuations Library [10] implements them using bytecode instrumentation, and Project Quasar [12] uses them to implement fibers, which are similar to threads but without the performance overhead, as a Java virtual machine extension. Neither requires extending the language itself.

6   Conclusion

We identified and described a set of interfaces to customize and extend a traffic simulation software package. As a mechanism for the user to implement custom behavior using these interfaces, previous versions of the software relied on a system of settable factory properties on multiple levels, which had grown over time as the need for more such interfaces developed. Its main drawback was that the responsibility for creating objects in the correct order was left to the users: They would have to find a point in the control flow late enough so that all dependencies necessary to create an instance of a custom class would be available, but early enough so that the instance itself would not yet have been requested. Alternatively, the creation of the entire object graph would have to be done in user code, which would introduce duplicate code over different configurations, and expose all dependencies of all components, requiring all configuration code to change whenever a constructor signature changed.

For this paper, that mechanism was developed into a plug-in system. It was implemented using dependency injection provided by the Guice framework. This solves the problem of mutable factory properties, unspecified order of object creation, and public visibility of dependencies. All components are constructed at startup time, in an order induced by the dependency graph, and with a check on completeness and uniqueness. The construction process and the resulting component graph are inspectable. This can be used to draw object graphs visualizing the system configuration, which can be saved with the simulation output, so that the precise configuration used to produce a simulation run is transparent. The described mechanism has already been used externally to develop a car-sharing model based on MATSim [9].

References

1. Balmer, M., Rieser, M., Meister, K., Charypar, D., Lefebvre, N., Nagel, K., Axhausen, K.: MATSim-T: architecture and simulation times. In: Bazzan, A., Klügl, F. (eds.) Multi-Agent Systems for Traffic and Transportation, pp. 57–78. IGI Global (2009)
2. Dubernet, T.: The new MATSim routing infrastructure. In: Presentation at the MATSim User Meeting, Zurich (2013)
3. Fowler, M.: Inversion of control containers and the dependency injection pattern, January 2004. http://martinfowler.com/articles/injection.html
4. Gandrud, C.: Reproducible Research with R and RStudio. CRC Press, Boca Raton (2015)
5. Google, Inc.: Guice. https://github.com/google/guice
6. Grether, D., Nagel, K.: Extensible software design of a multi-agent transport simulation. Procedia Comput. Sci. **19**, 380–388 (2013). http://www.sciencedirect.com/science/article/pii/S1877050913006601
7. Horni, A., Axhausen, K.W., Nagel, K. (eds.): The Multi-Agent Transport Simulation MATSim. Ubiquity, London (in press). http://matsim.org/the-book
8. Johnson, R., Hoeller, J., Donald, K., Sampaleanu, C., Harrop, R., Risberg, T., Arendsen, A., Davison, D., Kopylenko, D., Pollack, M., et al.: The Spring framework - Reference documentation. http://docs.spring.io/spring/docs/current/spring-framework-reference/pdf/spring-framework-reference.pdf
9. Laarabi, H., Bruno, R.: A generic software framework for car-sharing modelling based on a large-scale multi-agent traffic simulation platform. In: Pre-proceedings of the 1st Workshop on Agent Based Modelling of Urban Systems (ABMUS), Singapore (2016)
10. Mann, M.: Continuations library. http://www.matthiasmann.de/
11. Nagel, K., Axhausen, K.W.: Some history of MATSim. In: Horni et al. [7], Chap. 46. http://matsim.org/the-book
12. Parallel Universe: Quasar. http://docs.paralleluniverse.co/quasar/
13. Project Reactor: Reactor. http://projectreactor.io/
14. Rieser, M., Horni, A., Nagel, K.: Let's get started. In: Horni et al. [7], Chap. 2. http://matsim.org/the-book
15. Strippgen, D.: Integrating the CUDA simulation into the MATSim framework. In: Investigating the Technical Possibilities of Real-time Interaction with Simulations of Mobile Intelligent Particles, Berlin (2009). http://opus.kobv.de/tuberlin/frontdoor.php?source_opus=2364

A Generic Software Framework for Carsharing Modelling Based on a Large-Scale Multi-agent Traffic Simulation Platform

Mohamed Haitam Laarabi[✉] and Raffaele Bruno

Institute for Informatics and Telematics (IIT),
Italian National Research Council (CNR), Pisa, Italy
{haitam.laarabi,raffaele.bruno}@iit.cnr.it
http://www.iit.cnr.it/

Abstract. Over the last decade, numerous carsharing systems have been deployed around the world. Yet, despite this success, net profit margins of carsharing services are still insufficient due to a complicated demand modelling and high expenses for fleet redistribution. To address these problems, different carsharing paradigms (e.g., one-way versus free floating), operational models and pricing schemes have been proposed. In order to assess the effectiveness of these models and strategies, realistic simulation tools are needed that account for the main parameters that affect system performance. To this end, we have developed a generic software framework that caters for several flavours of carsharing services, such as hybrid systems where both one-way and free floating modes coexist. In addition, the proposed framework accounts for electric vehicles, power sharing capabilities, smart charging policies, booking services, fleet redistribution and membership management. Our tool is based on MATSim, an open-source platform for multi-agent traffic simulation. To validate our simulation model we will use a case study based on data from the 2006 Lyon conurbation household travel survey, which provides information about more than three million trips.

Keywords: Carsharing · Electric vehicle · Multi-agent systems · Traffic simulation · MATSim

1 Introduction

Worldwide, the sharing economy is rapidly gaining momentum and it is typically identified with an economic model in which communities of people share access to goods and services, beyond one-to-one or singular ownership. Sharing economy can take a variety of forms, but shared transport systems are one of the fastest growing trends in terms of users and revenues. A recent study by Roland Berger Strategy Consultants [3] has shown that the most popular shared transport services, namely carsharing, ride-sharing, bike-sharing and shared-parking, experience market annual growth rates between 20% and 35%; revenues are expected to reach between 2 and 6 billion dollars for 2020.

© Springer International Publishing AG 2017
M.-R. Namazi-Rad et al. (Eds.): ABMUS 2016, LNAI 10051, pp. 88–111, 2017.
DOI: 10.1007/978-3-319-51957-9_6

Carsharing is not a novel concept but over the last decade, worldwide participation to carsharing has steadily grown and today carsharing services operate in hundreds of cities around the world. Various types of carsharing paradigms have been proposed, including two-way, one-way, and free floating systems. Both in two-way and one-way carsharing, shared vehicles can be picked up only at designated locations (called stations). In two-way carsharing (e.g., Zipcar, Modo), customers are required to drop-off the vehicle at the station where they have initially picked it up. This constraint is dropped in one-way carsharing. Examples of one-way carsharing are Autolib, Ha:Mo ride, CITIZ. A further step towards maximum flexibility for the users is represented by free floating carsharing (such as Car2go, DriveNow, Enjoy), in which the concept of stations disappears and cars can be picked up and dropped off in any public parking within the area covered by the service. While free floating systems provide customers with higher flexibility than station-based solutions, the latter have the advantage of facilitating access to parking spaces, which are typically scarce resources in congested and densely populated cities. It is worth mentioning that even free-floating carsharing systems have sometimes dedicated on-street and municipal parking-lot spaces within dense city regions.

Despite the success of carsharing services and the expected exponential growth of the carsharing market [3], the economic viability of carsharing services is still an open issue due to asymmetric demand-offer problems (i.e. the unbalanced offer and demand of vehicles) and the high costs for fleet redistribution. It is important to point out that the planning and operation of carsharing systems is a complex task because it is very difficult to accurately model the dynamics of demand and supply processes. In fact, the availability of vehicles in a carsharing system is intrinsically dependent on trips that are demanded by the customers and vice-versa. In addition, there are several operational conditions that add uncertainties to the system about the future location of vehicles, e.g., how different pricing schemes impact users' decisions. Several optimisation approaches have been proposed to decide how to relocate vehicles in order to satisfy future (known a priori or predicted) customer demands [10,13,18]. Dynamic pricing schemes have been also proposed to incentivise users to leave vehicles at locations in which there is a shortage of vehicles [5,15,16]. However, the efficiency of these solutions has not been convincingly demonstrated because existing analytical and simulation models of carsharing systems are limited in scope or based on simplified assumptions. Furthermore, they leave out some of the most important characteristics that affect the performance of real systems, such as service booking or traffic congestion.

The main purpose of this work is to develop a modular, expandable and easily customisable simulation model of carsharing systems, which considers all the main characteristics of existing and future carsharing services. Key features of our framework are summarised in Fig. 1 and described in the following. First, we base the implementation of our framework on MATSim [1], a popular open-source and agent-based traffic simulation platform, which supports dynamic traffic assignment, large scenarios and detailed modelling of transportation networks.

Our objective is to develop a relatively independent core model that includes all basic functionalities of a general carsharing system and to implement specific strategies as external components. In this way, the carsharing system can be easily customised without affecting the core model. It is important to point out that our simulation tool accounts for all the main characteristics of real carsharing services, including fleet redistribution and membership management, booking policies, and electric vehicles. Finally, our model is not limited to conventional station-based or free-floating carsharing systems, but it also includes emerging carsharing paradigms, such as hybrid systems, as well as new types of electric cars that can be stacked together. Specifically, in hybrid carsharing systems both free-floating and one-way usage modalities may coexist (e.g. if a station facility is full the customer may be allowed to leave the car on any available on-street parking). Furthermore, electric car prototypes have been recently released or are under development that can be folded together when parked or driven as a stacked train, such as MIT's Bit Car [17], EO Smart [4], or ESPRIT vehicle [8]. It is expected that the adoption of these vehicles in next-generation carsharing services can significantly improve the system manageability, for instance by allowing advanced power sharing policies or more efficient redistribution mechanisms. However, it is necessary to develop more advanced models to study the performance of such sophisticated carsharing systems, and this is one of the targets of our simulation platform.

As a preliminary validation of the capabilities of our contribution to the MATSim framework we used the city of Lyon as case study. Specifically, we set up a simulation scenario using data from the 2006 Lyon conurbation household travel survey, which provides information about more than three million trips, and data from the Bluely system, a full electric one-way carsharing service that is operated in the city of Lyon.

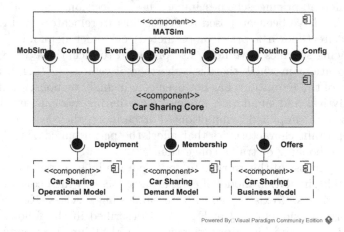

Powered By: Visual Paradigm Community Edition

Fig. 1. An overview of carsharing system that consists of three main layers: MATSim, carsharing core and carsharing models

The rest of this paper is organised as follows. In Sect. 2 we overview the MATSim framework and discuss the limitations of existing models of carsharing. Section 3 is devoted to the description of the software architecture and functionalities of our proposed framework. Finally, Sect. 4 presents the case study we will be using for model validation and discusses the ongoing work.

2   Background on MATSim and the Carsharing Model

2.1   A Brief MATSim Description

The modelling of traffic simulation can be carried out at different levels of detail. One common approach is to model traffic as an aggregated flow of cars based on Origin-Destination matrix [14]. While it is a straightforward approach and does not require considerable computing resources, it does not allow the modelling of individuals' preferences and a detailed analysis of temporal-spatial traffic characteristics. In contrast, agent-based traffic simulation considers each individual as an agent, and in the case of MATSim the travel demand is described through an activity-based model [1]. This model describes individuals' travel choices with plans containing information on their daily activities such as time and location of activities to be performed and transport mode to be used in order to travel from one location to another. This activity-chain can be assigned to each individual with specific socio-demographic attributes. Then, simulation is executed to characterise the traffic interactions between the different individual travel choices, which are constrained by a space-time network. Each of these activity-chains or plans are evaluated with a score at the end of each iteration, which contributes to the selection of plans for the next iterations. The replanning concept is based on a genetic algorithm where only fittest plans are kept and might undergo mutations. The latter is a way for individuals to improve the score of their plans by varying, for instance, transport mode, routes or departure time. The simulation continues to iterate until it relaxes as depicted by Fig. 2. Finally, MATSim enables the simulation of large scale scenarios by leveraging queue-based models of traffic flows, which are significantly faster than microscopic continuous-time traffic models (e.g. car-following models) [12]. Specifically, each link of the road network is represented as a queue that adopts a First In First Out service discipline.

It is then possible, with such a traffic simulation platform, to account for specific attributes and mobility decisions that dynamically influence the travel choices of individuals, which is needed to accurately model a carsharing system. In the following, we will discuss the existing carsharing contribution in MATSim to clarify its base concept and features, as well as its limitations.

2.2   Current Carsharing Contribution

The carsharing model had been introduced into MATSim since 2008 [6] and it has been applied in different studies over the years, such as [5, 7]. Three different types of carsharing services are considered by this existing carsharing contribution:

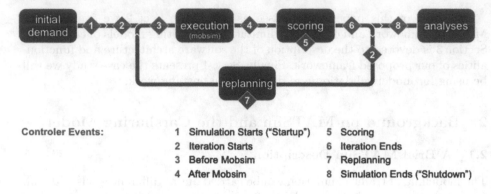

Fig. 2. The structure of the simulation controller of MATSim [19]

- Two-way, or round-trip, where a vehicle needs to be returned to the station from where it was picked up.
- One-way, where a vehicle can be dropped off at any station of the service.
- Free-Floating, where a vehicle can be picked up and dropped off at any station within the service area.

In the case of one-way carsharing service, the simulation model is portrayed graphically by Fig. 3 and summarised by the following steps:

1. *Booking Vehicle*: after the agent finishes an activity, it starts looking for the closest station, within a search distance radius, that has an available (i.e., non-booked) vehicle. If an available vehicle is found then the agent books it, and this makes the vehicle immediately unavailable to other agents;
2. *Access Walk*: agent walks from its current location (e.g. home) to the selected station;
3. *Pick Up*: agent picks up the vehicle and frees the parking spot;
4. *Booking Spot*: agent looks for the closest station to his final destination with an available parking space and books it, which makes the spot unavailable for others;
5. *Drive*: agent drives the vehicle to the destination station while interacting with other vehicles on the network;
6. *Drop Off*: Agent drops off the vehicle on the booked spot, which terminates the rental period;
7. *Egress Walk*: agent starts walking towards the location of his next activity;
8. Finally, agent carries out the remainder of the daily plan.

In case of either no vehicle is available or no parking spot can be found, the agent aborts its plan and consequently the controller assigns the worst score to the plan. The individual can also decide to use other modes such as public transport, bike or private car.

Regarding the behavioural model, agents use a scoring function that assesses their daily activity plans. In general, activities are evaluated positively with

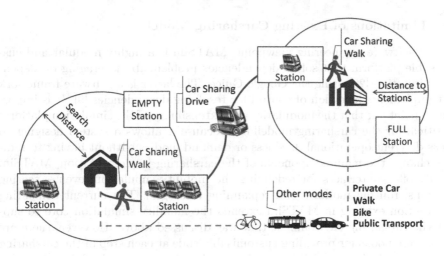

Fig. 3. Graphical representation of the simulation model of the carsharing contribution.

a utility function, whereas travelling is evaluated negatively with a dis-utility function [6]. As far as the carsharing transportation mode is concerned, the travel disutility function is composed of the following components:

- Access & Egress travel time cost;
- Carsharing usage constant;
- Rental time cost;
- Travel distance cost;
- Rental monetary cost;

In addition to the scoring, the behavioural model of the carsharing contribution is based on two different replanning strategies: *Carsharing Subtour Mode Choice Strategy* and *Random Trip To Carsharing Strategy*. The former one changes the transportation mode of all the legs of a sub-tour[1] to a different mode from a list of possible modes [6]. Note that certain transportation modes, called chain-based modes in MATSim, require that a specific resource (e.g., a private car or a bike) is available all along the sub-tour (e.g., an agent can not drive his car back from work to home if he had not previously parked it there). The second strategy is to incite individuals to use the carsharing service by substituting randomly a leg mode, which should not be a chain-based mode, by a carsharing mode.

---

[1] A sub-tour is any sequence of activities which starts and ends at the same location. For example, the chain home – work – shop – work – leisure – home (where both work activities are performed at the same location) contains two sub-tours: home-work-leisure-home and work-shop-work.

2.3   Limitations of Existing Carsharing Models

From a software engineering viewpoint, MATSim is a highly modular and customisable platform that solves dependencies problems by leveraging on dependency injection [20] using the Google Guice. The latter is a software framework
that implements inversion of control for resolving dependencies [9]. It is important to point out that the modularity and extensibility of the simulation platform
is critical for the carsharing modelling, because it allows a system designer to
assess different operational, business or demand models without having to radi-
cally change the main components of the carsharing implementation. MATSim
already offers interfaces for redefining the mobility simulation, events, scoring
functions, routing modules and replanning strategies. The current carsharing
contribution existing in MATSim extends the mobility simulation core to support the carsharing environment that was discussed above. However, there are
no software hooks for providing customisable code at each step of the carsharing
simulation, which would allow users to implement more easily different strategies for booking, pick up, drop off, access & egress and driving. Furthermore,
carsharing stations are currently implemented as simple containers of vehicles.
Whereas, stations represent a critical component of a carsharing system (e.g.,
to support smart charging policies of electric vehicles). Thus, it might be more
appropriate to consider station as a special type of stage activity[2] within a complex trip. Finally, a realistic simulation of a carsharing system would require
to consider also real-time fleet relocation, stations with charging infrastructure,
more sophisticated booking and membership management mechanisms (e.g., for
implementing dynamic pricing schemes).

Based on the limitations of the current carsharing contributions (both in
terms of architecture and functionalities) we have designed a new simulation
model of carsharing that ensures the independence of the operational, business
and demand sub-models from the core components of the system (Fig. 1). In the
following section, we describe in details the proposed framework.

3   A New Modelling Framework for Carsharing

3.1   Carsharing System Modelling

As explained above, the main goal of this work is to develop a simulation framework for carsharing that not only considers all main operational aspects of a
real carsharing service, but should be also sufficiently flexible to accommodate
the needs of next-generation carsharing systems (e.g. hybrid carsharing schemes,
stackable vehicles, etc.). A prerequisite for flexibility is to design the corresponding software architecture in such a way that the "core" model is separated from the
specific operational strategies. In fact, this approach facilitates system designers

---

[2] A stage activity is an activity part of a trip journey, such as public transport station,
but is not considered as trip end as it is the case for default activities e.g. Home,
Work etc.

to assess and compare different models. However, before discussing our proposed software architecture, let us first introduce all the key new features of our modelling framework for carsharing. Then, the following section will be devoted to explain how each of these general functionalities is implemented within the different software modules that compose our proposed carsharing model.

- Conventional, floating and charging stations: In our framework a station is a set of parking spaces that can be organised according to a specific physical layout and spatial constraints (e.g., to model a FIFO approach for vehicle pick up and drop-off). Each station keeps track of both demand and usage patterns and maintains information about vehicle availability and status (e.g., non-operational, booked, charging, etc.). A special type of stations, called floating stations, have been also implemented. Specifically, a floating station is a kind of virtual station that is used to model a vehicle dropped off anywhere else than a conventional station (e.g. to model a system that allows customers to leave the rented vehicles on on-street parking if the destination station is full). This features helps in modelling a variety of hybrid carsharing services in which both one-way and free floating carsharing approaches are employed. Finally, a station can be equipped with a charging infrastructure to enable the modelling of electric vehicles. We have implemented a variety of charging spot models, including multiple outputs multiple cables charging (MOMC) spots. MOMC spots have multiple cables which can charge several electric vehicles simultaneously, enhance the utilisation of the charging infrastructure and reduce investment costs [11]. Note that if a vehicle runs out of battery during the mobility simulation, then the plan is aborted and the vehicle disappears from the simulation.
- Electric and stackable vehicle: A shared vehicle can be an electric or hybrid car with associated specific energy consumption models. In case of electric vehicles, we assume that a vehicle is available only if the state of charge is above a certain threshold. An important novelty of our modelling framework is to allow the simulation of stackable vehicles, i.e., vehicles that can be mechanically and electrically connected and can be driven as a road train. This new generation of electric vehicles is expected to have a significant impact on the performance of future carsharing systems, especially for more efficient fleet relocation. For instance, in the European Project ESPRIT [8] is currently ongoing the prototyping of a lightweight electric vehicle for short trips in urban areas that can be stacked together in a road train of up to eight vehicles, seven being towed (see Fig. 4 for an illustration of the ESPRIT prototype vehicle). This makes easier

Fig. 4. ESPRIT stackable electric vehicles.

to redistribute them to locations where they are most wanted (a single staff can relocated multiple vehicles simultaneously). Furthermore, when parked at the stations they can be charged through the train electric connection and support dynamic load balancing. This can increase the carsharing operators' revenues by reducing the cost of installation (only one charging supply equipment to serve multiple parking spaces), while supporting, due to their small size, the growing demand for charging spots.

In practice, in our framework a stackable vehicle is modelled as a trailer that is assigned to a head vehicle to form a road train. Thus, when a road train is being relocated to a different station, the vehicle to be relocated should be detached from the station and attached to the head vehicle.

– Vehicle booking: The booking procedure is a critical management task for the carsharing provider. While the possibility to reserve a vehicle helps carsharing providers to predict future demands, they are also mandated to ensure vehicle availability at the requested time, which makes vehicle relocation even more compelling. In our framework, the booking procedures are executed during the mobility simulation for agents who have chosen to use carsharing as one of their transportation modes. We support two types of booking services: *early* booking and *immediate* booking. With early booking an agent can place a booking request a few hours before the desired starting time of the carsharing trip (e.g., up to 12 h). In this case, the booking process requires the starting time, as well as the source/destination of the trip. As better explained in the following, the booking system provides the customer with a single option or with multiple offers depending on the rental model and the relocation strategy that is implemented (user-based vs. operator based). It is worthwhile to mention that an available vehicle means that a vehicle is not booked, operational and its state-of-charge is above a critical threshold. Since both the source and destination are provided, the booking system can estimate the amount of required energy to successfully complete the trip. In case of insufficient battery, the system warns the agent during the booking process.

With immediate booking, the agent searches for an available vehicle at the time he needs it. Then, he may decide to make a *Full Booking* with both a vehicle to pick up and a parking space at the destination. If the agent accepts one of the offers he received from the carsharing system, he should receive a confirmation and starts the access walk towards the source station. Otherwise, the user might ask for another offer. The agent can also decide to drive to his destination without pre-booking a parking space at the final station, or booking it later on during the rental period, which is considered as *Partial Booking*. At this stage the only required information is the source of the trip. In the case of immediate booking, the booked vehicles are immediately made unavailable for subsequent customers and considers the walking time needed to reach the start station. Note that the plan of the agent is aborted if he declines all received offers, unavailability of vehicles, booking time expiration, etc. The plan abortion results in assigning to that plan the worst score.

– Real-time vehicle relocation: The largest part of the carsharing modelling lies in the mobility simulation, where individuals have to book, search for available vehicles, walk to/from stations and drive. In the mobility simulation is also implemented the modelling of the fleet relocation procedures. Two different approaches are modelled: operator-based and user-based [18]. In operator-based solution a separate staff is assumed that is dedicated to the relocation activities. In this case, the relocation strategy consists of decisions made by the system manager on which vehicles to relocate and how to assign staff to task relocation. The possibility to use stackable vehicles adds additional degrees of freedom (and complexity) in the decision process. On the contrary user-based relocation strategies make use of monetary incentives or bonus models for suggesting to customers alternative destinations than the preferred ones. It is also possible that an already driving customer is asked to pick up a second vehicle with him (taking advantage of the stackable capabilities of vehicles), thus also contributing to the rebalancing the system supply. To study the trade-off between incentive schemes for user relocation and staff planning for relocation is part of our future work.

- Rental model: The definition of different dynamic pricing schemes and rental models is supported to assess the impact of tariffs and monetary incentives discount on the performance of the carsharing service and its decision support system (e.g., user-based relocation, free-floating trips, multiple offers). In the rental model we also include the membership management. This includes the specification of the behavioural model of each customer, which specifies how that customer reacts to system offers and booking constraints.
- Demand model: Typically, the demand model is concerned with the generation/import of the transportation network, activity locations, synthetic population and their initial travel plans. We have extended the conventional demand model to include features that are relevant to the carsharing model, such as personal preferences of carsharing usage, characteristics of shared vehicles, station and charging infrastructure.
- Agent behaviour model: In our framework, the first stage of agents behaviour during mobility simulation is the *access walk*, which includes the walking leg towards the carsharing station. Before starting the walking leg, the agent performs the booking. Once an agent reaches the location of the selected vehicle, an event is triggered to start the second stage of the carsharing mobility simulation, i.e., the *carsharing drive*. As described above, in the case of immediate booking, the agent can provide a destination point but it is up to the agent to drop off the vehicle at the suggested stations or anywhere else. Furthermore, the carsharing system might invite an agent to take a second car with him. Then, the agent starts the driving leg towards the destination. The plan is aborted when an agent declines an offer, does not find a drop-off station or the vehicle runs out of energy. Once an agent drops off the vehicle the third and last stage of the carsharing mobility simulation starts, i.e., the *egress walk*. The agent starts walking to the next activity or next trip (in the case of last kilometre carsharing). The rental is ended and summarising trip information are logged.

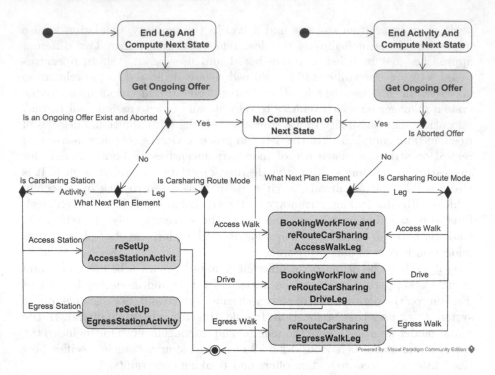

Fig. 5. General workflow of the agent's behaviour.

For the sake of completeness and to better illustrate the sequence of agent's decisions that are made during the mobility simulation, in Fig. 5 we show the workflow of the mobility simulation with a UML activity diagram. The white boxes refer to MATSim's default agent workflow, while the grey boxes refer to the carsharing sub-workflow. As shown in the diagram, each iteration of the mobility simulation consists in processing an element of the agent activity plan iteratively. Therefore, at the end of an activity or a leg the agent reflects about the next step. For instance, when an agent completes the execution of the access station activity, he has to pick up the car and starts driving. The agent behaviour model offers the flexibility not only to pick up and drop off in stations, but also nearby an activity location. Therefore, an agent can undertake not only direct trips — station to station — but also indirect trips where the agent can drop off vehicle nearby a shopping mall, for example, so that he picks it back up later on.

Conventional transportation modes (private cars, public transports, bikes, walking) are handled by the *MATSim default flow*. When a leg uses the carsharing mode the workflow described in Fig. 6 is invoked. First of all, the flow starts with booking verification since agents who choose plans that contain carsharing legs can decide to make an early booking or an immediate booking. In the former case, the simulation has already all the booking information (departure station, destination station, trip time), and the agent can immediately start the

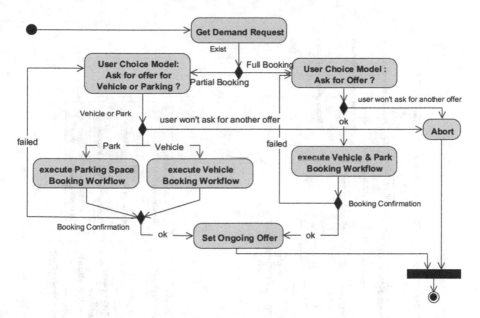

Fig. 6. Booking workflow.

access. In the latter case, which is shown in Fig. 6 the agent first searches for an available car, asks for an offer and books the vehicle if the offer is accepted. If the offer is declined or no car is available the travel plan is aborted and he obtains the worst score. Regarding the booking model, on the one hand the system can suggest personalised offers to each individual, for instance to incentivise users to participate to the vehicle relocation program. On the other hand, each agent is characterised by his own preferences regarding carsharing use. For instance, some agents would prefer to minimise travel costs by carsharing, which makes them more willing to drop-off the vehicle at a less favourite station. While other agents would prefer comfort and maintain their favourite departure and destination stations or accept to drive in a free floating mode.

3.2 Software Architecture

The design of a software architecture that is sufficiently flexible and independent from the carsharing operational model will require lightweight containers that enable to assemble components into a cohesive system. These containers are governed by a common pattern that characterises the way the components wiring is performed, and it is referred to as *Inversion of Control* (IoC) or more specifically as *Dependency Injection* [9]. This concept will be more apparent within the new modelling framework for carsharing with a UML Component Diagram, as shown in Fig. 7. Three main layers can be identified on the diagram. First, the MATSim layer is the base software component for traffic simulation, which, in turn, is based largely on the dependency injection design pattern [20]. The second

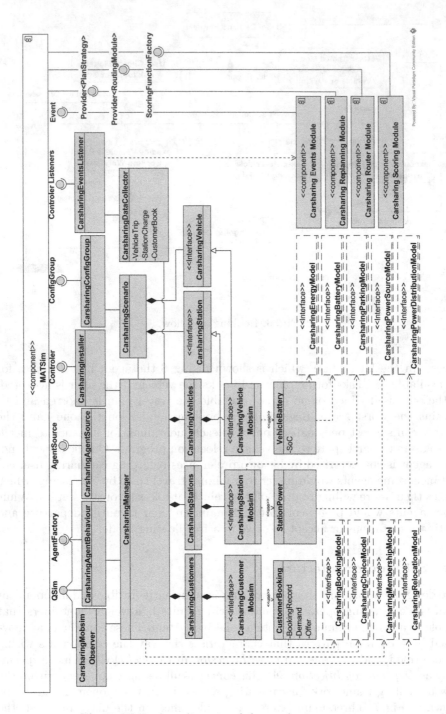

Fig. 7. UML class diagram of the carsharing system.

layer consists of the core modules (the grey boxes in Fig. 7) of the carsharing model, which set the environment for the simulation. In other words, it is an interface that translates the carsharing operational models into a traffic simulation, which is then controlled by the specific rules of the carsharing system. The third layer is a set of interfaces ready to be implemented (dashed boxes in Fig. 7) that describe the operational models the system designer wants to assess, the demand model to simulated and the customer choice model to be considered. These three layers are wired by inversion of control, so that MATSim retains the control to the carsharing system and, in turn, it injects dependency into the third layer. In addition, every component of the system core is disaggregated and control is centralised within the carsharing manager. In the following we present the main software components of our framework.

- Carsharing Scenario: Represents the data structure that should be constructed, in principle, before installation of the carsharing module. It contains initial deployment of stations and vehicles, carsharing configuration module, car network and MATSim scenario.
- Carsharing Manager: It serves as an access point and for the carsharing scenario. Basically, it contains a mapping of customers and vehicles, in addition to a tree data structure for stations with geolocated information. Each of the three key features of the carsharing systems (customers, fleet, stations) are represented with a generic interface that injects dependency into the multiple instances that implement those interfaces. For instance, a station can be either a conventional charging station or a floating station but its representation is based on the same model. Stations are also characterised by power supply information and a vehicle container model.
  Similarly, vehicles can have different features too with a specific energy consumption and balancing model. Customers entity help to keep track of the carsharing usage, since the customer is identified by an id, geographic coordinates and socio-demographic information which can be monitored not only over iterations but even over entirely different simulations set-ups. The manager has also access to all the models, booking service as well as to the logging service that generates the carsharing event file for post-analysis.
- Carsharing Agent Behaviour: Describes an agent behaviour work flow, therefore it has access to the carsharing manager and governed by the mobility simulation.
- Carsharing Agent Source: Responsible for physical deployment of carsharing fleet in the car network.
- Carsharing Events Listener: It captures fired carsharing event, during mobility simulation. Data collection is basically undertaken at this level. This component can be easily extended through class inheritance.
- Models: They represent interfaces for energy, relocation, demand, rental, user choice and vehicle models, which help at injecting customized models into the carsharing core.
- Carsharing Mobsim Observer: This class offers plan view of the simulation and run in parallel with mobility simulation steps. It can be extended to included further controls and handling, as the operator-based relocation.

- Carsharing Installer: A utility class for installation of the carsharing module. It can be customized by inserting new models, observer, and/or events listener.
- Carsharing Data Collector: By default, this class collects information about trips, charging at stations and customer booking. Then it writes them out in a file predefined in the carsharing configuration group.
- Component modules: These components offer direct usage of MATSim's replanning, routing and scoring modules, and can be easily customized.

4   Validation and Ongoing Work

To validate our modelling approach of carsharing systems we use a real-world scenario for the city of Lyon. Our test case is built using real traffic demands for the metropolitan area of Lyon based on data from the 2006 Lyon conurbation household travel survey. More precisely, the traffic demand is originally provided in terms of two OD matrices, representing the travel modes and travel purposes between 148 different traffic zones in the metropolitan area of Lyon. As shown in Fig. 8, we focus our study only on Lyon downtown, because this is the service area of Bluely, a one-way station-based carsharing provider that operates in Lyon. The simulated area includes 56 zones (in the figure zone borders are shown with black polygons). According to the travel survey, during a typical working day, almost 3 million trips have an origin or destination within the considered 56 zones.

As discussed [2], generating plausible daily activity chains from OD matrices is a complex task and it generally requires the integration of census and

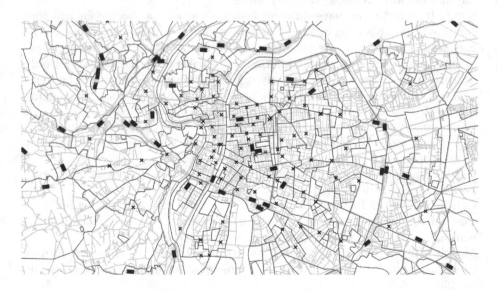

Fig. 8. Lyon Scenario: simulating the Bluely service in Lyon downtown. The diagram shows the road network in the Via traffic visualiser. Carsharing stations are depicted as crosses, while rectangles are shared vehicles.

socio-demographic data from various sources, as well as simplifying assumptions. For instance, census data can be used to generate a synthetic population, including population groups (e.g., children, workers, non-workers, pensioners), spatially distributed among zones and household compositions. Similarly business census data can provide the number of workplaces, as well as shopping, leisure and education facilities, which can be randomly deployed within each zone. For simplicity we have only used the OD matrices to derive a preliminary travel demand for the Lyon scenario. More precisely, OD matrices are used to derive the trip shares between each pair of zones and to assign a *purpose* to each trip (i.e., home-work-home, or home-education-home, and home-leisure-home). Then, we also assume that the temporal distribution of opening times and durations of each activity type is known. Finally, we assign an agent to each trip departing from a zone and we randomly locate the agent in the initial zone. The total number of agents in our simulation is 100,000. Following these steps, we have obtained the modal share depicted by Fig. 9.

Regarding the station infrastructure of the carsharing system, we consider the locations of the real Bluely stations (104 stations within Lyon downtown), all equipped with a charging point. In each scenario, the total number of parking spaces in the carsharing network is assumed to be two times the fleet size. Then, parking spaces are uniformly assigned to each station. The carsharing membership is assumed to be a function of the distance to the carsharing stations: all agents who execute their activities in facilities which have one or more stations within a predefined search distance, are considered to be members and potential users of the carsharing system. Specifically, the considered search distance in this case study is 500 m, which made 20% of the simulated agents holders of the

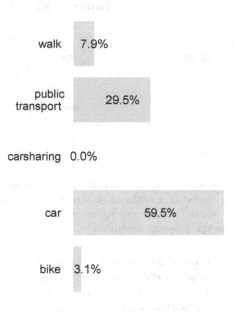

Fig. 9. Initial modal share

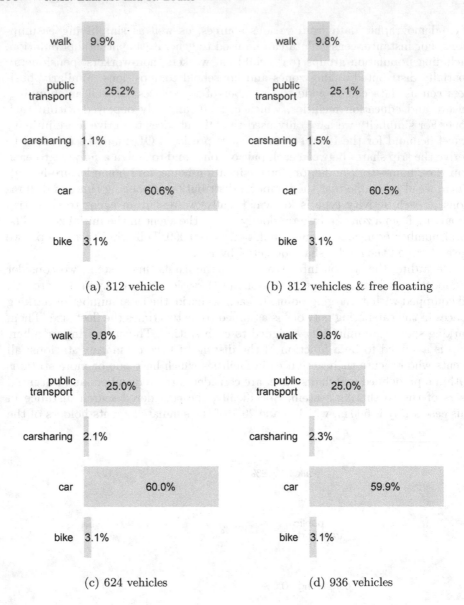

Fig. 10. The modal share after inciting carsharing members to use the carsharing mode, through a random mode choice as a replanning strategy to explore various solutions and combinations. The subtitle of each sub figure refers to the fleet size as a unique input variable to compare the different scenarios.

carsharing membership. Finally, we compare three different scenarios in which three, six and nine vehicles per station are deployed, as well as a fourth scenario where free floating is also allowed. The objective is to observe the performance of the carsharing system for various system capacities.

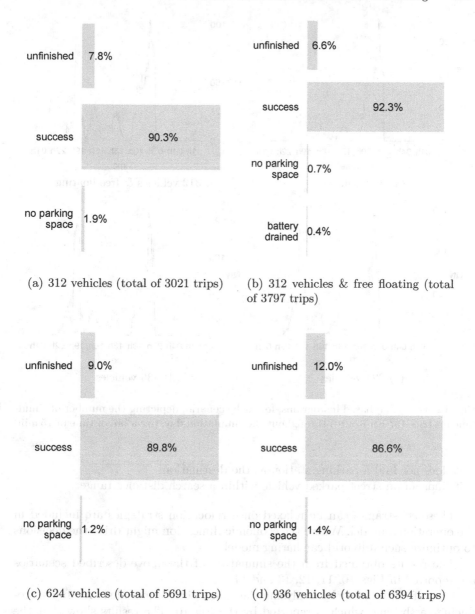

(a) 312 vehicles (total of 3021 trips)

(b) 312 vehicles & free floating (total of 3797 trips)

(c) 624 vehicles (total of 5691 trips)

(d) 936 vehicles (total of 6394 trips)

Fig. 11. Four pie charts describing the relative number of successful trips to the ones that failed due to 2 - unavailability of parking space or 4 - battery drained or 3 - other reasons such as end of simulation horizon.

The free floating capability has been constrained in such a way to ensure maximum performance in the absence of operator/user-based relocation. An agent, therefore, is constrained to opt for free floating offer if:

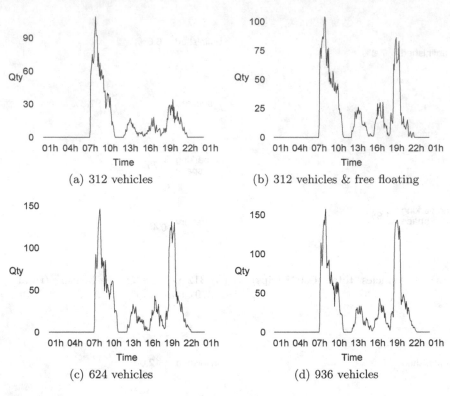

(a) 312 vehicles

(b) 312 vehicles & free floating

(c) 624 vehicles

(d) 936 vehicles

Fig. 12. Four time-based histograms, for each scenario, depicting the number of simultaneous trips (or En Route) throughout the simulation day, per a bin of time of 15 min.

– it does not find a parking station at the destination;
– it finds an on-street parked vehicle within a search distance range.

These constraints can be relaxed once relocation strategies are included in the operational model. Where the economic dimension might drive the decisions to optimize such a hybrid carsharing model.

The results obtained from the simulation of the above-described scenarios are reported in Figs. 10, 11, 12, 13 and 14.

First of all, we start by analysing the change in the modal share after introducing carsharing, which is reported by the Fig. 10. The results show that the carsharing mode is a *weak signal* in the transportation network, as the usage of carsharing is limited by the relatively small fleet of vehicles with respect to the number of travellers. We can also observe the proportional increase in modal share with respect to the increase of the carsharing fleet. For instance the modal share *doubles* when we doubled the fleet size to 624 vehicles, while it increased by 120% when fleet size was expanded to 936 vehicles. From operational perspective, one can observe a similar behaviour to a real world carsharing system,

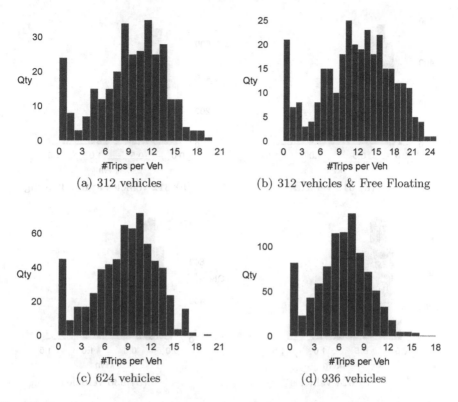

Fig. 13. Four histograms, for each scenario, depicting the number of trips (or rotation) per vehicle.

where it is not necessary to have a linear relationship between the size of the deployed carsharing fleet, and the carsharing usage/trips.

Regarding the scenario where agents are constrained to opt for dropping off or picking up an on-street vehicle, as detailed beforehand. The modal share also increased by 40% as shown on Fig. 10(b). This increase can be explained by the fact that free floating option has relaxed the constraints of necessity to drop a vehicle in one of the 104 carsharing stations. Thus, more agents were able to use carsharing system because they were allowed to drop the vehicles anywhere in the studied area. Since all the carsharing members have at least one station at proximity of each of the facilities where their activities are undertaken, the agents, then, were constrained to use a free floating vehicle because no parking space was available in the nearby station. In this way, even the on-street vehicles were dropped off within a radius of 500 m from a full station. Therefore, the agents willing to pick up a vehicle were again constrained to pick up from a station considered full as long as no on-street vehicle are parked in the neighbourhood.

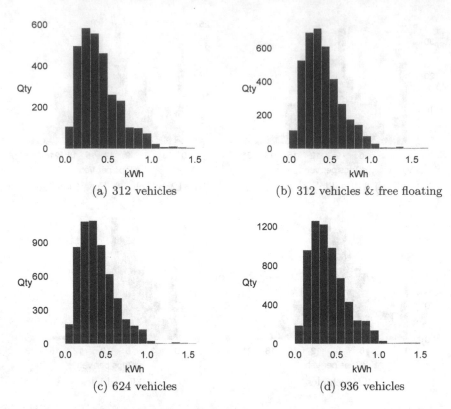

(a) 312 vehicles

(b) 312 vehicles & free floating

(c) 624 vehicles

(d) 936 vehicles

Fig. 14. Four histograms, for each scenario, depicting the amount of energy expressed in kilowatt-hour, which was consumed during a single trip.

We support the modal share with further details on the carsharing trips that actually have taken place after the replanning phase, as reported in Fig. 11. In fact, since there are 20% potential carsharing users, the number of agents who did not receive an offer after asking for the carsharing service, was not included in these charts. Having said that, we observe the evidence of clear increase of number of carsharing trips, as well as, the efficiency of the free floating scenario where relatively more successful trips have been recorded due to relaxation of the parking space constraint.

The results of Fig. 12 show the increasing number of simultaneous trips when expanding the fleet size. However, the highest number of simultaneous trips represent only 35%, 23% and 17% of the fleet, respectively, for the scenarios with 312, 624 and 936 vehicles. This means that the vehicles are not well distributed in the area, and the disparity grows higher by expanding the fleet while preserving the same distribution. This is another observed fact in real world systems, where spatial as well as temporal distribution of vehicles are key assets for the optimisation of the operational model.

Giving the simulated scenarios, a decision maker would wish to use this simulator to evaluate and measure the success of certain relocation strategies, either using a staff or through encouraging users to choose specific stations or to take a second car as a road train. Successful relocation algorithms would lead to an increase of carsharing usage, and notably to the increase of simultaneous trips, as an indicator of demand absorption during the day.

The trips histograms in Fig. 13 confirm the analysis drawn from the previous results. We note that, the number of rotations per vehicle is relatively high when comparing to real world systems. In other words, same vehicles are being reused again and again, while some are never used. Furthermore, we observe that the number of rotations decreases when the fleet is larger. While free floating increases the usage and rotation per vehicles due to the aforementioned constraints.

At last, the histograms in Fig. 14 report the amount of energy consumed per trip. These results are essential for vehicle design when it comes to battery capacity and usage. It is interesting to note that there are negligible differences between the results for different fleet size. This can be explained by observing that the energy consumption mainly depends on the mobility patterns of the carsharing trips. Thus, increasing the fleet size has not a significant impact on the length or travel time of carsharing trips.

5 Conclusion

The main contribution of this work is the development of a new simulation model of carsharing for MATSim, an urban-scale and activity-based multi-agent modelling framework of multi-modal transportation systems. Our module supports the modelling of various interrelated components of generic carsharing systems, including booking services, fleet redistribution, charging policies and membership management. In addition, we also included new carsharing paradigms such as mixed systems (free-floating and station-based), and stackable vehicles. To evaluate our model we used a scenario with real travel data from the city of Lyon.

As an ongoing work we intend to use our modelling framework for providing an initial estimate of the usage patterns of the carsharing service under different operational parameters and procedures. Specifically, we will assess the impact of the charging infrastructure and vehicle parameters (i.e., number of charging points, maximum charging power, battery capacity) on the operational time of electric shared vehicles. Our findings can provide a guidance to the system designers for deriving an optimal configuration of the charging station to minimise investment costs. In addition, we will provide a first analysis of simple heuristics for vehicle relocation. A first intuitive approach would be to relocate vehicles by moving them from full stations to empty stations at certain times of the day (e.g., peak hours) if the driving distance is below a given threshold (e.g., to limit battery consumption and to guarantee fast relocation). Alternatively, relocation could be carried out by those users, whose destinations are close to an area/station with an insufficient supply of vehicles. The amount of monetary incentives that are needed to encourage such users to participate in the relocation activity could be easily estimated.

Acknowledgement. This work has been partially funded by the ESPRIT project. This project has received funding from the European Union's Horizon 2020 research and innovation programme under grant agreement No. 653395.

References

1. Balmer, M., Cetin, N., Nagel, K., Raney, B.: Towards truly agent-based traffic and mobility simulations. In: Proceedings of the Third International Joint Conference on Autonomous Agents and Multiagent Systems, vol. 1, pp. 60–67, AAMAS 2004. IEEE Computer Society, Washington, DC, USA (2004). http://dx.doi.org/10.1109/AAMAS.2004.285, 00098
2. Balmer, M., Rieser, M., Vogel, A., Axhausen, K.W., Nagel, K.: Generating day plans based on origin-destination matrices. In: 5th Swiss Transport Research Conference, March 2005
3. Berger, R.: Roland Berger study on the market for car sharing in China: major potential for vehicle manufacturers and service providers|Press room|Roland Berger, July 2014. http://www.rolandberger.com/press_releases/Car_Sharing_in_China_2014.html
4. Birnschein, T., Kirchner, F., Girault, B., Yuksel, M., Machowinski, J.: An innovative, comprehensive concept for energy efficient electric mobility - EO smart connecting car. In: 2012 IEEE International Energy Conference and Exhibition (ENERGYCON), pp. 1028–1033, September 2012. 00003
5. Ciari, F., Balac, M., Balmer, M.: Modelling the effect of different pricing schemes on free-floating carsharing travel demand: a test case for Zurich, Switzerland. Transportation **42**(3), 413–433 (2015). http://link.springer.com/10.1007/s11116-015-9608-z
6. Ciari, F., Balmer, M., Axhausen, K.W.: Concepts for a large scale car-sharing system: modeling and evaluation with an agent-based approach. In: 88th Annual Meeting of Transportation Research Board, January 2009. http://www.researchgate.net/profile/Kay_Axhausen/publication/228952222_Concepts_for_a_large_scale_car-sharing_system_Modelling_and_evaluation_with_an_agent-based_approach/links/0deec517bbebe35452000000.pdf
7. Ciari, F., Schuessler, N., Axhausen, K.W.: Estimation of carsharing demand using an activity-based microsimulation approach: model discussion and some results. Int. J. Sustain. Transp. **7**(1), 70–84 (2013)
8. ESPRIT Project 2016, E.U.: Easily distributed personal rapid transit. http://www.esprit-transport-system.eu/
9. Fowler, M.: Inversion of control containers and the dependency injection pattern, January 2004. http://martinfowler.com/articles/injection.html#ServiceLocatorVsDependencyInjection
10. Jorge, D., Correia, G.H.A., Barnhart, C.: Comparing optimal relocation operations with simulated relocation policies in one-way carsharing systems. IEEE Trans. Intell. Transp. Syst. **15**(4), 1667–1675 (2014). http://ieeexplore.ieee.org/lpdocs/epic03/wrapper.htm?arnumber=6754142

11. Lindgren, J., Lund, P.D.: Identifying bottlenecks in charging infrastructure of plug-in hybrid electric vehicles through agent-based traffic simulation. Int. J. Low-Carbon Technol. **10**(2), 110–118 (2015)
12. Meister, K., Balmer, M., Ciari, F., Horni, A., Rieser, M., Waraich, R.A., Axhausen, K.W.: Large-scale agent-based travel demand optimization applied to Switzerland, including mode choice. Technical report, Zürich (2010)
13. Nourinejad, M., Zhu, S., Bahrami, S., Roorda, M.J.: Vehicle relocation and staff rebalancing in one-way carsharing systems. Transp. Res. Part E: Logistics Transp. Rev. **81**, 98–113 (2015). http://linkinghub.elsevier.com/retrieve/pii/S1366554515001349
14. Ortuzar, J., Willumsen, L.G.: Modelling Transport, 4th edn. Wiley, New York (2011)
15. Salies, E.: Real-time pricing when some consumers resist in saving electricity. Energy Policy **59**, 843–849 (2013). http://linkinghub.elsevier.com/retrieve/pii/S0301421513003030
16. Soltani, N.Y., Kim, S.J., Giannakis, G.B.: Real-time load elasticity tracking and pricing for electric vehicle charging. IEEE Trans. Smart Grid **6**(3), 1303–1313 (2015). http://ieeexplore.ieee.org/lpdocs/epic03/wrapper.htm?arnumber=6948246,00006
17. Vairani, F.: BitCar: design concept for a collapsible stackable city car. Thesis, Massachusetts Institute of Technology (2009). http://dspace.mit.edu/handle/1721.1/49717
18. Weikl, S., Bogenberger, K.: Relocation strategies and algorithms for free-floating car sharing systems. IEEE Intell. Transp. Syst. Mag. **5**(4), 100–111 (2013)
19. Zilske, M.: Controler structure. http://archive.matsim.org/book/export/html/271
20. Zilske, M., Nagel, K.: Software architecture for a transparent and versatile traffic simulation. In: Agent Based Modelling of Urban Systems, May 2016

Mapping Bicycling Patterns
with an Agent-Based Model,
Census and Crowdsourced Data

Simone Z. Leao[✉] and Chris Pettit

City Futures Research Centre, University of New South Wales, Sydney, Australia
{s.zarpelonleao,c.pettit}@unsw.edu.au

Abstract. As our cities continue to grow issues such as congestion, air pollution and population health are also on the increase. Active transport can play an important part in activating multi-benefits for citizens and the city. In this research we focus our attention on understanding the patterns and behaviours of bicyclists as a form of active transport. There are a number of data sources which can be used to analyse patterns of cycling across cities. With the advent of smart phones with GPS and cycling specification apps, crowdsourced approaches can be used to acquire fine scale individual cycle travel patterns. In this research we analyse such crowdsourced data acquired through the riderlog application with specific focus on the City of Sydney. We use this rich data source along with other a more traditional journey to work and household travel survey data to create an agent based model using the open source GAMA platform. The work in this paper is early work in building a more sophisticated Agent-Based Model (ABM) to understanding cycling patterns across the City of Sydney to hence we commence by first testing the simple hypothesis is the shortest distance the main criteria for commuting by bicycle?

Keywords: Agent-based modelling · Bicycling · Smartphone data · Census data · GIS

1 Introduction

Understanding the flows of people moving through the built environment is a vital source of information for the planners and policy makers who shape our cities. In this paper we focus on a novel application where we begin to build an agent-based model using a number of data sources to enhance our understanding in how people bicycle through the city. There are numerous sources with relevant information about bicycling in Australia. For the specific region of Sydney, for example, we can list the Journey to Work data, the Household Travel Survey and the Sydney Cycling Survey by the New South Wales Bureau of Transport Statistics, the Super Tuesday Bike Count by Bicycle Network, and bicycling tracks recorded by the RiderLog smart phone application (Table 1).

© Springer International Publishing AG 2017
M.-R. Namazi-Rad et al. (Eds.): ABMUS 2016, LNAI 10051, pp. 112–128, 2017.
DOI: 10.1007/978-3-319-51957-9_7

All this data is gathered for different purposes, following different procedures, having different levels of representativeness and contents, and being released in different formats. Although their differences may be complementary, and their integration would potentially allow a better portray of bicycling patterns, their differences make their integration very difficult through conventional statistical methods. If lack of data was an issue in the past, the overload of data with different purposes, contents and formats that are difficult to combine seems to have become a new challenging issue. However, such a rich tapestry of data offers opportunities to explore novel modelling domains such as agent-based modelling for understanding fine scale behaviour and patterns of travel through our built environment. Active transportation, such as bicycling and walking, is receiving increasing research interest due to its health and environmental benefits (Mueller et al. 2015). Many cities and countries are putting policies in place to implement infrastructure for a built environment that is supportive and motivational to safe and pleasant active transportation. In regards to bicycling, best practices are found in the Netherlands, where 27% of the trips are performed on bicycles, followed by Denmark (18%), and Finland, Germany, Sweden and Belgium (around 10%) (Pucher and Buehler 2008). Australia, similarly to the UK, USA and Canada, has bicycling accounting for about 1% of daily trips (Pucher et al. 2011). In the City of Sydney, the mode of transport share is in average 29% public transport; 25% private car; 25% walk; 3% bicycle; and 18% other (taxi, motorbike, truck, work at home, doesn't go to work, or not stated) (BTS-NSW 2011). Although walking is significant as an active mode of transportation used in the City of Sydney, bicycling is below expectations. Pucher et al. (2011) listed a number of factors that may lead to the low levels of bicycling in Sydney, including the lack of extensive bicycling lanes, particularly of lanes which are separated from traffic and dedicated to cyclists, and the disconnected structure of the existing bicycling network. Bazzan and Klugl (2013) presented a review on ABM applications for traffic and transportation, indicating the appropriateness of the platform's metaphor to the scope of issues addressed in transportation studies, and its advantages compared to aggregated models. More recently, computation developments on seamless integration of GIS (geographical information systems) into ABM and the possibility of agentification of geo-spatial features have significantly improved the capacity of ABM to portray more realistic processes and patterns of urban environments (Taillandier et al. 2012). ABM is a method under the umbrella of complexity. It is built upon the principles that emergence of macro-patterns come from individualised but interconnected micro-decisions. The concept of micromotives and macrobehaviour was already stated in the homonymous book published by Thomas Schelling in 1978. However, it was the advances in computing that allowed its translation into sophisticated computer models (Crooks et al. 2008). In ABM, autonomous agents interact with the environment and with each other through behavioural rules. Although the rules can be simple, the varied configurations of the environment and the agents may cause non-linear feedback, and result in surprising and unexpected results (Axelrod 2005). Agents can be people, vehicles, countries, or any other element that constitute a wider system under study. A review of the literature indicates that although there have been a number of studies on bicycling patterns, they have not generally used ABM simulation as part of their methodology. Most studies are focused on investigating route choices among cyclists, using different types of statistics and regression analysis to weight influencing factors. Broach et al. (2012), for example, based on GPS data for cyclists in Portland/USA found that the majority of cyclists, particularly commuters, try to optimise a shortest distance route. Topography, bicycling infrastructure, traffic volume, number of turns also influence choice, but in a much lower level than distance. The major effect of distance in bicycling route choice was also confirmed in Menghini's et al. (2010) study in Zurich. Pucher et al. (2011), comparing Melbourne and Sydney/Australia, identified a number of influencing factors to bicycling, including distance, topography, weather, urban density, traffic volume, etc. These factors were analysed individually against aggregated data, but not weighted among themselves. The literature also reveals that ABM applications to urban transportation are generally focused on vehicle or pedestrian movement, and not on bicycling (Davidson et al. 2007; Bazzan and Klugl 2013; Badland et al. 2013). Only a few recent studies, specifically on ABM, applied to bicycling were found in the literature, including two studies using ABM for wayfinding behaviour of cyclists (Rybarczyk 2014 and Snizek 2015), and an article modelling bicycle traffic on a regional scale (Wallentin and Loidl 2015). This study is focused on the application of agent-based modelling to the theme of bicycling as an active mode of transport in cities.

Table 1. Sources of bicycling data for Sydney and NSW, Australia

Data Input	Source	Description
Journey to Work Data (JTW)	Bureau of Transport Statistics NSW http://www.bts.nsw.gov.au/Statistics/Journey-to-Work#top	Journey to Work (JTW) data are derived from the five yearly Census of Population and Housing conducted by the Australian Bureau of Statistics (ABS), and enhanced by the Bureau of Transport Statistics NSW. It includes data on employment by industry and occupation, and method of travel to work at a fine geographical level known as the travel zone. This information is a valuable resource for the analysis and forecasting of employment, commuting patterns and land use changes.
Household Travel Survey	Bureau of Transport Statistics NSW http://www.bts.nsw.gov.au/Statistics/Household-Travel-Survey/default.aspx#top	5,000 randomly selected households are approached each year to participate in the survey.
Sydney Cycling Survey (SCS)	Bureau of Transport Statistics NSW http://www.bts.nsw.gov.au/Statistics/Cycling/Summary	The SCS surveys over 11,000 individuals from 4,000 households. It collects information about cydists, cycling trips, cycling participation and cycling mode share.
RiderLog	Bicycle Network	Crowdsourced Smart phone data on bicycle journeys-GPSX collected every two second

2   Proposed Bicycle Model

2.1   Study Area

Sydney centre is the largest employment area in Sydney's Metropolitan region, in NSW, Australia, concentrating the majority of commuting trips by all modes of transportation. Despite the known health and environmental benefits from active transportation, and some bicycling infrastructure in place, the share of bicycling is still very low in Sydney (Fig. 1). The study area used in this paper is concentrated in bicycling flows between the suburb of Randwick and Sydney Centre. The selection of such a small area is due to two factors: first, at a preliminary stage this research is focused on testing a methodology and the use of some databases, more than assisting in planning and management of bicycling infrastructure; this will be pursued in future research; second, in this area, the limited bicycling network coincides with the main transport network, and the topography is gentle, which can best suit the shortest distance criterion.

2.2   Model Purpose

The objective of this study is to develop and test a methodology based on ABM to integrate different available data on bicycling, and with the new generated

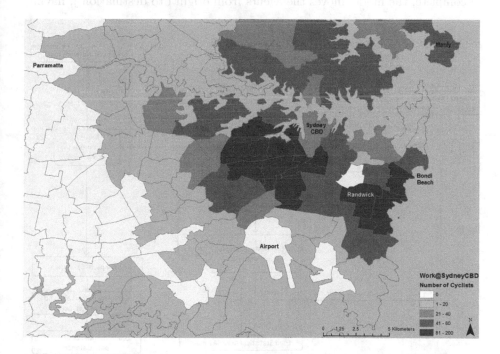

Fig. 1. Greater Sydney region showing number of cyclist living in statistical areas who work at Sydney CBD.

data, to better understand potential bicycling patterns. It is tested that the use of ABM can work as a platform to combine different data, overcoming their individual limitations and strengthening their complementarities. As a result of the simulation, the model should provide a portrait of how current cyclists commuting to work potentially distribute themselves across the city road network. Simulations will be validated with existing samples of bicycling tracks. In this preliminary stage, the simple hypothesis of shortest distance as the main criteria for commuting by bicycle is tested, as well considering independence among bicyclists (they do not influence each other).

2.3   Model Design

Figure 2 presents a flow chart with the inputs, main tasks and outputs produced by the proposed model. The model is developed using the open source GAMA 1.6.1 software. GAMA is a modelling and simulation environment for building spatially explicit agent-based simulations (Grignard et al. 2013). In summary, the model reads an Origin-Destination OD matrix aggregated by the Australian Bureau of Statistic's (ABS) statistical areas (SA2) and, using two nested loops, randomly allocates all commuters to their designated areas; then, it locates a destination for each commuter in a designated statistical area. Areas unsuitable for residence or employment are eliminated, respectively. When all the allocations are complete, the model moves the agents from origin i to destination j, having

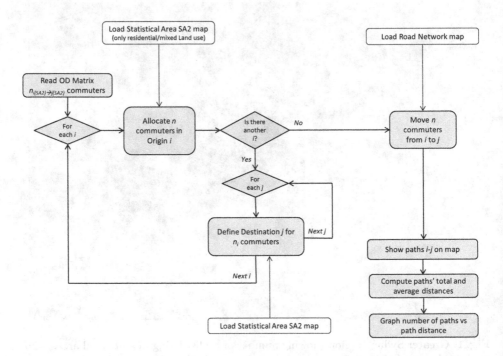

Fig. 2. ABM design for a simulating bicycling patterns

the road network as background, and shortest distance as criterion. Agents move with a speed randomly set between 8 and 14 Km/h. While moving the agents, the model draws the paths for visualisation, and also saves all paths as shapefiles for further analysis. Parameters are built-in to the model, so the user can change the number of cyclists or select Shapefiles for different origins and destinations with flexibility.

The conditions currently set by the model lead to limitations. Some of them are associated to speed, time, and agents allocation. The speed range used in the model was defined from actual speed recorded by cyclists in the RiderLog database. The model speed is defined by a minimum speed of 8 Km/h + a random value between 0 and 6 Km/h to accommodate different levels of fitness or cycling confidence. At the current stage of development, although cyclists can have different speed, this is constant along the whole cyclists path. Future version of the model should relate speed to other factors along the track, such as topography, traffic volume, number of intersections, type of cycling road infrastructure, etc. Currently, all agents start moving from home to work at the same time. They distribute across the road network because they have different origins and destinations, and they move with different speed. A further improvement for a revised version of the model should involve a random selection of departure time between commuting rush hours, such as between 7 to 9 am. This could provide a more realistic portrayal of cycling flows, and assist in analysing bicycling volumes along roads with significant amount of cyclists. It can also include the flow from work back home. Cyclists are allocated randomly in urban lots, in which a lot can have none, one or many cyclists. The allocation of agents at residences can be improved with additional cadastral information. Data on type of housing (single dwelling, small unit apartments, or large high rise apartments) together with number of residential units by lot can assist in a more realistic portray of residential density in an area.

2.4   Input Data: Journey to Work

The Journey to Work data from the NSW Bureau of Transport Statistics (BTS-NSW, 2011) provides information on the number of commuters for each pair of place of usual residence (PUR) and place of work (POW) aggregated by Statistical Area Level 2 (SA2), divided by principal mode of transport. This is called the origin-destination (OD) matrix. Based on this data for 2011, there are a total of 7,657 bicycling commuters who initiate or terminate their bicycling journeys within the City of Sydney. 57% are commuters who live outside the area, but cycle to the City of Sydney for work; 34% are commuters who live and work within the boundaries of the City of Sydney; the remaining 9% live in the area but cycle outside its boundaries for work. Figure 3 presents the spider diagram for commuting bicycling trips, where the lines indicate that there are commuters moving between Sydney Centre and the respective SA2, and the circle indicates the centroid of the SA2, with its size proportional to the number of cyclists. This OD matrix data is complete, since the JTW data covers the whole population. The number of commuters from one statistical area to another, divided by mode

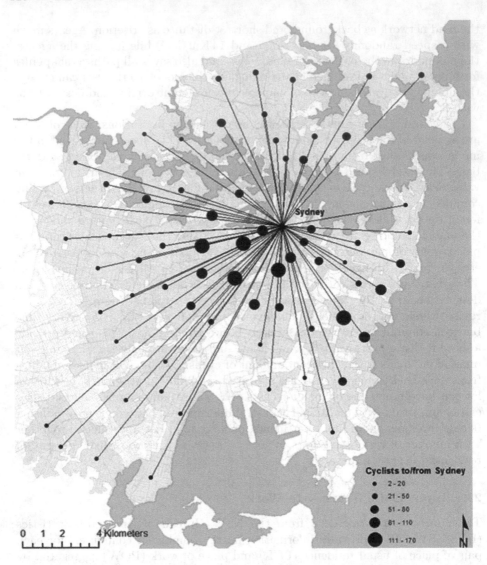

Fig. 3. Spider Diagram of the origin-destination links of cyclists to/from Sydney Centre from other SA2s The road network layer was obtained from NSWs Land and Property Information (LPI), and the statistical area boundaries (SA2) was obtained from the Australian Bureau of Statistics.

of transport, is robust information. However, this data is aggregated into large statistical areas, and no information is provided on distance, time, or itinerary of commuting trips. The agent-based model will be used here to provide this missing information.

3   Model Simulations

Figure 4 illustrates the simulation of the model, for commuting by bicycle between Randwick and Sydney Centre, as shown previously in the GAMA code. Considering 132 cyclists, as defined by the OD matrix for 2011, it shows the paths cyclists are likely to take if a shortest distance is the criterion. The shortest distance is defined through a network analysis on georeferenced road network, based on the length of each road segment and accumulated distance between origin and destination for alternative routes. The paths are marked in blue during

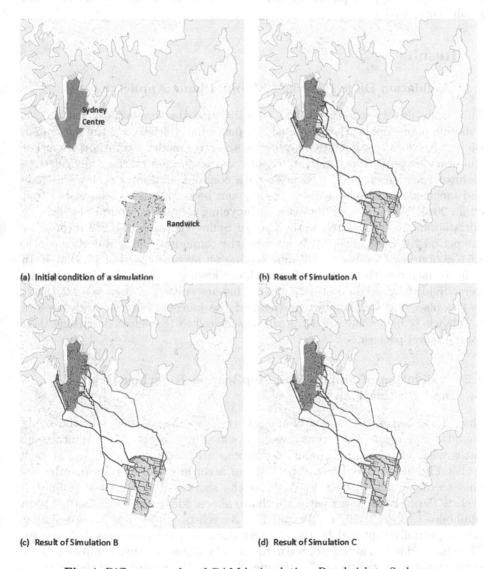

(a) Initial condition of a simulation

(b) Result of Simulation A

(c) Result of Simulation B

(d) Result of Simulation C

Fig. 4. Different results of GAMA simulation, Randwick to Sydney

the simulation for visualisation, and they are saved as shapefiles at the end of the simulation, allowing further spatial analysis in a GIS.

The initial conditions for the simulation, when residences and employment are allocated to each agent are presented in Fig. 4a. Results for three simulations of the model are presented in Figs. 4b, c and d, in which all agents reached their destination. Every simulation is slightly different because they rely on random values for residential and employment locations. However, since the random locations are restricted by specific boundaries (SA2s), although some differences are found at the micro level, the macro-behaviour seems to be very consistent. The identification of typical patterns required the model to be run several times, and results compared.

4   Results

4.1   Validation Data: RiderLog Mobile Phone Application

This study uses crowdsourced data for validating the simulations. RiderLog is a mobile phone application developed as part of an initiative of the Australian Bicycle Network to stimulate bicycling as an active mode of transportation. For voluntary users, it tracks individual rides and provides a platform for riders to monitor their progress. The Riderlog data contains attributes such as latitude and longitude so individual rider journey can be mapped and analysed (Pettit et al., 2016) The RiderLog database for bicycling commuting journeys which are initiated and/or terminated in the City of Sydney consists of 5,882 records for the period 2010–2014 (Fig. 5). In average, the commuters using RiderLog cycled 8.5 Km/journey (one way) in 35 min, having an average speed of 15.4 km/h. In order to facilitate the analysis of path choice among cyclists, bicycling patterns were divided by origin-destination pair, having statistical area level 2 (SA2) as the place tag for the start and end of the journey. For the study area of Randwick-Sydney, there are 37 records associated to 16 cyclists describing their spatial travel pattern.

4.2   Validation of Simulations: Replicating RiderLog Origins and Destinations

Since RiderLog is the data available on real bicycling journeys in the study area, the validation of the model was performed by using ABM to replicate the paths when identical origins and destinations are used for 16 cyclists. For each cyclist Fig. 6 compares the real path taken according to RiderLog (continuous line) to the simulated path by ABM as the shortest distance (dashed line). 8 cyclists (50%) have chosen paths which are almost identical to the shortest path (numbers 1, 3, 6, 7, 10, 11, 14 and 15). 3 cyclists (19%) have chosen similar paths, partially captured by the shortest distance path (numbers 4, 5 and 9). They have added an average of 800 m to the total distance, when compared to the shortest paths. 5 cyclists (31%) (number 2, 8, 12, 13 and 16) have chosen paths

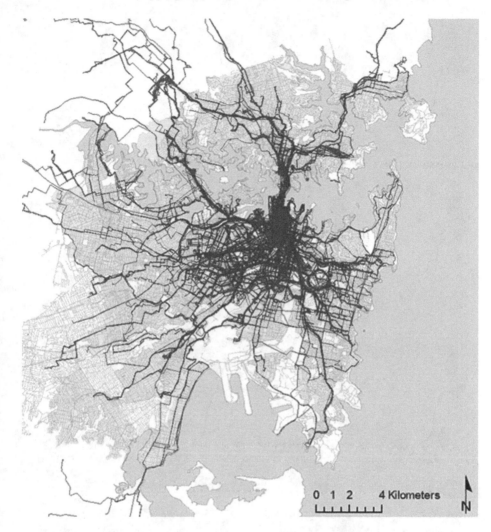

Fig. 5. Bicycling journeys to work, RiderLog 2010–2014

significantly different than the shortest paths. They generally increased the total journey distance in 1,300 m in average. Surprisingly, 2 cyclists (number 2 and 9) had real journeys shorter than the ABM shortest path (minus 110 and 240 m, respectively). These are probably shortcuts not captured by the digital road network used in the model, and reinforce the motivation of cyclists to reduce their journeys as much as possible. Overall, the simulations captured totally or partially 69% of the RiderLog bicycling journeys. This result is considered suitable in this preliminary stage of research, but it indicates that additional factors need to be included in the simulation if a more accurate portrait of bicycling patterns is desired.

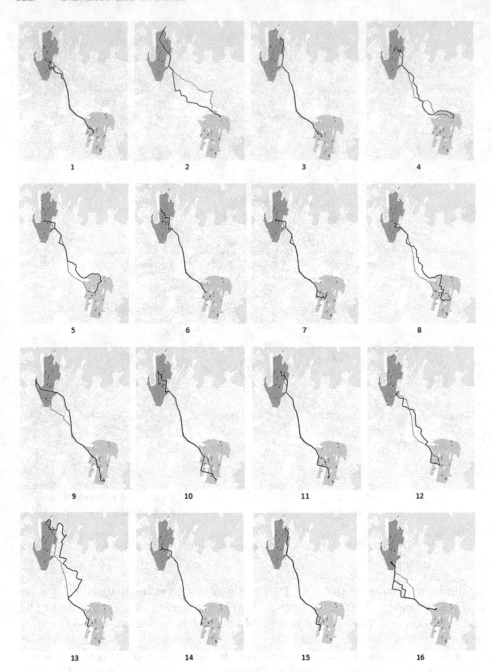

Fig. 6. Comparison between simulated shortest distance path (dashed line) and RiderLog recorded tracks (continuous line) for real cyclists for journeys from Randwick to Sydney, 16 cyclists

4.3   Assessment of Simulations: Bicycling Patterns According to ABS Journey to Work Data

Assuming the proposed model can reasonably portray bicycling patterns, it was run considering the total number of cyclists as per the ABS Journey to Work data: 132 people commute to work from Randwick to Sydney using bicycle as the main mode of transportation. Several simulations were performed for the study area, and a typical pattern was selected for analysis. The assessment of results was performed through a comparative analysis between the simulated bicycling patterns (ABM) and the RiderLog records for the same pair of origin-destination. The following parameters are compared: (1) a comparison between the two patterns (Fig. 7a and b); (2) the distribution of the percentage of cyclists by distance (Fig. 7c); (3) the average distance per journey (as well as minimum and maximum distance, and standard deviation); and (4) the proportion of RiderLog journeys that have been totally or partially captured by the simulation (Fig. 7d).

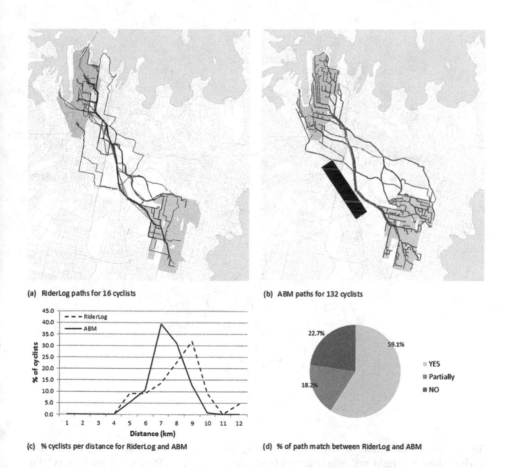

(a) RiderLog paths for 16 cyclists

(b) ABM paths for 132 cyclists

(c) % cyclists per distance for RiderLog and ABM

(d) % of path match between RiderLog and ABM

Fig. 7. Comparison between RiderLog and ABM simulation for the pair Randwick-Sydney

The comparison between RiderLog and ABM paths were developed in terms of proportion of common road segments; 100% for a complete match, and at least 2/3 (67%) for a partial match.

As shown in Fig. 7d, almost 80% of RiderLog paths were totally or partially captured by the ABM simulation. This is higher than the result for the validation in the previous section. It means that, when the total bicycling commuting population is simulated, including 132 people, the overall pattern is more similar to the sample of real journeys, due to the larger number of paths, and also

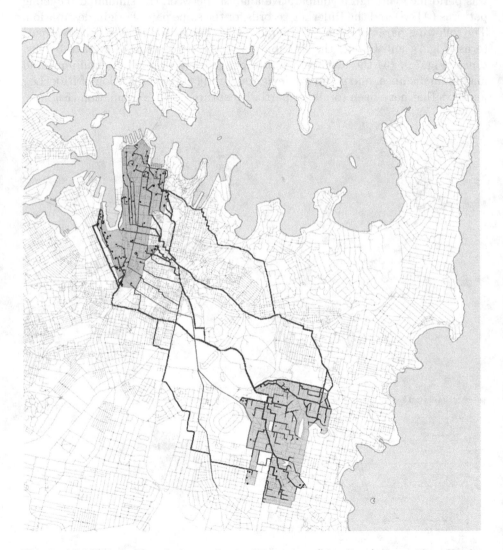

Fig. 8. ABM simulation of alternative cycling routes (blue lines) to avoid traffic disruption along the light rail construction (red line) for the pair Randwick-Sydney (Color figure online)

the more varied locations of origins and destinations. RiderLog paths are GPS tracked, therefore, the slight higher sharpness of the RiderLog paths (Fig. 7a) when compared to the ABM tracks (Fig. 7b) is caused by the influence of the GPS accuracy. ABM tracks align perfectly to the road network, since agents move along them in the model. The accuracy of the GPS do not affect the capacity of method to identify the track through the road network for comparison. The average distance per journey (one way) was 6.9 Km for the ABM simulation (min 4.4; max 9.0; st dev 1.0), while it was 7.8 Km/journey for the RiderLog sample (min 4.5; max 11.8; st dev 1.6). Figure 7.c plots the percentage of cyclists by distance for the two datasets. The distributions are proportionally similar, with a slight increase in the average distance for RiderLog, compared to the simulations. This is because, although a good visual correlation exists between the sample and the simulation (Fig. 7a and b), it is possible to notice that more than 20% of the paths were not captured by the simulation. This is associated with the fact that some cyclists have other criteria than short distance to select their path. The literature suggests safety, comfort and visual amenity as important aspects considered by cyclists (Pucher et al. 2011). Both sets of data indicate that part of Anzac Parade is used by most of the bicycling trips (it is part of 64% of the paths in the ABM simulation, and 70% of the RiderLog records). This is relevant, since the construction of a light rail is planned for this major urban highway, which will affect all types of traffic for a long period, including bicycling. The use of alternative routes can be tested with the ABM bicycling model. Figure 8 illustrates the context in which the light rail construction (red line) disrupt traffic, indicating which alternative routes, also considering the shortest possible distance, cycling commuters would use for their journey to work. The alternative routes have increased cycling distance in 19% in average when compared to the previous journeys through Anzac Parade (1.3 km, from 6.9 Km to 8.2 km). This increase could cause some decline in the share of cycling as a transportation mode in Randwick and other surrounding suburbs also affected by the light rail construction.

5   Discussion and Limitations

This study investigated the use of an ABM to produce a new database of bicycling commuting patterns through simulation, in order to overcome the limitations of the databases currently available. Census provides information of origins and destinations of all bicyclists, without detailing their itineraries. RiderLog, on the other hand, provides detailed information on bicyclist's itineraries; however, it is a sample of the population without known levels of representativeness. The proposed model combined the aggregated Census 2011 OD commuting data with the capacity of an ABM to randomise allocations and destinations under constraints and to emulate movement through a given network. Therefore, artificial cyclists, numbered and allocated according to the Census, cycled in the model from their potential residences to their potential work locations. It was assumed at this stage of the research that cyclists try to minimise their journey distance selecting the shortest length route. As a result, individual potential bicycling itineraries were designed by artificial agents representing an overall pattern in the study area in 2011 according to the Census journey to work data. For validation, a typical simulation among a large number of simulation runs is compared to the RiderLog journeys. A good level of match was found in the study area between the itineraries for the simulated (ABM) bicyclists and real bicyclists. Some differences are found in the micro-level at the start or end of the simulation due to the specific residential and employment allocations, however, the itineraries are significantly similar at the main intermediate parts of the trips along major roads. Using a metaphor of a tree: there are more similarities on the truck and main branches, that on the fine roots and small branches. For planning purposes, it means that such simulation results can be helpful to identify major bicycling routes that assist bicyclists to reach their destinations at the shortest distance. Improved safety can be implemented in those routes, for example, through the addition of bicycling lanes. Bicycling lanes separated from traffic are particularly recommended for roads with significant traffic volume and high speed limits. The combination of a policy implementing improved safety on shortest paths could lead to increasing cycling as a transport mode share. Differences between simulated and real bicycling itineraries were also found in a few proportion of trips, to which the criteria for route selection of real journeys were evidently not based on the shortest distance. Previous research support shortest distance as one of the most prominent factors for bicycling route selection, however it has also proven that some other factors such as topography and safety (traffic volume, congestion, and type of cycling infrastructure) can play a significant role. Future improvement of the proposed model should incorporate other motivations for the agents to choose their route to work. This can be informed by a detailed analysis of the factors affecting the decisions taken by the itineraries recorded in the RiderLog dataset, and their variations by socio-demographic, area, and ride distance.

6   Conclusions and Next Steps

This study indicates that a rich tapestry of data currently available offers opportunities to explore novel modelling domains such as agent-based modelling for understanding fine scale behaviour and patterns of travel through our built environment. Yet this is early work and there are a number of additional lines of enquiry being considered to advance this modelling, including the inclusion and testing against a larger geographical extent. This will mean we can draw upon a much larger resource of crowdsource bicycling data. We also plan on incorporating into the model Bicycle Count data derived from the Bicycle Network's Super Tuesday annual commuter bike count and also from the City of Sydney and other Councils bicycle count collections. The addition of additional spatial data including slope and the location of bicycle ways both shared and dedicated will also provide useful inputs for testing and refining the model. It is envisaged such a bicycling behaviour model will be useful in a practical sense. Land use and transport planners will be able to understand more clearly where bicyclists are travelling and how bicyclists are likely to behave when changes are made to the built environment as the city continues to grow. Subsequently, transport and land use planning strategies will be able to move beyond drawing five kilometre buffers around major centres as bicycle catchments. Through evidenced based approaches as supported by modelling and data visualisation, more comprehensive plans can ultimately be undertaken to properly plan for high quality bicycling infrastructure to support citizens and visitors who wish to use this active transport mode to move about our cities.

References

Axelrod, R.: Advancing the art of simulation in the social sciences. In: Rennard, J.-P. (ed.) Handbook of Research on Nature Inspired Computing for Economy and Management. Idea Group, Hersey (2005)

Bazzan, A.L.C., Klugl, F.: A review on agent-based technology for traffic and transportation. Knowl. Eng. Rev. **29**(3), 375–403 (2013)

Broach, J., Dill, J., Gliebe, J.: Where do cyclists ride? A route choice model developed with revealed preference GPS data. Transp. Res. Part A: Policy Pract. **46**(10), 1730–1740 (2012)

BTS-NSW, Bureau of Transport Statistics NSW, Journey to WorkData (2011). http://www.bts.nsw.gov.au/Statistics/Journey-to-Worktop

Crooks, A., Castle, C., Batty, M.: Key challenges in agent-based modelling for geospatial simulation. Comput. Environ. Urban Syst. **32**(6), 417–430 (2008)

Grignard, A., Taillandier, P., Gaudou, B., Vo, D.A., Huynh, N.Q., Drogoul, A.: GAMA 1.6: advancing the art of complex agent-based modeling and simulation. In: Boella, G., Elkind, E., Savarimuthu, B.T.R., Dignum, F., Purvis, M.K. (eds.) PRIMA 2013. LNCS (LNAI), vol. 8291, pp. 117–131. Springer, Heidelberg (2013). doi:10.1007/978-3-642-44927-7_9

Menghini, G., Carrasco, N., Schussler, N., Axhausen, K.W.: Route choice of cyclists in Zurich. Transp. Res. Part A: Policy Pract. **44**(9), 754–765 (2010)

Mueler, N., Rojas-Rueda, D., Cole-Hunter, T., Nazelle, A., Dons, E., Gerike, R., Gotschi, T., Panis, L.I., Kahlmeier, S., Nieuwenhuijsen, M.: Health impact assessment of active transportation: a systematic review. Prev. Med. **76**(July), 103–114 (2015)

Pettit, C.J., Liekse, S., Leao, S.: Big bicycling data processing: from personal data to urban applications. In: ISPRS XXIII Congress, Prague, 12–19 July 2016

Pucher, J., Buehler, R.: Making cycling irresistible: lessons from the Netherlands, Denmark, and Germany. Transp. Rev. **28**(4), 495–528 (2008)

Pucher, J., Garrard, J., Greaves, S.: Cycling down under: a comparative analysis of bicycling trends and policies in Sydney and Melbourne. J. Transp. Geogr. **19**(2), 332–345 (2011)

Rybarczyk, G.: Simulating bicycle wayfinding mechanisms in an urban environment. Urban Plan. Transp. Res. **2**(1), 89–104 (2014)

Schelling, T.C.: Micromotives and Macrobehavior. Harvard University Press, Cambridge (1978)

Snizek, B.: Mapping cyclist's experiences and agent-based modelling of their wayfinding behaviour. PhD Thesis, Department of Geosciences and Natural Resource management, University of Copenhagen, June 2015

Taillandier, P., Vo, D.-A., Amouroux, E., Drogoul, A.: GAMA: a simulation platform that integrates geographical information data, agent-based modeling and multi-scale control. In: Desai, N., Liu, A., Winikoff, M. (eds.) PRIMA 2010. LNCS (LNAI), vol. 7057, pp. 242–258. Springer, Heidelberg (2012). doi:10.1007/978-3-642-25920-3_17

Wallentin, G., Loidl, M.: Agent-based bicycle traffic model for Salzburg City. J. Geogr. Inf. Sci. 1, 2015 (2015)

Davidson, W., Donnelly, R., Vovsha, P., Freedman, J., Ruegg, S., Hicks, J., Castiglione, J., Picado, R.: Synthetsis of first practices and operational research approaches in activity-based travel demand modelling. Practice 41(5), 464–488 (2007)

Badland, H., White, M., MacAulay, G., Eagleson, S., Mavoa, S., Pettit, C., Giles-Corti, B.: Using simple agent-based modelling to inform and enhance neighbourhood walkability. Int. J. Health Geographics 12(58), 1–10 (2013)

Transportation in Agent-Based Urban Modelling

Sarah Wise[1]([✉]), Andrew Crooks[2], and Michael Batty[1]

[1] Centre for Advanced Spatial Analysis, University College London,
90 Tottenham Court Road, London W1T 4TJ, UK
s.wise@ucl.ac.uk
[2] Department of Computational and Data Sciences, College of Science, George Mason
University, Research Hall, 4400 University Drive, MS 6B2, Fairfax, VA 22030, USA

Abstract. As the urban population rapidly increases to the point where
most of us will be living in cities by the end of this century, the need
to better understand urban areas grows ever more urgent. Urban simulation modelling as a field has developed in response to this need, utilising developing technologies to explore the complex interdependencies,
feedbacks, and heterogeneities which characterise and drive processes
that link the functions of urban areas to their form. As these models
grow more nuanced and powerful, it is important to consider the role of
transportation within them. Transportation joins, divides, and structures
urban areas, providing a functional definition of the geometry and the
economic costs that determine urban processes accordingly. However, it
has proved challenging to factor transportation into agent-based models
(ABM); past approaches to such modelling have struggled to incorporate
information about accessibility, demographics, or time costs in a significant way. ABM have not yet embraced alternative traditions such as
that in land use transportation modelling that build on spatial interaction in terms of transport directly, nor have these alternate approaches
been disaggregated to the level at which populations are represented as
relatively autonomous agents. Where disaggregation of aggregate transport has taken place, it has led to econometric models of individual
choice or microsimulaton models of household activity patterns which
only superficially embody the key principles of ABM. But the explosion in the availability of movement data in recent years, combined with
improvements in modelling technology, is easing this process dramatically. In particular, agent-based modelling as a methodology has grown
ever more promising and is now capable of emulating the interplay of
urban systems and transportation. Here, we explore the importance of
this approach, review how transportation has been factored into or omit-
ted from agent-based models of urban areas, and suggest how it might
be handled in future applications. Our approach is to take snapshots of
different applications and use these to illustrate how transportation is
handled in such models.

Keywords: Agent-based modelling · Urban systems · Urban modelling

© Springer International Publishing AG 2017
M.-R. Namazi-Rad et al. (Eds.): ABMUS 2016, LNAI 10051, pp. 129–148, 2017.
DOI: 10.1007/978-3-319-51957-9_8

1 Introduction

From the time when the first cities emerged some 5000 years ago, the manner in which populations physically transported themselves was governed by prevailing technology. Taken in conjunction with the key social and economic objectives which shaped and drove the development of cities, transportation has defined the way the city interacts for the whole of their existence. Until the invention of the internal combustion engine in the late 18th century, the fastest transportation was based on horse and carriage, while the distance travelled by populations to and from work was limited to how far one could walk within an hour. Economic landscapes and city systems were thus conditioned geometrically by these distances. Moreover, within cities the polarisation of activities involving local movement to and from their market centres imposed a limit on the density of traffic: the average speed of traffic in the largest cities from ancient Rome to Elizabethan London, and even to contemporary times has never been greater than about 10 km an hour on the local street systems (Morris 1994).

Until the invention of the railways, the technologies utilised for urban transportation had barely changed over thousands of years (Schobert 2014). The industrial revolution enabled mass transportation using the first public systems, and facilitated private means of travel such as the automobile, allowing cities to break out of the straightjacket imposed by non-automated technology. In the last 200 years, transportation has dominated cities in ways that have enabled them to grow dramatically, to sprawl across vast areas only limited by the time taken to travel and the restrictions imposed by time required at work. In the early 19th century, this meant that for the first time cities could grow well beyond their previous population limits of about 1 million persons; this nexus is changing once again as new information technologies are increasingly being used to complement and substitute for more material forms of transportation of people and goods (Batty 2013).

Cities can only grow if the requisite transportation is in place, and problems of rapid growth depend on getting the balance between private versus public transportation right (UN-Habitat 2010). This dynamic is particularly pronounced in the developing world, where the fastest growing cities now exist. Most cities with populations greater than 2 million persons require some form of mass transit or subway system. Much of London's explosive growth in the Victorian era necessitated the development of new technologies to support its expansion, such as the London Underground system and Bazalgette's remarkable public sanitation works, both systems which are still in active use. Cities and regions thus depend fundamentally in terms of their spatial structure on flows between activities and the populations that create and operate them, which are profoundly shaped by the physical networks that connect them together. For over 200 years, economists have argued that space itself is a critical factor in determining how industries locate and how cities function. Markets bring demand and supply together through a clearing mechanism which provides a functioning system in which prices and rents determine how land is allocated in the production and consumption of economic and social activities. Distance and its usual formalisation as an inferior good - which in general suggests that on balance, we want less of it rather then more of it - is the basic arbiter of how cities are structured. Transportation is central to this and is enshrined in the basic notion best articulated by Tobler (1970) in his famous first law of geography: "... everything is related to everything else, but near things are more related than distant things". Transport is intrinsic to this principle or law and it appears directly or indirectly in most models of urban systems.

Not all models incorporate transportation. However, in particular those developed using systems dynamics (see Forrester 1969) - and thus appropriate conceptions of distance and transport - are key to the way urban models must operate (Batty 1971). Brockmann and Helbing (2013) make this point simply and elegantly, showing that the seemingly chaotic spread of disease can be easily modelled as a simple function of what they term "effective distance". Thus, as transportation networks structure and dictate an emergent cost of movement, it is important to bring them to bear when we attempt to study processes that rely on distance and interaction.

Modelling cities is a Herculean task, and historically researchers who might have wished to include transportation in their models faced a variety of challenges to incorporating transport data. Access to data has always been an obvious limitation, as has been the way we embody networks into such models. Even as tools and data have become more accessible, theoretical conundrums remain with respect to how we determine where to draw the line of abstraction in attempting to understand transportation. For example, accessibility has changed with the advent of new technologies, and researchers must choose whether to include socioeconomic factors such as car ownership or bus usage in their model. Some researchers have tried to get around the problem of transport by drawing upon Simon's (1996) concept of the near-decomposability of systems, in which parts of a system interact among themselves in clusters or subgraphs, with interactions among subsystems being relatively weaker or fewer but not negligible. This is what Forrester (1969) articulated in his Urban Dynamics model, in which transport became insignificant due to the fine spatial granularity of the model. Essentially he abstracted the problem into one of interacting regions so that the model might focus on activities solely with one such region. In fact, many agent-based models focus on urban problems without really addressing the question of transportation, omitting it as a factor in processes such as gentrification, regeneration, urban sprawl, crime, agricultural land use, land markets, and disease models as we will highlight in this chapter.

In the remainder of this chapter, we first identify how transport enters a wide array of models of urban systems, pointing to agent-based models as having quite rudimentary conceptions of transportation embedded within them. Section 2 will give an overview of how land use transportation interaction (LUTI) models, disaggregate economic choice models (sometimes called discrete choice), and microsimulation models all incorporate transport directly, and give an overview of agent-based modelling with its contrasting approach. This variety of approaches to transportation within the existing literature sets the context for a discussion of the current state of the field. In Sect. 3, we lay out a framework for understanding the complexity of the transportation models utilised by existing agent-based models, which we utilise as a guide in application domains in Sects. 3.1, 3.2 and 3.3. The chapter concludes with Sect. 4, a summary and outlook for the field of agent-based modelling and transportation.

2   Simulation Models for Urban Transportation

The first computer models of urban systems were based on transportation and emerged in the early to mid-1950s in parallel with the development of mainframe computers for transactions processing in government and business. The development of the digital computer was closely linked to scientific applications in which transport was an early focus, as were location-allocation, input-output modelling, and commodity and trade flow analysis. The first operational models were built in 1955 for policy analysis for the Chicago Area Transportation Study (Boyce and Williams 2015). These models were essentially aggregative simulations of flows of traffic between what came to be called origins and destinations, invariably defined by dividing the city into small zones. The models in question originated from analogies between classical Newtonian physics and human flows using ideas about gravitation and potential. In this, the inverse square law was central; thus from the very beginning of the discipline, distance became the key organising factor of transportation modelling.

   These models became the basis for the standard four stage transport model which is still today the workhorse of transportation planning (Ortuzar and Willumsen 2011). Models were built to generate trips within small zones (the first stage); gravity models were then used to distribute flows between origin and destination zones according to distance and the attraction of these zones (the second stage); the flows were then split into different modes using econometric type statistical models (modal split, the third stage); the resultant flows were assigned to the network (the fourth stage) so that congestion could be evaluated and the network changed if necessary. These models are highly aggregate in that they simulate total flows on different modes of transit networks and their segments, usually at peak hour. They are only implicitly dynamic, as they simulate only a total number of trips taken at the peak hour: in this sense, they are equilibrium models (Batty 2008). As they were developed, they came to be disaggregated in terms of trip types and trip maker categories and a new theory based on how typical travellers - or agents - made choices between different locations emerged. These discrete choice models are consistent with more aggregate gravity-spatial interaction styles of models; their populations as agents do not communicate with one another. However, such models do attempt to represent the system at the level of the behavioural unit (Ben-Akiva and Lerman 1985), albeit with respect to generic probability distributions applicable to any individual trip maker.

   The development of discrete choice modelling in the 1970s gave way to microsimulation models of traffic. These essentially model the decisions of the household or trip-makers in households with respect to their daily activity patterns, representing the city in complete detail with all agents being represented (or in the case of really massive systems, with a sample percentage, usually 10 percent, of the individuals represented (Horni et al. 2016). In these models, the agents again do not communicate, influencing one another indirectly through the congestion they generate for one another with its resulting cost to the household activity budget. The best example of these kinds of models is MATSIM which was developed from the US initiative in the TRANSIMs model in the early 1990s (Horni et al. 2016). More recent work (Padgham et al. 2014) has explored the integration of a Belief-Desire-Intention decision making component within MATSIM, allowing the model to incorporate more nuanced behaviours and interactions.

Aggregate, disaggregate, and household activity microsimulation transport models quickly spawned extensions to land use modelling, which in turn have generated their own tradition by fusing ideas about density, rents, housing markets, economic base and input-output analysis with locational decision-making. These have come to be called LUTI models and, in general, operate by separating out transport from land use but taking standard four stage transport models and linking these through a loose coupling to their land use equivalents. Some such as UrbanSim have attempted to specify populations at the individual, agent-based level (Waddell 2002); these are often referred to as agent-based equivalents of urban models (Batty 2012). They again do not incorporate communication, thus making coordination or purposive (joint) action impossible to model.

Historically, then, there have been many different kinds of transport models, many of which are relatively top-down, aggregate, or non-interactive. More modern approaches such as microsimulation or agent-based modelling have sought to rectify the dynamics which elude older models. Agent-based modelling (ABM) is a simulation methodology which breaks a system down into individual actors, or agents, which interact with one another and with their environment based on their own individual attributes and behavioural rules (Epstein and Axtell 1996; Miller and Page 2007; Cederman 2002). They are distinct from microsimulation models, in which large random samples of a population of individuals are progressively advanced through statistical transitions based on their individual attributes (see Crooks and Heppenstall 2012). The line between microsimulation and ABM is indeed very blurred, as there exist microsimulation models which incorporate minimal social networks to guide their decision-making (e.g. the demand for eldercare as modelled in Gilbert and Troitzsch 2005) and ABMs in which interaction occurs exclusively through environmental variables (e.g. the most basic, baseline implementation of the SugarScape model of Epstein and Axtell 1996). On the other hand, the two approaches are moving towards a more common ground as microsimulation models add more behavioural and spatial interaction between individual units and ABM add both space and demographic characteristics to their agents (Birkin and Wu 2012). In this work, we proceed with the definition of ABM that requires explicit interaction among agents for a model to be considered an ABM. In the interests of length, we will leave microsimulation and household activity models of transport such as MATSIMs to one side (see Horni et al. 2016 for more information), focusing exclusively on how transportation is represented in agent-driven models that do not attempt to model the transportation system or the transportation planning process per se.

In light of this individual focus, it is important to address a factor of individually-oriented models which is frequently elided, namely the unit of behavioural representation. Agent-based models that directly address the transportation system are usually conceived in terms of the movement of persons and the way they interact with one another; this tends to exclude vehicles which often remove the personal, interactive element of ABM in favour of fixed route systems which promote mixing. Accordingly, most ABMs for transport have tended to abstract from the transportation system per se, and in the following work, we will demonstrate several of these kinds of models relating to crime, segregation, and disease within cities. An exception to this general trend is in pedestrian modelling, where the agents are mainly pedestrians (although other elements of the built environment may be treated as fixed or mobile agents; e.g. Torrens 2014). In such models, agents come into physical contact and also generate crowding, flocking, and herding effects that emerge from their interactions. Sometimes these sorts of models are coupled to decision-making sequences that pertain to the social and economic context, such as movement to purchase goods in shopping centres; there can be quite complex linkages between agents, goods, and the transport of these to other locations that feature in such models (Heppenstall et al. 2012).

All of these dynamics can be more powerfully addressed thanks to the growing supply of data. With increasing availability of the kind of fine-grained data that allows for high-quality agent-based models to be applied to systems, ABM can be applied to a growing range of locations and contexts. In particular, as we will see, ABM tends to be much more detailed with respect to particular sectors of the urban system where there is much more emphasis on detailed behavioural mechanisms that are composed of a variety of rules that define the ways in which such models function. ABM offers us a new lens through which we can focus on human populations as individuals and groups in models - and through which we can critically simulate their physical and social movements in ways that were never possible before. Given the promise of this new technology, in the following sections, we explore the relationship between transportation and ABM, presenting broad categories of models to better explore how the same processes have been addressed by different researchers.

One final point is worth making before we review transportation in ABM, and it involves networks. As transport models largely abstract from the transport network in terms of the way models of transport flow are articulated and only load these flows back onto networks for operational purposes, the network has never been the subject of any exhaustive analysis in transportation modelling. Not so in ABM, where the network itself in terms of its structure is often central to the way agents interact. In ABM, trends of feedback and emergence which are reflected in network processes can be key drivers of higher-level patterns. In this sense, we would argue that ABM is much more closely linked to network science and its developments than traditional transportation modelling that has never focussed on the morphology of the network per se.

3   Tiers of Complexity in Agent-Based Modelling

Our review here will present examples of how agent-based models have been developed for a range of urban dynamic processes which tend to focus on individual sectors of the urban system in which transportation plays a key role. In the following section, we will highlight agent-based models which successfully incorporate transportation, and especially models which utilise network properties to give more focussed understandings of transportation and distance. In fact, unlike the complete models discussed in Sect. 2, the models reviewed here are not built around transportation per se, as transportation is not privileged in these models over and above any other activities or features. It is important to reiterate that we will not be addressing cellular automata or other styles of models which lack either purposive agents or interactions, as these necessarily treat transportation as, at best, a fixed and invariant process. Our focus is thus on quite a narrow range of model types, namely those which deal with transportation in emergent phenomena arising from the interactions and feedbacks among agents.

In order to more conveniently compare and contrast models, we will distinguish among models by defining a notional measure of the complexity, specifically orientated to transport models. Thus a model in which the entities or agents move freely across a continuous space or lattice includes only the most basic sense of transport; they represent space and include an implied understanding of distance, but nothing more. We call this Tier 0 complexity. Pursuing a more detailed understanding of interaction, a Tier 1 model is one in which movement is structured by a network or some other topological features. Thus for example, if a model of housing choice includes not only information that a home is near a public transit station, but is able to consider the betweenness or centrality of that station within the network, the agent's understanding of the desirability of that property is accordingly enriched. More complex still is a Tier 2 model, in which a network's edges are weighted to reflect their costs and/or benefits. Cost may be economic: a model which ignores the relative cost of a toll road fails to capture the true impact of the road on the system. Cost could also allow the agent to plan based on their personal costs due to having or lacking certain attributes: if one has access to an automobile rather than public transit alone, new parts of the network are opened and/or closed to the agent. These models may include multiple costs/benefits per edge, such as the cost in terms of time, money, unpleasantness (e.g. overfull commuter trains), pollution, and so forth. Finally, at the most complex end of the scale are Tier 3 models, which incorporate information about edges with weights that vary over different dimensions of the simulation. Driving agents can plan their day around traffic surges, for example; similarly, agents might avoid a particularly busy commuter train, stringing together a chain of public transit links to arrive at their destination in slightly

Table 1. Different tiers of transport complexity for ABM

Tier	Qualities	Examples
0	Spatial environments without constraints on movement	Agents move between home work, and other location types at a constant speed on a lattice
1	Environment constrained topologically, e.g. by a network or areas of exclusion	Agents move between home, work etc. locations at a constant speed along a road/rail/walk network
2	Topological environmental structures incorporating weights which constrain movement	Agents move between home, work, etc. locations along a transport network, minimising an economic cost function
3	The weights of the topological structure vary over the different dimensions of the simulation	Agents move between home, work etc. locations along a network with fluctuating traffic levels, minimising a cost function with economic and temporal components

more time but greater comfort. These Tier 3 models are examples of the full behavioural richness agents could emulate. At the time of writing, the authors were unaware of any agent-based model that could achieve this level of complexity. It is included here to give a sense of future research directions with respect to agent-based modelling and transportation models. The tiers are presented in Table 1 for reference. However, it should be noted that agent-based models that focus purely on transportation have been excluded from this review as the focus is on more partial subsystems of the urban system and their processes and dynamics. With this notional index of transportation complexity, we will present a number of models, identifying the origins of the model, the context to which it is applied, the entity being modelled, the spatial and temporal scales of the simulation, the modes of transit included, and some discussion of the index of transport complexity. The entities being modelled may be, for example, individuals, households, groups, or spatial areas - in short, the units within the model which are able to exhibit heterogeneous behaviours, which is one of the hallmarks of agent-based modelling. The spatial scale of the model is the size of the physical area being modelled (e.g. inside a building, neighbourhood, city, region, country, and so forth). Temporal scale is used here to mean the mapping of ticks of the simulation to units of time.

3.1   Models of Criminal Activity

Crime represents a high-stakes and high-profile urban issue, one for which it can be difficult to justify experiments en vivo. As such, many researchers have attempted to use ABM in this context. The field of crime science holds that crime is emergent from the interactions among potential offenders, potential targets, and guardians of the potential targets (Cohen and Felson 1979), making a methodology which can simulate the behaviours of each even more attractive. It thus implies that ABM is highly applicable in that the source of the activity itself is a product of the interactions between different kinds of agents. Different models have incorporated movement and behaviour in a variety of ways as we show in Table 2.

Table 2. Typical applications of ABM to crime

Author	Application	Entity	Spatial scale	Temporal scale (units)	Transportation	Transport complexity
Dray et al. (2008)	Crime	Individuals	City	36 months (days)	Pedestrian	0
Melo et al. (2006)	Crime	Individuals	City	1 month (minutes)	Pedestrian	0
Groff (2007)	Crime	Individuals	City	1 month (minutes)	Road	1
Wise and Cheng (2016)	Crime	Individuals	Neighbour-hood	1 month (minutes)	Road	2
Malleson and Birkin (2012)	Crime	Individuals	Neighbour-hood	1 month (minutes)	Road, Rail, Bus	2

For example, Dray et al. (2008) have developed a series of simulations that explore the impact of three different street-level policing interventions (random patrols, hot-spot policing, and problem-oriented strategies), specifically exploring how problem-oriented policing influences a drug market. Their work situates officers and civilians within an abstract lattice environment of "street blocks" representing an urban area, through which they are free to move. Similarly, Melo et al. (2006) use a grid of cells in their simulation of police patrol routes. Their work similarly treats the agents as pedestrians who move among points of interest. Groff (2007) presents a more complicated model in terms of transportation, utilising real road network data in her study of street robbery. Her work models the police randomly moving through the environment and arresting offenders as they encounter them, informed by and influenced by the real road networks of Seattle, Washington. In particular, she compares the impact of including the real road network in place of a grid or lattice, finding that the road network structure significantly impacts the outcome of the model. The introduction of even a road network enables the model to pick out simple transport dynamics.

In a similar vein, the work of Wise and Cheng (2016) includes the real road network of an area of London in the simulation of police patrolling activity. Car-based police officers interact with traffic lights, which vary the cost of travel depending on the timing of their arrival; officers also weight the cost of roads based on whether or not they are responding to an emergency call and may ignore traffic laws. The richness of path costs is even more clearly displayed in the work of Malleson and Birkin (2012), in which burglars move around an environment, familiarising themselves with neighbourhoods and selecting targets to burgle. Malleson and Birkin's model includes transport by road, rail, and bus, even going so far as to denote which roads are car or pedestrian accessible. This range of available transit influences the agent's familiarity with different parts of the city, a critical dynamic in the burglary target selection process. These more nuanced models are more capable of capturing the important spatial dependencies associated with crime and policing, and suggest the importance of including these factors in models.

In all these varieties of crime model, transportation is key but this is largely because crime involves intrinsic mobility with detection occurring in mobile contexts through policing and criminals invariably moving to points where crime is committed. So far there has been little thought about cybercrime and its agent-based characteristics but this like many urban activities in the digital age is an undiscovered country when it comes to simulation, as much because such crime is at first sight invisible. What is important here is that the kind of aggregate dynamics of transportation as reflected in mainstream flow modelling is simply not a feature of this style of ABM where transport is one of many features of the system being represented but by no means the sole focus of such simulations.

To an extent, many of these kinds of ABM depend upon pedestrian modelling, which is arguably the archetypal agent-based model in the social sciences. These models are frequently motivated by the sole factor of determining how pedestrians move, assuming that their purpose can be determined by their direction and their contact with other pedestrians and related fixed obstacles. Many such models are highly geometrical in that the interaction between agents and the obstacles in their environment of movement is purely physical; this is the main reason why such models have been in the vanguard of ABM. Adding behavioural factors that determine the rationale for movement is much more complicated and to date, most developments have avoided such extensions except for applications such as those noted here in crime. Good reviews of the state of the art focussing first on relations to more conventional traffic flow modelling and second in relation to more rule-driven modelling are in the papers by Bellomo and Dogbe (2011) and the thesis by Zachariadis (2014).

3.2   Models of Disease Transmission and Diffusion

As cities grow denser, the potential cost of epidemic disease looms larger. Historically, researchers have modelled the spread of disease using mathematical models (e.g. network propagation in Brockmann and Helbing (2013), or system dynamics (Brailsford et al. 2009). These models tend to omit dynamics such as variable individual susceptibility to disease, and struggle to incorporate space meaningfully. The particular attributes of space, distance, and interaction are incredibly important in understanding the spread of disease, as the variable transmission patterns of influenza versus cholera versus sexually transmitted infections (STIs) suggest. An important consideration when describing how diseases spread is the fact that space can be extremely local and relational - a patient might be infected on a bus as she travels through an area, without that area ever experiencing a reported case. The "location" of the transmission event is the bus, which is a mobile space, and any intervention would need to take that dynamic into account. To some extent some crime patterns are affected in the same way, crimes being committed in mobile situations and not registered or recorded at the point where they take place. Aleman et al. (2011) note that while contact in public spaces is an important part of the mixing that produces epidemics, ABM of disease contexts have struggled to incorporate public transit into models of urban disease epidemics (Table 3).

The simplest models track the movement of susceptible individuals through space, as they proceed through the environment without constraint. Linard et al. (2008) present a simulation of exposure to malaria in southern France,

Table 3. Typical applications of ABM to disease in cities

Author	Application	Entity	Spatial scale	Temporal scale (units)	Transportation	Transport complexity
Linard et al. (2008)	Disease	Individuals (Human, Animal, Insect)	Region	1 Year (weeks)	Pedestrian	0
Perez and Dragicevic (2009)	Disease	Individuals	Neighbourhood	1 Month (hours)	Public transit	1
Simoes (2012)	Disease	Individuals	Country	2 Years (days)	Abstract	1
Aleman et al. (2011)	Disease	Individuals	City	1 Day (minutes)	Subway	2
Crooks and Hailegiorgis (2014)	Disease	Individuals	Region	Months (minutes)	Roads	2

in which humans periodically appear in locations where mosquitoes are common and animals move randomly around the environment. While there are both rural and urban areas, there are no connections among them to structure movement or the spread of disease.

Perez and Dragicevic (2009) present a more complicated model in which individuals with measles move among points of interest based on the road network. The authors associate the road network with public transit, but do not clarify how the individuals are grouped or their movements structured by the road network. In a similar vein, Simoes (2012) presents a model of individuals who are infected with mumps. These susceptible individuals exist within neighbourhoods through which they may move via a random graph; the neighbourhoods are connected to other neighbourhoods through their own random graph, with the urban centres themselves being connected to other urban centres throughout the country. Aleman et al. (2011) have a more complicated model of the available public transit, which allows individuals to select their path based on the minimal times taken, but the dynamics of the model are not influenced by any other costs or assumptions. Thus such movement is channelled through the connected networks but otherwise unstructured.

More complex models of the agent-based interactions between disease and movement patterns do exist. Crooks and Hailegiorgis (2014) present a model in which individuals travel around an environment trying to minimise their distance travelled, while being constrained by the carrying capacity of the network edges. Thus, individual efforts to move throughout space are limited and influenced by the movements and choices of others. Further, agents make choices based on the distances between them and the desired targets of their activities, choosing where and when to move in a way that is inherently informed by distance and accessibility. Thus, agents experience a more variable set of weights which significantly impacts the amount of exposure they have on other (potentially infected) individuals, with concordant ramifications for rates of infection.

3.3   Models of Urban Change

As noted in the introduction to this chapter, changes in transportation technologies have allowed cities to grow at an accelerating pace. Early theorists brought broad, abstract, macro and micro models to bear on the problem, utilising mathematical structures based on micro economic considerations to understand the complex functioning of cities. Alonso (1964), for example, posited that residential location choices were a trade-off for individuals attempting to allocate fixed budgets to optimise factors such as the size of the house, their household budget for other goods, and the distance of the residence from the city centre. In this model, the distance of the house from the city centre is a de facto representation of transportation costs. The trade-off among the optimised factors in Alonso's model drives higher-level residential patterns; it represents one of the first efforts to explore how different preferences interacted to produce the patterns and structures that characterise cities. As well as forming the basis of modern urban economics, such theories set the context for various applications of agent-based models of housing markets, an early example being the NBER (National Bureau of Economic Reseach) urban simulation models developed by Ingram et al. (1972) in Harvard in the 1970s and early 1980s. More recently, agent-based models have been developed to explore processes including urban growth, land markets, gentrification, and regeneration.

Models like Alonso's effort to understand residential patterns have given rise to further research into why such growth occurs, and in particular how the role of land markets shape the development of cities. Land markets are said to exist "once land is traded as a commodity" (UN-ESCAP 1998), and represent an important driver and shaper of urban form. The pricing of that commodity, obviously, is partially driven by features such as the accessibility of a piece of land via various forms of transit. A particularly interesting aspect of land markets is that, unlike labour or capital markets, land is immobile and finite. Currently less than five percent of the earth's surface is urban; with urban populations predicted to grow to 5 billion by 2030, the urban footprint will still account for less than 10 percent of the surface (Seto et al. 2011). Understanding land markets is important as such markets heavily influence where people can live, and how they will change their cities in the near future.

At a finer spatial scale, another important aspect of cities is the process of how neighbourhoods change over time. Areas are developed due to many factors, accessibility being one of the most important as areas change and decline. For example, affluent households sometimes move to suburbs for the better opportunities offered by modern housing (e.g. Burgess 1927); this leads to higher rates of rental tenancy in vacated houses. In another trend, landlords of inner city properties might under-maintain their properties, which leads to rapid depreciation in some neighbourhoods. If an area has declined, it has the possibility of being gentrified under certain conditions, gentrification being defined as "the transformation of a working-class or vacant area of the central city into middle-class residential and/or commercial use (Lees et al. 2008). While gentrification has a relatively long history, it was not until Smith's (1979) Rent Gap Hypothesis appeared that aspects of gentrification could be explored in a model. The theory attempts to show that certain areas are gentrified based on the dynamics of residential property values and location - in particular, how accessible the area is to other parts of the city, as abstracted by distance from the urban centre (an abstraction inspired by the work of Burgess (1927) and Hoyt (1939)). Thus, in the dynamics of urban change at a range of spatial and temporal scales, accessibility, distance, and transport all shape the space within which people make decisions about housing and land purchases. We show a collection of agent-based models which demonstrate these dynamics and processes in Table 4.

Some of these models are derived from classic theories and are relatively naïve in their inclusion of the impact of transport on urban systems. Many of the residential location models have been developed which are in essence simple agentisations of classic theories, such as von Thünen's location theory of residential development by Sasaki and Box (2003) or Alonso's (1964) land rent theory by Crooks (2007). In such models, the agentisation process allows for dynamic behaviours to be added to static theories, but the representation of

Table 4. Typical applications of ABM to urban change

Author	Application	Entity	Spatial scale	Temporal scale (units)	Transportation	Transport complexity
Sasaki and Box 2003	Landuse allocations	Farmers	Region	Decades (years)	Abstract	0
Crooks 2007	Land rents	Households, Businesses	Region	Decades (years)	Abstract	0
Filatova et al. 2009	Land markets	Buyers, Sellers	Region	Abstract (ticks)	Abstract	0
Magliocca et al. 2011	Land markets	Consumer, Developer, Farmer	Region	Abstract (ticks)	Abstract	0
Gilbert et al. 2009	Housing markets	Buys, Sellers, EstateAgents, Property	Neighbour-hood	Abstract (ticks)	Abstract	0
Diappi and Bolchi 2008	Gentrification	Owner, Landlord, Tenant, Developer, Property	Neighbour-hood	Decades (years)	Abstract	0
Liu and O'Sullivan 2016	Gentrification	Household	Region	Decades (years)	Abstract	0
Torrens 2006	Urban growth	Households, Employers, Developers, Planners	Region	Decades (years)	Roads	1
Xie et al. 2007	Urban growth	Households	Region	Decades (years)	Roads	1
Jackson et al. 2008	Gentrification	Renters	Neighbour-hood	2 Years (months)	Roads	2
Torrens and Nara 2007	Urban regeneration	Property, Resident, Market	Neighbour-hood	Decades (years)	Roads	2
Jordan et al. 2014	Residential mobility	Households, Houses	Neighbour-hood	Decades (years)	Roads	2
Haase et al. 2010	Land markets	Households	City	Decades (years)	Roads	2

distance or transportation cost is understandably simplistic. The work of Filatova et al. (2009) and Magliocca et al. (2011) deal with the buying, development and selling of land, while Gilbert et al. (2009) represent specific properties:
all represent space as a continuous area without associated variable costs (i.e.
distance from the transport network). As with models of classic land market
theories, simulations which implement traditional models of gentrification (e.g.
Diappi and Bolchi 2008; Liu and O'Sullivan 2016) have tended to include only a
Cartesian sense of distance into the model. They represent Tier 0 complexity, in
that they acknowledge that physical space impacts the functioning of the system
but ignore variable costs of any kind.

Torrens (2006) and Xie et al. (2007) are two examples of urban change models
which include slightly more developed representations of transport. In both models, the agents themselves are rather abstract. For example, the Torrens (2006)
model simulated urban sprawl around Lake Michigan, abstracting the various
agents that impact growth - such as Households, Employers, Developers, Planners - into a category called "agents of change". Similarly, the model of Xie et
al. (2007) explored the change from rural to urban land-use in the Wuxian City
region of China, with agents representing developers and townships (collections
of households). In both models, transportation is only considered with respect
to the development potential of the land. For example, in Torrens (2006), the
presence of nearby existing roads made the development of land more likely.

Xie et al. (2007) modelled transportation infrastructure more explicitly,
incorporating the distance from the potential site of development to the economic activity of the town centres into the likelihood of area development. Such
abstraction of agent types and the use of transportation is understandable in that
such models are extensions of the more widely used Cellular Automata modelling
style often used to explore land use change and urban growth (e.g. Clarke et al.
1997). The key difference between these models and CA is that the emphasis is
more on the decision making process of the agents, rather than a probability of
a cell transitioning from one land use to another. These models of change take
place over the course of years, and include notions of distance or transportation in only a topologically constrained fashion, making them arguably Tier 1
in terms of transport complexity.

More spatially informed models of urban change also exist. For example,
Jackson et al. (2008) model a potentially gentrifying neighbourhood in part of
Boston, representing variable location costs to the agents based on the agent's
characteristics and their impact on the area's relative accessibility. Torrens and
Nara's (2007) work in Salt Lake City, Utah, similarly assesses the qualities of
different locations based on accessibility to a bundle of different resources, taking the work further by considering the interaction between the household's
socioeconomic status and that bundle of accessibilities. Jordan et al. (2014) similarly weight the attractiveness of different housing options based on whether
the household in question had a car and, accordingly, what their relative transportation options would be. Other models like Haase et al. (2010) study economic
decline, again factoring in variable distances and travel costs based on household

type. These examples can be said to achieve Tier 2 complexity, as the cost of the distance is more or less important based on the attributes of the households. These represent some of the most advanced examples of transport complexity in ABM currently being simulated.

4   Discussion: The Growing Importance of Transportation in ABM

The work presented here is a brief snapshot of a variety of ways researchers have chosen to think about and study urban system dynamics as they are influenced by transportation in the context of agent-based modelling and how this relates to the broader field of transportation modelling. Different researchers have adopted different assumptions about how space, closeness, and accessibility shape the environment in which agents operate. It is important, then, to understand how the social, physical, informational, and market dynamics which drive these processes are assumed to be influenced by transport distance rather than naive distance. These assumptions have been shown to have impacts for the dynamics of these models: different fidelities of physicality and mobility implied by transport result in different patterns of movement and behaviour, and therefore in a sense represent different models altogether (e.g. Groff 2007). Thus, researchers need to be explicit in their assumptions, precise in their descriptions of transit and movement, and open with their implementations of movement and transport.

It is important to note that one of the tiers of transportation complexity introduced in Sect. 3, that of Tier 3, could not be found in the reviewed literature. This finer-grained understanding of transit has yet to be achieved in agent-based models, and we suggest that future researchers consider designing their simulations with these specifications in mind. One potential way of overcoming this is the merging of microsimulation and agent-based modelling techniques, an emerging research agenda given form by Birkin and Wu (2012). An example of this move toward unity is reflected in the recent work of Horni et al. (2016), which exemplifies the way that the MATSim framework is seeking to blend techniques to better capture traffic dynamics as a function of demographic and physical qualities within a study area. The achievability of incorporating more and more complex models of road, pedestrian, public transit, rail, air, and informal transport within agent-based models of processes influenced by transport will only grow with increasing data accessibility. Even simple models will be increasingly powerful in this era of new and fine-grained data. Specifications such as the General Transit Feed Specification (GTFS) will allow researchers to capture an ever-growing range of information about public transit, and the flowering of sensor technology will provide new information about cars and pedestrians. Turning this data into meaningful information and comparing it with simulated data will push the boundaries of the technologies even further, and help us to understand the true nature of the processes at work. The interplay between simulation and observation has the potential to identify new dynamics, discard disproven correlations, and measure the interaction among them. The synthesis of these new forms of modelling and data represents a major challenge as well as an incredible opportunity to explore the true processes at work in these complex systems, which have thus far eluded us.

Incorporating a more focussed presentation of distance and closeness requires that agent-based models must become both more complicated and more complex. The linking together of diverse models and processes is a major current theme in agent-based modelling, and the broader field of modelling more generally (see, for example, Jha et al. 2004; Wang et al. 2016, for applications of models which bridge technologies). This speaks to a larger concern about how generalisable models are, and whether it is advisable or, practically speaking, possible to combine them. These points of complicatedness and complexity must be considered separately.

In terms of being complicated - that is, ungainly to implement and test - there are steps that researchers can and arguably should be taking to ensure that models can be integrated with one another. Focusing more on building frameworks rather than one-off constructions or proofs of concept can allow for reasonably well-validated transport systems to be incorporated into models in general which seek to study more expansive, transport-informed systems. Indeed, abstracting transportation out of the model design process could actually have the effect of simplifying many models and facilitating the docking of the different models as the pieces of the simulation become more modular. This is something that has already been achieved in alternative transport models built by engineers and planners and what is now needed is some form of synthesis that combines the best of each (Boyce and Williams 2015). Their 'complicatedness' is a problem which can be dealt with by abiding by responsible best practices with simulation design.

The complexity of these models is arguably a greater concern. In discussing complexity here, we mean the way in which the components of the model combine to create higher-level effects which are absent from the individual components. This is, obviously, the core and indeed purpose of ABM, but it raises questions of model parsimony. The simulator cannot model the world in all of its complexity, and must at some point accept some level of abstraction as a cut-off. With the increasing availability of nuanced data tracking transport information across wide regions at the granularity of seconds, there exists the temptation to create slavishly detailed simulations of transport. Researchers must consider what tier of transport complexity is really required for each of the processes they are incorporating into the model, and ensure that the model constructed is the cleanest and simplest model possible (but no simpler). Ideally, integration between different types of models will allow researchers to optimise on the strengths of different methodologies. Whether this is best accomplished through an explicitly integrated series of standards or simply by stringing together the output of one model into another in a loose coupling remains to be seen. The assumptions researchers make, however, must be clear and the treatment of space and transport well-considered, lest the double-edged sword of complexity threaten the interpretability of the results.

Transportation models that have been built primarily for simulating predicted future traffic flows and land use locations do provide a sense of how transport is considered as a completely integrated system within cities. But most of the models have been extremely aggregative, and in this sense are not able to address detailed policy-making objectives (e.g. socio-economically informed access to transit). Moreover, as they have always attempted to simulate the most aggregative of activities, they fail to address detail that is often needed when individual subsystems or sectors of the city system become the subjects of analysis and policy (e.g. regeneration schemes). Even where these models have been disaggregated to the household level, the straightjacket in which householder behaviour with respect to travel is considered narrows the scope that is possible in testing new kinds of scenario and focuses still on traffic flows, capacity, and congestion. There are however, several features of more aggregate transport models that can be incorporated in ABM. In particular summaries of transportation flows and levels of mobility are incorporated in a variety of indices of accessibility as we outlined in the previous section. Accessibility measures combine various indicators of geometry, distance, travel costs and locational benefits in such a way that they are consistent with underlying transportation flow modelling. Moreover, combined with much more detail about transportation networks, ABM do have some real possibilities for simulating transport at a much finer behavioural and spatial resolution than anything hitherto. The current stumbling block is that most agent-based models that incorporate transportation do so in ways that are not easily scalable to more comprehensive systems where many sectors such as crime, health, policing and so on are considered in an integrated way.

From this brief review, it is clear that agent-based show promise with respect to modelling aspects of urban systems but explicit transportation is often lacking and that some synthesis is required with respect to integration. Already transport per se is being rapidly broadened to embrace concerns about mobility in general, but in ABM some of the physicality of existing transport models needs to be modelled explicitly, to reflect the fact that transport at the end of the day involves physical movements and infrastructures. Of course the idea that much of transport in the future will be ethereal - by email, social media and so on - does not make this notion any less real but simply expands the transport herein to embrace the virtual as well as physical. Agent-based models will be central to expanding these horizons so that policy can truly begin to reflect some of the challenges raised by transportation issues in the future city.

References

Aleman, D.M., Wibisono, T.G., Schwartz, B.: A nonhomogeneous agent-based simulation approach to modeling the spread of disease in a pandemic outbreak. Interfaces **41**(3), 301–315 (2011)

Alonso, W.: Location and Land Use: Toward a General Theory of Land Rent. Harvard University Press, Cambridge (1964)

Batty, M.: Modelling cities as dynamic systems. Nature **231**, 425–428 (1971)

Batty, M.: Fifty years of urban modelling: macro-statics to micro-dynamics. In: Albeverio, S., Andrey, D., Giordano, P., Vancheri, A. (eds.) The Dynamics of Complex Urban Systems: An Interdisciplinary Approach, pp. 1–20. Springer Physica-Verlag, New York (2008). doi:10.1007/978-3-7908-1937-3_1

Batty, M.: A generic framework for computational spatial modelling. In: Heppenstall, A.J., Crooks, A.T., See, L.M., Batty, M. (eds.) Agent-based Models of Geographical Systems, pp. 19–50. Springer, New York (2012). doi:10.1007/978-90-481-8927-4_2

Batty, M.: The New Science of Cities. MIT Press, Cambridge (2013)

Bellomo, N., Dogbe, C.: On the modeling of traffic and crowds: a survey of models, speculations, and perspectives. SIAM Rev. **53**(3), 409–463 (2011)

Ben-Akiva, M., Lerman, S.R.: Discrete Choice Analysis: Theory and Application to Travel Demand. MIT Press, Cambridge (1985)

Birkin, M., Wu, B.M.: A review of microsimulation and hybrid agent-based approaches. In: Heppenstall, A.J., Crooks, A.T., See, L.M., Batty, M. (eds.) Agent-Based Models of Geographical Systems, pp. 51–68. Springer, New York (2012). doi:10.1007/978-90-481-8927-4_3

Boyce, D.E., Williams, H.C.W.L.: Forecasting Urban Travel: Past, Present and Future. Edward Elgar Publishing, Cheltenham (2015)

Brailsford, S.C., Berchi, R., De Angelis, V., Mecoli, M.: System dynamics models to assess the risk of mosquito-borne diseases and to evaluate control policies. Discussion Papers in Centre for Operational Research, Management Science and Information Systems, University of Southampton, Southampton, UK (2009)

Brockmann, D., Helbing, D.: The hidden geometry of complex, network-driven contagion phenomena. Science **342**(6164), 1337–1342 (2013)

Burgess, E.W.: The determinants of gradients in the growth of a city. Publ. Am. Sociol. Soc. **21**, 178–184 (1927)

Cederman, L.E.: Endogenizing geopolitical boundaries with agent-based modeling. Proc. Nat. Acad. Sci. U.S.A. **99**(Suppl 3), 7296–7303 (2002)

Clarke, K.C., Hoppen, S., Gaydos, L.J.: A self-modifying cellular automaton model of historical urbanization in the San Francisco Bay area. Environ. Plann. B **24**(2), 247–261 (1997)

Cohen, L.E., Felson, M.: Social change and crime rate trends: a routine activity approach. Am. Sociol. Rev. **44**(4), 588–608 (1979)

Crooks, A.T.: Experimenting with cities: utilizing agent-based models and GIS to explore urban dynamics. Ph.D. thesis, University College London, London, England (2007)

Crooks, A.T., Hailegiorgis, A.B.: An agent-based modeling approach applied to the spread of cholera. Environ. Model. Softw. **62**, 164–177 (2014)

Crooks, A.T., Heppenstall, A.J.: Introduction to agent-based modelling. In: Heppenstall, A.J., Crooks, A.T., See, L.M., Batty, M. (eds.) Agent-Based Models of Geographical Systems, pp. 85–105. Springer, New York (2012). doi:10.1007/978-90-481-8927-4_5

Diappi, L., Bolchi, P.: Smith's rent gap theory and local real estate dynamics: a multi-agent model. Comput. Environ. Urban Syst. **32**(1), 6–18 (2008)

Dray, A., Mazerolle, L., Perez, P., Ritter, A.: Policing Australia's "heroin drought": using an agent-based model to simulate alternative outcomes. J. Exp. Criminol. **4**(3), 267–287 (2008)

Epstein, J., Axtell, R.: Growing Artificial Societies: Social Science from the Bottom Up. Brookings Institution, MIT Press, Cambridge (1996)

Filatova, T., Parker, D., van der Veen, A.: Agent-based urban land markets: agent's pricing behavior, land prices and urban land use change. J. Artif. Soc. Soc. Simul. **12**(1) (2009). http://jasss.soc.surrey.ac.uk/12/1/3.html

Forrester, J.W.: Urban Dynamics. MIT Press, Cambridge (1969)

Gilbert, N., Hawksworth, J.C., Swinney, P.A.: An agent-based model of the English housing market. In: Association for the Advancement of Artificial Intelligence (2009). http://www.aaai.org/Papers/Symposia/Spring/2009/SS-09-09/SS09-09-007.pdf

Gilbert, N., Troitzsch, K.: Simulation for the Social Scientist. Open University Press, Milton Keynes (2005)

Groff, E.R.: Situating simulation to model human spatio-temporal interactions: an example using crime events. Trans. GIS **11**(4), 507–530 (2007)

Haase, D., Lautenbach, S., Seppelt, R.: Modeling and simulating residential mobility in a shrinking city using an agent-based approach. Environ. Model. Softw. **25**(10), 1225–1240 (2010)

Heppenstall, A.J., Crooks, A.T., See, L.M., Batty, M. (eds.): Agent-Based Models of Geographical Systems. Springer, New York (2012)

Horni, A., Nagel, K., Axhausen, K.W. (eds.): The Multi-Agent Transport Simulation MATSim. Ubiquity, London (2016)

Hoyt, H.: The Structure and Growth of Residential Neighbourhoods in American Cities. Federal Housing Administration, Washington (1939)

Ingram, G.K., Kain, J.F., Ginn, R.: The Detroit Prototype of the NBER Urban Simulation Model. NBER, New York (1972)

Jackson, J., Forest, B., Sengupta, R.: Agent-based simulation of urban residential dynamics and land rent change in a gentrifying area of Boston. Trans. GIS **12**(4), 475–491 (2008)

Jha, M., Moore, K., Pashaie, B.: Emergency evacuation planning with microscopic traffic simulation. Transp. Res. Rec. **1886**(1), 40–48 (2004)

Jordan, R., Birkin, M., Evans, A.: An agent-based model of residential mobility assessing the impacts of urban regeneration policy in the EASEL district. Comput. Environ. Urban Syst. **48**, 49–63 (2014)

Lees, L., Slater, T., Wyly, E.: Gentrification. Routledge, New York (2008)

Linard, C., Poncon, N., Fontenille, D., Lambin, E.F.: A multi-agent simulation to assess the risk of malaria re-emergence in Southern France. Ecol. Model. **220**(2), 160–174 (2008)

Liu, C., O'Sullivan, D.: An abstract model of gentrification as a spatially contagious succession process. Comput. Environ. Urban Syst. **59**, 1–10 (2016)

Magliocca, N., Safirova, E., McConnell, V., Walls, M.: An economic agent-based model of coupled housing and land markets (CHALMS). Comput. Environ. Urban Syst. **35**(3), 183–191 (2011)

Malleson, N., Birkin, M.: Analysis of crime patterns through the integration of an agent-based model and a population microsimulation. Comput. Environ. Urban Syst. **36**(6), 551–561 (2012)

Melo, A., Belchior, M., Furtado, V.: Analyzing police patrol routes by simulating the physical reorganization of agents. In: Sichman, J.S., Antunes, L. (eds.), Multi-Agent-Based Simulation VI, Germany (2006)

Miller, J., Page, S.: Complex adaptive systems: an introduction to computational models of social life (2007)

Morris, A.E.J.: History of Urban form: Before the Industrial Revolutions, 3rd edn. Longman, London (1994)

de Dios, O.J., Willumsen, L.G.: Model. Transport, 4th edn. John Wiley, New York (2011)

Padgham, L., Nagel, K., Singh, D., Chen, Q.: Integrating BDI agents into a MAT-Sim simulation. Front. Artif. Intell. Appl. **263**, 681–686 (2014). doi:10.3233/978-1-61499-419-0-681

Perez, L., Dragicevic, S.: An agent-based approach for modeling dynamics of contagious disease spread. Int. J. Health Geographics **8**, 50 (2009)

Sasaki, Y., Box, P.: Agent-based verification of von Thünen's location theory. J. Artif. Soc. Soc. Simul. **6**(2) (2003). http://jasss.soc.surrey.ac.uk/6/2/9.html

Schobert, H.H.: Energy and Society: An Introduction, 2nd edn. CRC Press, Boca Raton (2014)

Seto, K.C., Fragkias, M., Güneralp, B., Reilly, M.K.: A meta-analysis of global urban land expansion. PLoS ONE **6**(8), e23777 (2011)

Simoes, J.: An agent-based/network approach to spatial epidemics. In: Heppenstall, A.J., Crooks, A.T., See, L.M., Batty, M. (eds.) Agent-Based Models of Geographical Systems, pp. 591–610. Springer, New York (2012). doi:10.1007/978-90-481-8927-4_29

Simon, H.A.: The Sciences of the Artificial, 3rd edn. MIT Press, Cambridge (1996)

Smith, N.: Toward a theory of gentrification: a back to the city movement by capital not people. J. Am. Plann. Assoc. **45**(4), 538–548 (1979)

Tobler, W.: A computer movie simulating urban growth in the Detroit region. Econ. Geogr. **46**(2), 234–240 (1970)

Torrens, P.M.: Simulating sprawl. Ann. Assoc. Am. Geogr. **96**(2), 248–275 (2006)

Torrens, P.M.: High-fidelity behaviors for model people on model streetscapes. Ann. GIS **20**(3), 139–157 (2014)

Torrens, P.M., Nara, A.: Modelling gentrification dynamics: a hybrid approach. Comput. Environ. Urban Syst. **31**(3), 337–361 (2007)

UN-ESCAP: Urban land policies for the uninitiated. United Nations Economic and Social Commission for Asia and the Pacific, New York, NY (1998). http://www.unescap.org/huset/land_policies/index.htm

UN-Habitat: State of the cities 2010–11 - cities for all: bridging the urban divide. UN-Habitat, Nairobi, Kenya (2010). http://www.unhabitat.org/content.asp?cid=8891&catid=643&typeid=46&subMenuId=0&AllContent=1

Waddell, P.: UrbanSim: modeling urban development for land use, transportation, and environmental planning. J. Am. Plann. Assoc. **68**(3), 297–314 (2002)

Wang, H., Mostafizi, A., Cramer, L.A., Cox, D., Park, H.: An agent-based model of a multimodal near-field tsunami evacuation: decision-making and life safety. Transp. Res. Part C Emerg. Technol. **64**, 86–100 (2016)

Wise, S., Cheng, T.: How officers create guardianship: an agent-based model of policing. Trans. GIS (2016). doi:10.1111/tgis.12173

Xie, Y., Batty, M., Zhao, K.: Simulating emergent urban form: desakota in China. Ann. Assoc. Am. Geogr. **97**(3), 477–495 (2007)

Zachariadis, V.: Modelling pedestrian systems. Doctoral Thesis, UCL (University College London), London (2014). http://discovery.ucl.ac.uk/1435418/

Applications

Simulation-Aided Crowd Management: A Multi-scale Model for an Urban Case Study

Luca Crociani[1], Gregor Lämmel[2(✉)], and Giuseppe Vizzari[1]

[1] Complex Systems and Artificial Intelligence Research Centre,
University Milano-Bicocca, Milan, Italy
{luca.crociani,giuseppe.vizzari}@unimib.it
[2] Institute of Transportation Systems,
German Aerospace Center (DLR), Berlin, Germany
gregor.laemmel@dlr.de

Abstract. Safety, security, and comfort of pedestrian crowds during large gatherings are heavily influenced by the layout of the underlying environment. This work presents a systematic agent-based simulation approach to appraise and optimize the layout of a pedestrian environment in order to maximize safety, security, and comfort. The performance of the approach is demonstrated based on annual "Salone del mobile" (Design Week) exhibition in Milan, Italy. Given the large size of the scenario and the proportionally high number of simultaneously present pedestrians, the computational costs of a pure microscopic simulation approach would make this hardly applicable, whereas a multi-scale approach, combining simulation models of different granularity, provides a reasonable trade off between a detailed management of individual pedestrians and possibility to effectively carry out what-if analyses with different environmental configurations. The paper will introduce the scenario, the base model and the alternatives, discussing the achieved results.

Keywords: Crowd management · Multi-agent simulation · Pedestrian simulation · Optimal environment layout

1 Introduction

The management of pedestrian crowds is a crucial task when organizing large gatherings such as festivals, sports events, or religious celebrations. Three main reasons for an active crowd management are: safety, security, and comfort.

- Regarding safety, situations leading to high pedestrian density should be avoided, in particular for bidirectional pedestrian flows or for crossing pedestrian streams.
- Security considerations deal with unforeseen threats to the event attendees that would require e.g. fast evacuation of large venues.
- Related to safety and security is the comfort of visitors. Comfort considerations include the avoidance of long waiting times (e.g. at ticket counters) and the reduction of high density situations.

© Springer International Publishing AG 2017
M.-R. Namazi-Rad et al. (Eds.): ABMUS 2016, LNAI 10051, pp. 151–171, 2017.
DOI: 10.1007/978-3-319-51957-9_9

Obviously, these three key concepts are closely related and should be seen as mutually dependent. The present work proposes an integrated simulation based appraisal and optimization approach to improve safety, security, and comfort of attendees of large events. The current contribution demonstrates the approach based on an 'offline' scenario of the annually "Salone del mobile" exhibition in Milan, Italy. The overall event attracts more than 200,000 visitors[1] every year. The location is the main fairgrounds of Milan, but its importance and number of visitors led to the creation of a spin-off called "Fuori Salone" that organizes many related events in the city center during the fair week. The case study that will be analyzed in this paper describes the scenario of an important event belonging to the Fuori Salone, named "Tortona Design Week." It is located in the surrounding area of the Porta Genova train and metro station of Milan. The estimated number of visitors is also quite significant, around 115,000 in total during the 6 days of the event[2].

This paper is an extension of the work presented in [13], where the scenario of the Tortona Design Week has been analyzed by means of the multi-scale modeling approach proposed in Sect. 3. Unlike the previous paper, the modeling approach is more thoroughly discussed here, with the presentation of further validation tests showing the plausibility of the results achieved in the case study. In particular, the model is tested in two benchmark scenarios, representing a bottleneck situation and a staircase, which are composing elements of the case study scenario (the overall pedestrian bridge is a bottleneck reached through staircases at its ends). In addition, the case study has been enriched with an additional environmental modification solving the congestion issues: the staircases, representing the real bottlenecks of this scenario, are enlarged according to the results and evidence provided by the validation tests.

2   Related Works

In the simulation context, (pedestrian) travel behavior is usually modeled at three different levels [24,34]. Plans and final objectives are formulated at the *strategic level*. At the *tactical level*, a set of activities to complete the plan is created. The physical execution of the activities is performed at the *operational level*. Approaches to simulate the operational level can be divided into three classes.

– Macroscopic models treat the crowds as a flow of densities where individual pedestrians are not represented but rather considered as gas or liquids (see, e.g., [20,23]). For macroscopic models, the computational burden increases rather with the size of the simulated area than with the number of simulated pedestrians. Thus, macroscopic models can be efficient for the simulation of

---

[1] http://salonemilano.it/en-us/VISITORS/Salone-Internazionale-del-Mobile/
Exhibition-fact-sheet.

[2] http://www.tortonadesignweek.com/.

large crowds in small spaces. However, since individual pedestrians are not represented by those models, scenarios with complex origin-destination-relations seem to be hard to model.

- In contrast, microscopic models are constructed from the individual's point of view, where each and every traveler follows his/her own plan. Some microscopic models treat space as a continuous entity (e.g. force based models [11,22]), others take a discretized view of the environment (e.g. cellular automata (CA) [3,8]). Most microscopic models are built as simulations with a fixed time step size. Recently, a model with adaptive time step size has been proposed in order to speed up computation [39]. Another way to speed up the computation is to apply the concept of discrete event simulation [29].

- A third class of simulation models is often referred to as mesoscopic models. One example is the queue simulation model [30]: in this approach, pedestrians are still treated individually, but the environment is represented as a graph of interconnected FIFO queues. This implies a simplification of the environmental representation and a reduction of the computational costs for the management of the simulation process. The representation of the physical movement at the operational level is simplified and the approach is less effective at representing turbulences due to conflicts, for instance when the situation comprises crossing streams [32].

Hybrid coupling (or multi-scale modeling in general) has been applied to different scientific fields and combines the advantages of models with different granularity in spatial representation, striving to achieve good overall computational properties with the possibility to zoom in on spots requiring more details in the model. This is valid both for extremely small areas, like biological systems [15], that include a very high number of interacting entities in a potentially small space, as well as for urban and territorial scale socio-economic systems [40].

In the transportation field, early approaches deal with the vehicular traffic only. Hybrid couplings of macroscopic and microscopic models are proposed by [4,17,21]. Examples for the hybrid couplings of mesoscopic and microscopic models are [6,7]. Approaches from the pedestrian domain include [1,10]. A basic requirement for hybrid modeling is a consistent transfer of travelers (e.g. pedestrians or vehicles) between the involved simulation models. In the pedestrian domain, this requires that fundamental properties like flow and speed are conserved over the models' boundaries. A respective approach is discussed in [32]. Recently, this approach has been demonstrated in a case study on an inter- and multi-model evacuation [27].

The strategic and tactical level of behavior deals with the navigation in complex environments, and a key feature is the ability to find feasible paths from any origin to any destination. An apparent solution to this problem is the shortest paths solution. It can be computed, e.g. by Dijkstra's shortest path algorithm [16]. However, since the shortest path solution neglects congestion, often longer but faster paths exists: although humans are not necessarily always able to find optimal solutions, the shortest path approach sometimes fails at representing the ability of some pedestrians to select a longer trajectory for preserving a higher walking speed. Those faster but longer paths can be found by an iterative best response dynamics [9]. In the pedestrian context, a corresponding macroscopic modeling approach is proposed in [24]. A mesoscopic modeling approach is presented in [31]. In the microscopic context, applications of best response dynamics started only recently. An application to tactical level of behavior is discussed in [26]. A systematic approach, where all three levels of behavior are explicitly modeled and path finding is solved by an iterative approach, is proposed in [12].

Pedestrian simulation models are often applied in the evacuation context. Newer works also deal with the appraisal of pedestrian environments regarding their performance under normal conditions in order to optimize crowd management strategies (e.g. [14]).

3   A Multi-scale Model for the Simulation of Urban Scenarios

The development of a multi-scale model has been proposed for two main purposes. On the one hand, the simulation system should provide a very detailed representation of parts of the scenario in which more complex behaviors can take place. On the other hand, a mesoscopic approach can be used to design and simulate large parts of the urban environment that are not affected by such complex dynamics but are still fundamental for the analysis of the overall scene. Hence the system described here is composed of two models with two different scales of detail: (i) a 2d microscopic model based on a discrete representation for a detailed yet optimized reproduction of pedestrian environments; (ii) a queue model that is used for the simulation of other relevant city roads. Such integration between these models leads to a quite powerful approach, capable of performing analysis in urban scenarios, considering multiple modes of transportation and performing simulations in a relatively fast way.

Considering computational costs is quite relevant since the multi-scale system applies an iterative approach to manage the agents' strategic model. The iterative approach moves the overall behavior either towards a Nash equilibrium (NE) or to the system optimum (SO) depending on the applied cost function. In this way it is possible both to predict what will happen in the scenario on a normal day (with the NE) and to have information about the minimum average travel time of the whole crowd (with the SO). One might argue that implementing the optimal flows configuration is still an issue, since it implies that some people take a detour without perceiving relevant congestion on the shorter way. The desired behavior could be induced by the usage of adaptive bottlenecks (e.g. automatic bollards) that make, depending on the current situation, detours more attractive to some of the people. The development of such a concept represents the overall idea behind this work and it will be subject of future research.

The components of the multi-scale model and their integration will be now briefly presented. For a in-depth discussion of the CA model, refer to [12].

3.1   The Discrete Microscopic Model

The model is a 2-dimensional Cellular Automaton with a representation of the space as a grid of square cells. The $0.4 \times 0.4\,\mathrm{m}^2$ size of the cells describes the average space occupation of a person [41] and reproduces a maximum pedestrian density of 6.25 persons/m^2 which covers the values usually observable in the real world. Basically, a cell of the environment can be one of two types, *walkable* or *obstacle*, meaning that it will never be occupied by any pedestrian during the simulation.

Intermediate targets can also be introduced in the environment to mark the extremes of a particular region (e.g. rooms or corridors) which act as decision points for the routing choice of agents. Final goals of the discrete environment are its open edges, i.e., the entrances/exits of the discrete space that will be linked to roads. Since the concept of region is fuzzy and the space decomposition is a subjective task that can be tackled with different approaches, the configuration of their position in the scenario is not automatic and is left to the user.

Employing the floor field approach [8] and spreading one field from each target "either intermediate or final" allows to build a network of the environment. In this graph, each node denotes one target and the edges identify the existence of a direct way between two targets (i.e. passing through only one region). To allow this, the floor field diffusion is limited by obstacles and cells of other targets. An example for an environment with the overlaid network is shown in Fig. 1. The open borders of the microscopic environment are the nodes that will be plugged to the other network of the mesoscopic model.

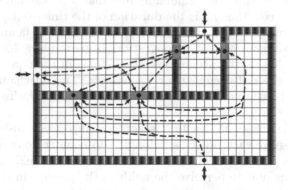

Fig. 1. Sample scenario with its network representation. While the blue cells represent intermediate targets, the outside arrows describe the links with the outside network that will be simulated with the mesoscopic model.

To integrate the network with the one of the mesoscopic model and to allow the reasoning at the strategic level, each edge a of the graph is firstly labeled with its length l_a, describing the distance between two targets δ_i, δ_j in the discrete space. This value is computed using the floor fields as:

$$l_a(\delta_1, \delta_2) = Avg\left(FF_{\delta_1}(Center(\delta_2)),\ FF_{\delta_2}(Center(\delta_1))\right) \tag{1}$$

where $FF_\delta(x, y)$ gives the value of the floor field associated to a destination δ in position (x, y); $Center(\delta)$ describes the coordinates of the central cell of δ and Avg computes the average between the two values and provides a unique distance. Together with the average speed of pedestrians in the discrete space (explained below), l_a is used to calculate the free speed travel time of the link $T_a^{free} = \frac{l_a}{s_a}$.

With a simple probabilistic choice, similar to the one proposed in [8], the pedestrian movement towards one target is reproduced with the floor fields values. This allows to avoid obstacles and other pedestrians in a very simple way, but it is not enough to generate plausible dynamics, i. e. by respecting the fundamental relation about local density and flow.

For the achievement of a realistic microscopic model, the idea of [18] has been extended to 2-dimensional models. The model works on the basis of 3 simple rules that allow the calibration to fit the fundamental diagram of 1-directional and 2-directional flow. The movement rules are summarized as follows:

- **Movement rule:** A pedestrian cannot change his/her position before τ_m seconds,
- **Jam rule:** If a cell is occupied at time t by the pedestrian p, every pedestrian $\bar{p} \neq p$ cannot occupy that cell before time $t + \tau_j$,
- **Counter-flow rule:** If two pedestrian in two consecutive cells at time t are in a head-on conflict, then they will swap their position at time $t + \tau_m + \tau_s$.

The first rule describes the minimum time that a pedestrian can employ to move forward one cell, thus τ_m is the duration of the time-step.

The second rule manages the dynamics in presence of jamming, implying additional time to move in case of congestion. In particular, this rule has been implemented by letting the agents produce a *trace* in their previous position, which will keep the cell occupied for τ_j seconds. This mechanism is able to translate back the effects of congestion as observed, generating the so-called *density waves*.

The third rule defines an agents position exchange mechanism, but the way that agents recognize each other as belonging to counter-flows needs clarification. The agents of this model, in addition to the floor field related to their current target, are able to perceive the fields of the persons in their immediate vicinity. With this information, they can understand if the surrounding agents are "probably" moving in the opposite direction. Hence they are able to opt for moving towards the position occupied by the counter-flow pedestrian and, if this agent performs the same choice, start the position exchange at the end of the step. This action will need $\tau_m + \tau_s$ s. In [12] it is shown how, by varying the value of τ_m and τ_s with the local density, it is possible to fully calibrate this model to fit the fundamental diagrams of pedestrian 1-directional and 2-directional flow.

In summary, these rules enable the model to produce feasible simulations of pedestrian motion in planar environments. Nonetheless, the simulation of a complex environment might need consideration of particular elements, such as stairs, which implies at least a lower speed of the agents. To overcome this issue, the definition of the environment has been enriched by introducing the possibility to mark the borders of stairs, which will affect the agent's speed by multiplying their $\tau_m \times 2$, i.e. they will move one time-step over two. With the assumed $\tau_m = 0.30$ s, pedestrians will have a free flow speed of 1.3 m/s in flat areas and of 0.65 m/s on stairs, in accordance with the average speed observed in the real world [41]. At the network level, the links describing the area of a staircase are labeled with the respective free speed travel time.

More advanced approaches to manage arbitrary speeds have already been proposed in the literature, using stochastic methods that do not imply a complete synchronization of the agents (e.g. [2]). For the model and the application proposed here, though, this simple and efficient approach is considered effective and further developments on this aspect might be subject of future directions.

Finally, in order to respect the dynamics among the mesoscopic and microscopic models, the connection at the borders of the pedestrian environment are managed with so-called *transition areas*, which temporarily host the agents before they enter the "real" environment. Therefore, when the agents pass from the mesoscopic model to the discrete environment, they have a temporary *double* presence in both models, which allows to extend the influence of eventual congestion from one model to the other one [32].

3.2 Validation of the Microscopic Model

The presented model is validated against fundamental diagrams related to 1-directional and 2-directional flows in a planar scenario, using empirical data from laboratory experiments described in [42,43]. For the analysis of the properties of the model and other details about its calibration, refer to [12,18]. In this section, advances in the validation procedure will be presented to demonstrate the reliability of the model for the application presented in Sect. 4.

Validation of stairs. An advancement proposed in this paper aims at a simplified simulation of stairs. To validate this new component, it is important to evaluate the flow of pedestrians generated by the model at different densities. Experimental studies focused on the performances of stairs (e.g. [5]) in fact recognize a fundamental diagram with significantly lower values of flows than in the case of a normal corridor. The relation between density and flow generated by the model is analyzed by simulating a benchmark scenario representing a staircase of 10×3.2 m^2. Each level of density is globally configured with individual simulations of 1 h each, in which the staircase is made toroidal by keeping the simulated pedestrians inside (i.e. closed boundary conditions). Every time an agent reaches the extreme of the staircase, its average velocity is calculated with the travel time as $\nu = \frac{corridorLength}{travelTime}$ m/s. The flow associated to the global density ρ is then computed as $J = \nu \cdot \rho$.

A comparison between the fundamental diagrams generated by the model in a planar corridor and in the staircase scenario is illustrated in Fig. 2(a), describing

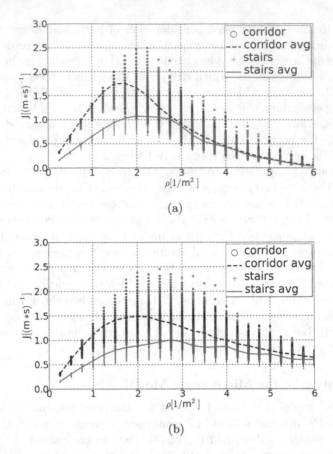

Fig. 2. Fundamental diagrams generated by the model in case of 1-directional (a) and 2-directional flow (b). An effect of transparency is used with the color of points, to emphasize the frequency of the distribution among the provided range. (Color figure online)

results for 1-directional flow, and 2(b), for the 2-directional case. Note that with this configuration of the model, no influence of the direction of movement in the stairs has been introduced, hence all pedestrians share a unique desired speed also in the case of 2-directional flow inside staircases. The achieved results are in agreement with observations in the real world (see [5]) and, as expected, the overall flow is below the one generated in planar environments.

Bottleneck flow. Since the dynamics simulated in the application scenario are mainly affected by the presence of a bottleneck, the behavior of the model in presence of physical restrictions must be discussed as well. This property has been analyzed empirically by testing another benchmark scenario composed of a rectangular room divided by a wall, with an opening at the center configuring a bottleneck of fixed width ω. A set of simulations is then configured by varying

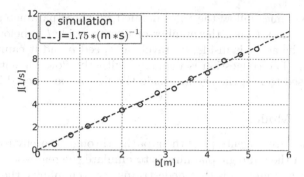

Fig. 3. Average flow observed in the bottleneck tests.

ω in the discrete range [0.4,5.2], achieved by subsequently increasing the width by one cell. 350 agents are initialized at one extreme of the scenario at the beginning of the simulation and have to reach the other part. At each second the flow in the bottleneck is computed and all measurements are averaged for each simulation. Outflow data is stored only once the simulation is in a *steady state*, i. e. the agents have reached the bottleneck, generating a stable outflow. For this scenario it has been observed that the steady state is achieved between 5 and 35 s into the simulation, for all tested widths ω. Average steady state flows for simulations are shown in Fig. 3.

As is visible by the dotted line, the model is generating a specific outflow from bottlenecks of 1.75 $\frac{pers}{m \cdot s}$. This is also in line with what is generally observed in reality; results are a bit lower than those of more recent observations coming from experiments with wide bottlenecks [33], although these results fit with other datasets (e. g. [37]) and can therefore be considered acceptable.

3.3   The Mesoscopic Model

The overall system is implemented within the MATSim framework[3]. The standard simulation approach in MATSim is based on a queueing model based on [38]. Originally, the model was designed for the simulation of vehicular traffic only, but later it has been adapted for the additional consideration of pedestrians [31]. The network is modeled as a graph with links describing urban streets and nodes describing their intersections. In the pedestrian context, "streets" also include sidewalks, ramps, etc. Links behave like FIFO queues controlled by the following parameters:

– the length of the link l;
– the area of the link A;
– the free flow speed $\hat{v}$;
– the free speed travel time t_{min}, given by $l/\hat{v}$;
– the flow capacity FC;
– the storage capacity SC.

---
[3] http://www.matsim.org.

Thus the dynamics follow the rules defined by these parameters. An agent is able to enter a link l until the number of agents inside l is below its storage capacity. Once the agent is inside, it travels at speed $\hat{v}$ and it cannot leave the link before t_{min}. The congestion is managed with the flow capacity parameter FC, which is used to lock the agents inside the link to not exceed it.

3.4   Strategic Model

At the strategic level, agents plan their paths through the environment. Normally, the aim of the strategic planning is to emulate the real-world pedestrians' behavior. A fair assumption is that pedestrians try to minimize the walking distance when planning their paths. In the simulation context, the shortest path solution is straightforward to compute e.g. by Dijkstra's shortest path algorithm [16]. However, it is well known that the shortest path solution neglects congestion and thus the shortest path solution is not necessarily the fastest one. In particular, commuters who repeatedly walk between two locations (e.g. from a particular track in a large train station to a bus stop outside the train station) often try to iteratively find faster paths. If all commuters display that same behavior, they might reach a state where it is no longer possible to find any faster path. If this is the case, then the system has reached a state of a Nash [35] or user equilibrium w.r.t. individual travel times. This behavior can be emulated by applying an iterative best-response dynamic [9] and has been widely applied in the context of vehicular transport simulations (see, e.g., [19,25,36]). In the pedestrian context, this concept is still new albeit some preliminary works exist as discussed in Sect. 2. Related to the Nash equilibrium is the system optimum. But unlike the Nash equilibrium, the system optimum does not minimize individual travel times but the system (or average) travel time. Like the Nash equilibrium, the system optimum can also be achieved by an iterative best response dynamic, but based on the marginal travel time instead of the individual travel time. The marginal travel time of an individual traveler corresponds to the sum of the travel time experienced by her/him (internal costs) and the delay that he/she impose to others (external costs). While it is straightforward to determine the internal costs (i.e. travel time), the external cost calculation is not so obvious. An approach for the marginal travel time estimation and its application to a mesoscopic evacuation simulation is discussed in [28]. Based on this, [12] propose an adaption of the approach to microscopic simulation models. In the present work, the external costs are estimated in the same way as proposed in [12]. The following gives a brief description of the approach. As discussed, both the mesoscopic and the microscopic model are mapped on the same global network of links and nodes. A link can either be in a congested or in an uncongested state. Initially, all links are considered as uncongested. A link switches from the uncongested state to the congested state once the observed travel time along the link is longer than the free speed travel time. Vice versa, a link in the congested state switches to the uncongested state as soon as the first pedestrian is able to walk along the link in free speed travel time. Every pedestrian that leaves a given link while it is in the congested state imposes external costs to the others. The amount of the external costs corresponds to the time span from the time when the pedestrian under consideration leaves the congested link till the time when the link switches to the uncongested state again.

In this work, the iterative search of equilibrium/optimum follows the logic of the iterative best response dynamic and is described by the following tasks:

1. Compute plans for all agents
2. Execute the multi-scale simulation
3. Evaluate executed plans of the agents
4. Select a portion of the agents population and re-compute their plans
5. Jump to step 2, if the stop criterion has not been reached

The stopping criterion is implemented as a predetermined number of iterations defined by the user. This is because the number of iterations needed for the system to reach a relaxed state depends on the complexity of the scenario and is not known a priori. In the underlying context, one hundred iterations gives a good compromise between relaxation and run-time.

Initial plan computation is performed with a shortest path algorithm. In the subsequent iterations, the agents try to find better plans based on the experienced travel costs. Depending on the cost function, the agents learn more convenient paths either for them individually (relaxation towards a Nash equilibrium) or for the overall population (relaxation towards the system optimum).

4 Analysis of an Urban Scenario

4.1 The Scenario of the Tortona Design Week

The Tortona Design Week is a yearly exhibition that is organized in the area surrounding the Porta Genova train station in Milan. The estimated number of visitors for the 6 days of the event is about 115,000 people, mostly evenly distributed, with peaks on Friday and Saturday nights.

Figure 4 illustrates the real world scenario with the location of the event and the directions of flows. The larger part of the incoming flow of pedestrians arrives from the station square, where entrance/exit of a subway station are also located. The main issue with this scenario is the connection between the square and the event location. In fact, in these surroundings, the only viable connection is a pedestrian bridge three meters in width, which makes alternative routes unattractive for visitors.

Consequently, the congestion on the pedestrian bridge is very high and the traveling times become long. In addition to comfort, the overcrowding on the bridge might imply safety issues. This motivated the analysis discussed here, which will explore three main simulation scenarios.

4.2 Experiments

For the performed experiments, the population of agents has been instantiated according to two normal distributions, which split a total of 15,000 pedestrians

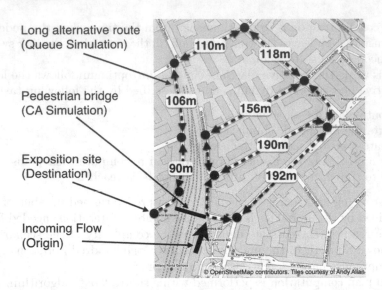

Long alternative route
(Queue Simulation)

110m

118m

Pedestrian bridge
(CA Simulation)

106m

156m

190m

Exposition site
(Destination)

90m

192m

Incoming Flow
(Origin)

© OpenStreetMap contributors. Tiles courtesy of Andy Allan

Fig. 4. The location of the event and the possible paths from the train and subway stations. The pedestrian bridge is simulated by the CA model and the longer alternative route by the queue model.

among the two origin/destination points (cf. Fig. 4): the square in front of the train station and the event location. The distribution of agents from the train station has been centered one hour before the other one in the simulation time-line, to achieve an earlier incoming flow towards the event. Both distributions are configured with a standard deviation of 30 min.

The dimensions of the simulated environment motivates for the usage of the multi-scale approach: as shown in Fig. 4, the area surrounding the pedestrian bridge is represented with the detailed 2-dimensional discrete model as a rectangular area of 100.8×41.2 m^2, since it is the area affected by complex pedestrian flows and interactions. The outer connecting streets, which will not be affected by congestion, have been modeled as 1-dimensional queues, to improve the computational efficiency as well as to simplify the task for the scenario configuration. The dimensions and proportions of the environment, in addition to the roads lengths—also in the Figure—have been extracted from Google Earth software. The pedestrian bridge is composed of a single 35 m long span preceded by two 10 m long runs of stairs at its extremes. The west staircase is perpendicular to the flat walkway and connected with an additional flat component of 3×3 m^2, while the east run of stairs is parallel and directly linked to the walkway. To improve the understanding of the setting, a satellite picture of the part of the scene represented with the microscopic model is shown in Fig. 5.

Initially, two versions of the environment have been designed by means of the microscopic model: a baseline that approximates the real setting and an alternative one that proposes an extension of the handrail along the pedestrian bridge,

Fig. 5. Satellite view of the area simulated with the microscopic model (picture taken from Google Earth).

in order to physically separate the directions of flows. The two environments are used to configure five case studies:

- real world setting, all agents traveling the shortest path (SP_NONSEP);
- real world setting, at the Nash Equilibrium (NE_NONSEP);
- alternative scenario, with shortest path (SP_SEP);
- alternative scenario, at the Nash Equilibrium (NE_SEP);
- alternative scenario, at the System Optimum (SO_SEP);

The simulation of the first two scenarios showed that the performance of the real setting is quite low with the assumed population of agents. The 2-directional flow on the bridge, in fact, starts generating some congestion on stairs at the east side of the bridge after around 1 h and 20 min of simulated time (near the peak of the incoming flow to the event). The congestion continues to grow with the increasing frequency of arrival of the counter-flow agents, reaching full congestion of the pedestrian bridge and its nearby after about 2 h and 10 min (see Fig. 6(a)). The congestion heavily affects the traveling times and around 3 h are needed to reach a complete discharge of the bridge, achieving the end of the simulation around time 4 h and 21 min.

With the progression of the iterations, the long traveling times induce the choice of the agents to the alternative route, gradually solving the congestion. At the Nash Equilibrium state for this environment, the jamming is almost solved and the average traveling time has been decreased to 329 s (see Table 1). Nonetheless, the maximum traveling time is still relatively high, due to the length of the alternative route not allowing a complete dispersion of the congestion.

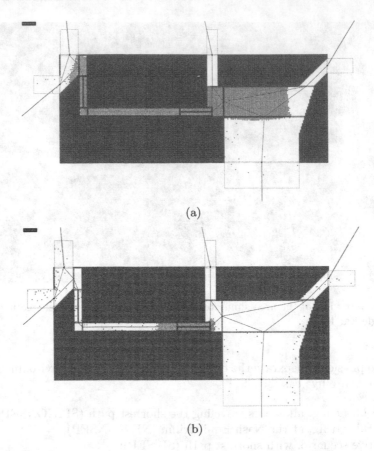

(a)

(b)

Fig. 6. Screenshots from the simulation of the real world setting, with the SP (a) and NE (b) scenario. The blue agents are directed towards the event, the red ones to the station square. The associated network is superimposed on the scenario. Both screenshots are taken at about 2 h and 10 min of simulated time. (Color figure online)

A comparison of the histograms of Fig. 8(a) and (b) shows that the distribution of traveling times significantly differs: at the Nash equilibrium state two peaks are recognizable, identifying the initial portion of the population that succeeds in performing the plan without encountering congestion and another large part that experience a limited congestion that shifts the traveling times to around 600 s.

The simulation of the second environment shows that the proposed modification that separates the flows is quite effective, despite its simplicity. In this way, conflicts on the bridge are prevented and jamming occurs only in front of the access ramps (stairs) with minor effects. Thus the longer route has no advantage in terms of travel time and the Nash equilibrium becomes equal to the shortest path solution. The respective travel times are approximately less than half as long as the ones achieved in the real environment (see the Table 1). The average

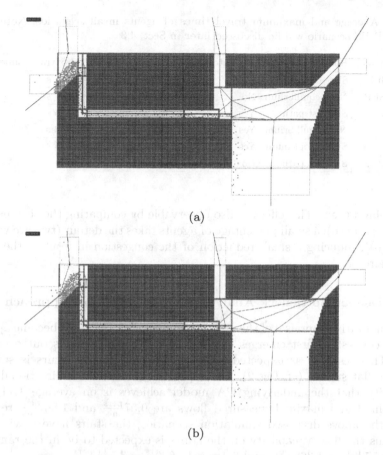

(a)

(b)

Fig. 7. Screenshots from the simulation of the alternative setting, with the SP/NE scenario (a) and the SO one (b). The same color is applied to the agents, regarding their destination. Screenshots are taken at about 2 h and 40 min of simulated time. (Color figure online)

and maximum travel times for the Nash equilibrium simulation are higher than for the shortest path solution. This is not a particular finding and is rather due to the stochastic nature of the model. Overall, the relative distribution of travel times (Fig. 8(c) and (d)) share the same trend and data range.

With this configuration of the environment and pedestrian flows, however, the Nash equilibrium state is different from the system optimum. The system optimum results in lower average and maximum travel times. The difference is more evident in the histogram of the travel times distribution in Fig. 8(e). Firstly, the number of agents which reached the destination in the box corresponding to the smallest travel time is increased by about 500 individuals. Moreover, there is an additional local distribution peak at around 600 s, (probably) generated by the individuals that opted to take the detour in order to make room for

Table 1. Average and maximum travel times of agents in all scenarios. Note: the SP_NOSEP_BS scenario will be discussed later in Sect. 4.3

Scenario name	Routing strategy	Separated flows	Avg. travel time	Max travel time
SP_NONSEP	Shortest path	No	458 s	3,173 s
NE_NONSEP	Nash equilibrium	No	329 s	2,485 s
SP_SEP	Shortest path	Yes	237 s	1,898 s
NE_SEP	Nash equilibrium	Yes	239 s	2,132 s
SO_SEP	System optimum	Yes	232 s	1,625 s
SP_NOSEP_BS	Shortest path	No	162 s	215 s

people behind them. This effect is also observable by comparing the screenshots in Fig. 7(a) and (b): a small percentage of agents takes the detour (two are visible in Fig. 7(b)), inducing a small reduction of the congestion in front of the west access staircase.

4.3 A Deeper Bottleneck Analysis and Optimization Approach

From a qualitative appraisal of the visualizer movies (cf. Fig. 6), it became apparent that congestion first emerges at the stairs before it spreads out over the bridge. This result is as expected since the specific flow at stairs is smaller than on a flat surface (cf. Fig. 2). To be precise, the specific bidirectional flow at capacity that the underlying CA model achieves is on average $1.11 \frac{pers}{m \cdot s}$. The minimal and maximal measured flows are $0.57 \frac{pers}{m \cdot s}$ and $1.56 \frac{pers}{m \cdot s}$ respective. In the above discussed simulation scenarios, the stairs have a width of 2.4 m, thus the flow at capacity on the stairs is expected to be in the range of $2.4 \, m \times 0.57 \frac{pers}{m \cdot s} = 1.368 \frac{pers}{s}$ and $2.4 \, m \times 1.56 \frac{pers}{m \cdot s} = 3.744 \frac{pers}{s}$.

Based on the assumed two shifted normal distributions of the pedestrians departure times, the peak inflow of pedestrians for all scenarios is $q_{max} = 2 \frac{pers}{s}$. Although the stairs are able to manage a flow of $2 \frac{pers}{s}$ on average, there might be fluctuations where the flow on the stairs drops below q_{max}. Those fluctuations result in rapidly accumulating densities and lead to total flow breakdowns and congestion, which then spread over the whole area. Once the congestion starts spreading, the system can no longer recover. However, based on the specific flow on stairs, even the SP_NONSEP scenario seems to be almost feasible. This also explains why it only takes a few pedestrians taking the detour in the NE_NONSEP scenario to avoid the total congestion of the bridge.

Based on this consideration, another scenario has been set up. The new scenario, denoted as SP_NONSEP_BS, is similar to SP_NONSEP with one small but important difference. In the SP_NONSEP_BS scenario, the stairs have been broadened by 0.4 m to a total width of 2.8 m. Thus, the flow at capacity on the stairs is expected to be in the range of $2.8 \, m \times 0.57 \frac{pers}{m \cdot s} = 1.596 \frac{pers}{s}$ and $2.8 \, m \times 1.56 \frac{pers}{m \cdot s} = 4.368 \frac{pers}{s}$.

The SP_NONSEP_BS run results in an average travel time of 162 s and a maximum travel time 215 s. These results are significantly better than those of

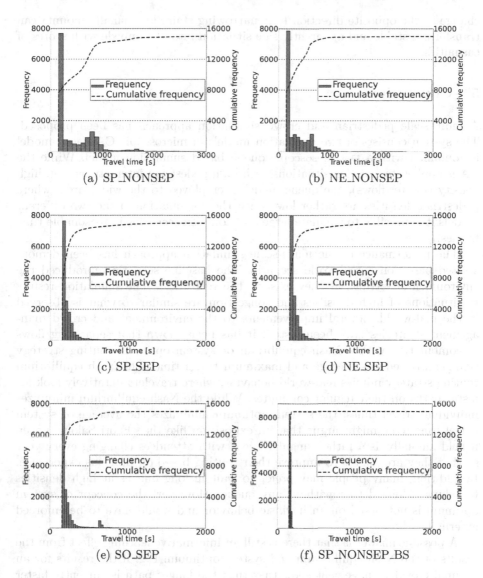

Fig. 8. Travel time histograms for the various scenarios. Note, scales for plot (a) and (b) are different to other plots.

the other scenarios (cf. Table 1 and Fig. 8(f)). From a visual appraisal, even the SP_NONSEP_BS run produces some minor congestions at the stairs. However, because of the broadened stairs, the system is always able to recover from these perturbations.

These results not only show that small structural changes can significantly improve the overall situation, but more importantly that a small structural change in the opposite direction (e.g. narrowing stairs by a small amount) can transform a stable and apparently safe situation into a stampede with scores of casualties.

5 Conclusion

A multi-scale pedestrian and crowd simulation approach has been proposed. The system consists of two simulation models: a microscopic CA based model is combined with a fast mesoscopic queue based simulation model. While the CA is applied to complex situations with high pedestrian interactions (e.g. high density counter-flows), the queue model is employed to the wider area, where pedestrian densities are rather low. With the combination of the two different models it is possible to simulate large and complex scenarios in reasonable time frames.

The performance of the multi-scale simulation approach has been demonstrated based on a real-world scenario. The baseline scenario reproduced the environmental settings as they exist in the real-world. The simulation results in situations of high densities and congestion are similar to what is observed in the real-world. Several improvements to the environment and crowd management strategies have been tested. It has been shown that separating flows in combination with a Nash equilibrium or system optimum routing strategy significantly reduces average and maximum travel time. The Nash equilibrium routing strategy mimics real-world behavior, where travelers iteratively look for faster paths on their regular commutes. While the Nash equilibrium minimizes individual travel times, the system optimum minimizes the average or system travel time. One might argue that an exposition like the "Fuori Salone", even if held annually, is a rather singular event with attendees changing every year so that they are unable to improve their routing based on previous experience. In addition, many people may prefer to wait in long queues at high densities to taking a long detour without any queue. Moreover, the concept of system optimum is not based on an intrinsic behavior and would have to be enforced externally.

A possible answer is that there is still an informative learning effect from the results of the Nash equilibrium and system optimum. E.g. if the results for an optimal crowd management show that that the longer path is currently faster and this could be communicated, then the acceptance would increase. In order to establish such a system, one would have to dynamically measure the incoming flow and direct the crowd dynamically onto the different paths.

However, the main insight—and probably also the most obvious one—is that separating flows in a crowded situation significantly improves the overall performance of the system. Indeed, even in the SP_SEP scenario, where everyone uses the shortest path, the average travel time is considerably decreased compared to any scenario with non-separated flows. The smaller average travel time is achieved by a higher average speed. Since there is a one-to-one mapping between speed and density, this also implies a lower average density. A lower average density definitely improves the comfort level for attendees and significantly contributes to safety and security. Finally, it must be stated that in the underlying scenario a rather long detour is required to avoid the crowded bridge. Thus, even for the SO_SEP scenario, only a few agents chose the long detour and thus all three scenarios with the separated flows (i.e. SP_SEP, NE_SEP, and SO_SEP) lead to very similar results.

Another important observation is that small changes in the layout of the environment can have significant impact on the overall performance. This has been demonstrated by the SP_NONSEP_BS scenario where the stairs have been slightly broadened. SP_NONSET_BS outperforms all other scenarios, even those with separated flows. Vice versa a change in the opposite direction (e.g. from SP_NONSEP_BS to SP_NONSEP) can have serious consequences on the overall situation. A recommendation from this observation is that for large-scale events, all pedestrian facilities should be operated well below capacity so that the system can recover from small local congestion.

Density aware cost functions for the routing strategies would be an interesting future direction for this research, with a routing solution that avoids densities above a certain threshold as a result. However, as for the system optimum, those routing solutions would have to be enforced by an active crowd management.

References

1. Anh, N.T.N., Daniel, Z.J., Du, N.H., Drogoul, A., An, V.D.: A hybrid macro-micro pedestrians evacuation model to speed up simulation in road networks. In: Dechesne, F., Hattori, H., Mors, A., Such, J.M., Weyns, D., Dignum, F. (eds.) AAMAS 2011. LNCS (LNAI), vol. 7068, pp. 371–383. Springer, Heidelberg (2012). doi:10.1007/978-3-642-27216-5_28
2. Bandini, S., Crociani, L., Vizzari, G.: An approach for managing heterogeneous speed profiles in cellular automata pedestrian models. J. Cell. Automata (in press)
3. Blue, V., Adler, J.: Emergent fundamental pedestrian flows from cellular automata microsimulation. Transp. Res. Rec. J. Transp. Res. Board 1644, 29–36 (1998)
4. Bourr, E., Lesort, J.B.: Mixing microscopic representations of traffic flow: hybrid model based on Lighthill-Whitham-Richards theory. Transp. Res. Rec. 1852, 193–200 (2003)
5. Burghardt, S., Seyfried, A., Klingsch, W.: Performance of stairs-fundamental diagram and topographical measurements. Transp. Res. Part C Emerg. Technol. 37, 268–278 (2013)
6. Burghout, W., Koutsopoulos, H., Andréasson, I.: Hybrid mesoscopic-microscopic traffic simulation. Transp. Res. Rec. 1934, 218–225 (2005)
7. Burghout, W., Wahlstedt, J.: Hybrid traffic simulation with adaptive signal control. Transp. Res. Rec. 1999, 191–197 (2007)
8. Burstedde, C., Klauck, K., Schadschneider, A., Zittartz, J.: Simulation of pedestrian dynamics using a two-dimensional cellular automaton. Phys. A Stat. Mech. Appl. 295(3–4), 507–525 (2001)
9. Cascetta, E.: A stochastic process approach to the analysis of temporal dynamics in transportation networks. Transp. Res. B 23B(1), 1–17 (1989)

10. Chooramun, N., Lawrence, P., Galea, E.: Implementing a hybrid space discretisation within an agent based evacuation model. In: Peacock, R., Kuligowski, E., Averill, J. (eds.) Pedestrian and Evacuation Dynamics 2010, pp. 449–458. Springer, Heidelberg (2011). doi:10.1007/978-1-4419-9725-8_40

11. Chraibi, M., Seyfried, A., Schadschneider, A.: Generalized centrifugal-force model for pedestrian dynamics. Phys. Rev. E **82**(4), 46111 (2010)

12. Crociani, L., Lämmel, G.: Multidestination pedestrian flows in equilibrium: a cellular automaton-based approach. Comput. Aided Civ. Infrastruct. Eng. **31**(2016), 432–448 (2016)

13. Crociani, L., Lämmel, G., Vizzari, G.: Multi-scale simulation for crowd management: a case study in an urban scenario. In: Osman, N., Sierra, C. (eds.) AAMAS 2016. LNCS (LNAI), vol. 10002, pp. 147–162. Springer, Heidelberg (2016). doi:10.1007/978-3-319-46882-2_9

14. Crociani, L., Manenti, L., Vizzari, G.: MAKKSim: MAS-based crowd simulations for designer's decision support. In: Demazeau, Y., Ishida, T., Corchado, J.M., Bajo, J. (eds.) PAAMS 2013. LNCS (LNAI), vol. 7879, pp. 25–36. Springer, Heidelberg (2013). doi:10.1007/978-3-642-38073-0_3

15. Dada, J.O., Mendes, P.: Multi-scale modelling and simulation in systems biology. Integr. Biol. **3**(2), 86–96 (2011)

16. Dijkstra, E.: A note on two problems in connexion with graphs. Numer. Math. **1**, 269–271 (1959)

17. Espié, S., Gattuso, D., Galante, F.: A hybrid traffic model coupling macro and behavioural micro simulation. Annual Meeting Preprint 06-2013, Transportation Research Board, Washington D.C. (2006)

18. Flötteröd, G., Lämmel, G.: Bidirectional pedestrian fundamental diagram. Transp. Res. Part B Methodol. **71**(C), 194–212 (2015)

19. Gawron, C.: An iterative algorithm to determine the dynamic user equilibrium in a traffic simulation model. Int. J. Mod. Phys. C **9**(3), 393–407 (1998)

20. Helbing, D.: A fluid dynamic model for the movement of pedestrians. arXiv preprint cond-mat/9805213 (1998)

21. Helbing, D., Hennecke, A., Shvetsov, V., Treiber, M.: Micro- and macro-simulation of freeway traffic. Math. Comput. Model. **35**, 517–547 (2002)

22. Helbing, D., Molnár, P.: Social force model for pedestrian dynamics. Phys. Rev. E **51**, 4282–4286 (1995)

23. Henderson, L.: The statistics of crowd fluids. Nature **229**(5284), 381–383 (1971)

24. Hoogendoorn, S., Bovy, P.: Dynamic user-optimal assignment in continuous time and space. Transp. Res. Part B Methodol. **38**(7), 571–592 (2004)

25. Krajzewicz, D., Erdmann, J., Behrisch, M., Bieker, L.: Recent development and applications of SUMO - Simulation of Urban MObility. Int. J. Adv. Syst. Meas. **5**(3&4), 128–138 (2012)

26. Kretz, T., Lehmann, K., Hofsäß, I.: User equilibrium route assignment for microscopic pedestrian simulation. Adv. Complex Syst. **17**(2), 1450010 (2014)

27. Lämmel, G., Chraibi, M., Kemloh Wagoum, A., Steffen, B.: Hybrid multi- and inter-modal transport simulation: a case study on large-scale evacuation planning. Transp. Res. Rec. (to appear)

28. Lämmel, G., Flötteröd, G.: Towards system optimum: finding optimal routing strategies in time-dependent networks for large-scale evacuation problems. In: Mertsching, B., Hund, M., Aziz, Z. (eds.) KI 2009. LNCS (LNAI), vol. 5803, pp. 532–539. Springer, Heidelberg (2009). doi:10.1007/978-3-642-04617-9_67

29. Lämmel, G., Flötteröd, G.: A CA model for bidirectional pedestrian streams. Procedia Comput. Sci. **52**, 950–955 (2015)

30. Lämmel, G., Grether, D., Nagel, K.: The representation and implementation of time-dependent inundation in large-scale microscopic evacuation simulations. Transp. Res. Part C Emerg. Technol. **18**(1), 84–98 (2010)
31. Lämmel, G., Klüpfel, H., Nagel, K.: The MATSim network flow model for traffic simulation adapted to large-scale emergency egress and an application to the evacuation of the Indonesian city of Padang in case of a tsunami warning. In: Timmermans, H. (ed.) Pedestrian Behavior, pp. 245–265. Emerald Group Publishing Limited (2009). Chap. 11
32. Lämmel, G., Seyfried, A., Steffen, B.: Large-scale and microscopic: a fast simulation approach for urban areas. Annual Meeting Preprint 14-3890, Transportation Research Board, Washington, D.C. (2014)
33. Liao, W., Seyfried, A., Zhang, J., Boltes, M., Zheng, X., Zhao, Y.: Experimental study on pedestrian flow through wide bottleneck. Transp. Res. Procedia **2**, 26–33 (2014)
34. Michon, J.: A critical view of driver behavior models: what do we know, what should we do? In: Evans, L., Schwing, R.C. (eds.) Hum. Behav. Traffic Saf., pp. 485–524. Springer, New York (1985)
35. Nash, J.: Non-cooperative games. Ann. Math. **54**(2), 286–295 (1951)
36. Raney, B., Nagel, K.: Iterative route planning for large-scale modular transportation simulations. Future Gener. Comput. Syst. **20**(7), 1101–1118 (2004)
37. Rupprecht, T., Klingsch, W., Seyfried, A.: Influence of geometry parameters on pedestrian flow through bottleneck. In: Pedestrian and Evacuation Dynamics 2010, pp. 71–80 (2011)
38. Simon, P., Esser, J., Nagel, K.: Simple queueing model applied to the city of Portland. Int. J. Mod. Phys. **10**(5), 941–960 (1999)
39. von Sivers, I., Köster, G.: Dynamic stride length adaptation according to utility and personal space. Transp. Res. Part B Methodol. **74**(30), 104–117 (2014)
40. Taillandier, P., Vo, D.-A., Amouroux, E., Drogoul, A.. GAMA: a simulation plat form that integrates geographical information data, agent-based modeling and multi-scale control. In: Desai, N., Liu, A., Winikoff, M. (eds.) PRIMA 2010. LNCS (LNAI), vol. 7057, pp. 242–258. Springer, Heidelberg (2012). doi:10.1007/978-3-642-25920-3_17
41. Weidmann, U.: Transporttechnik der Fussgänger - Transporttechnische Eigenschaftendes Fussgängerverkehrs (Literaturstudie). Literature Research 90, Institut füer Verkehrsplanung, Transporttechnik, Strassen- und Eisenbahnbau IVT an der ETH Zürich (1993)
42. Zhang, J., Klingsch, W., Schadschneider, A., Seyfried, A.: Transitions in pedestrian fundamental diagrams of straight corridors and t-junctions. J. Stat. Mech. Theor. Exp. **2011**(06), P06004 (2011)
43. Zhang, J., Klingsch, W., Schadschneider, A., Seyfried, A.: Ordering in bidirectional pedestrian flows and its influence on the fundamental diagram. J. Stat. Mech. Theor. Exp. **2012**(02), 9 (2012)

A National Heat Demand Model for Germany

Marcelo Esteban Muñoz Hidalgo[✉]

HafenCity University Hamburg, Überseealle 16, 20457 Hamburg, Germany
marcelo.hidalgo@hcu-hamburg.de

Abstract. Spatial microsimulation models can be used for the analysis of complex systems. In this paper we make use of a spatial microsimulation model for the estimation of heat demand for Germany at a NUTS–3 level. The presented model creates a synthetic building stock by re-weighting the national microdata sample to small areas (NUTS–3) statistics with help of the GREGWT algorithm. Using the GREGWT method we benchmark the microdata sample to three different aggregation units (a) the building level (i.e. number of buildings); (b) families/dwelling units; and (c) individuals.

The model takes into account the different climate regions defined on the national German 18599-DIN standard. In order to incorporate the climate data into the model, we make use of a quasi steady-state heat transfer model to compute the heat demand of the individual buildings. These type of models require a building geometry for the estimation of heat demand, in this case we do not have information of the individual building geometry but only about the building size, expressed as square meters. We define synthetic geometrical boxes for the computation of heat demand.

The described model is able to represent the national building stock at a microlevel. These type of models are essential for the assessment of policies targeting (a) the reduction of carbon emissions in the construction sector and (b) the increase of energy efficiency on heat distribution grids.

Keywords: GREGWT · Heat demand · Synthetic building stock · Spatial microsimulation

1 Introduction: The Need of a National Energy Demand Models at a Microlevel

Energy supply systems of most developed countries are facing a rapid transition towards carbon neutral infrastructures. Part of this transition has proven to be a decentralization of energy supply sources. This decentralization of supply has introduced many new actors into the system. This decentralization is not only a spatial decentralization but a decentralization of energy production capacities. We see a trend towards the supply of urban and rural areas through distributed systems with a much lower energy production capacity. In order to

© Springer International Publishing AG 2017
M.-R. Namazi-Rad et al. (Eds.): ABMUS 2016, LNAI 10051, pp. 172–188, 2017.
DOI: 10.1007/978-3-319-51957-9_10

understand this type of systems we need to develop models able to: (a) describe the distributed systems at their output aggregation level; (b) capture the diversity of the individual systems; and (c) integrate national policies influencing the development of these systems and the population affected by these policies.

The use of a spatial microsimulation model for the description of these complex systems is ideal. With a spatial microsimulation model we are able to generate a synthetic building stock benchmarked to small areas (NUTS–3 level). An internal validation of the model shows that it is performing with high accuracy (see Sect. 5.1). The synthetic building stock is enriched with energy relevant parameters– mainly heat transmission coefficients– needed for the computation of heat demand. With this enriched building stock we can perform many types of simulations. In this paper we simulate the monthly heat demand of the synthetic building stock. The spatial microsimulation model allows us to represent the entire building stock of Germany at a micro level with a monthly resolution. The simulation of heat demand at a higher temporal resolution can be achieved through the use of a thermal simulation model instead of the implemented quasi steady-state heat demand model.

An innovation of this model is the consideration of climate zones for the estimation of heat demand. We classify the individual small areas into predefined climate zones. A climate zone is defined by the monthly mean outside temperature and by its monthly solar radiation. Both variables are given as input to the heat demand model.

We structured the paper into five main sections: on Sect. 2 we make a brief description of the implemented heat demand model and the used input parameters, on this section we also describe the enrichment process of the microdata sample with energy relevant parameters; on Sect. 3 we describe the defined climate zones; on Sect. 4 we describe the implemented algorithm and procedure for the re-weighting of the enriched microdata; on Sect. 5 we present and discuss the main results from the performed simulation; we conclude the paper with Sect. 6 where we draw our conclusions from the simulation results and present an overview of the steps ahead as well as other possible applications of the developed model.

2   The Heat Demand Model

The computation of heat demand occurs at a micro level. We construct a synthetic building for each individual in the microdata sample, the resulting heat demand is divided by household-size. This means that we need to define a building geometry for each individual in the census. We use the average dwelling unit size from the microdata sample for the definition of number of stories of single family houses. E.g. if an individual from the microdata sample lives on a single family house with a floor space of $120\,m^2$ and the computed average dwelling unit size from the sample is $60\,m^2$, we define the geometry of the building as a two storey building, each storey with a floor space of $60\,m^2$. Multi-family houses are simulated as single storey buildings, e.g. each dwelling unit of the multi-family house is simulated as a one storey building.

Each individual on the microdata sample describes the building they live in with three characteristics: (1) dwelling unit size, in square meters; (2) construction year of the building; and (3) number of dwelling units on the building. With these three parameters we classify the microdata sample into building typologies. We make use of a well established building typology in Germany, the IWU typology [8,12]. This process allows us to enrich the microdata sample with energy relevant parameters. Out of the predefined typologies we take important parameters needed for the estimation of heat demand. Probably the most important parameters we take out of the building typology are heat transmission coefficients of building parts (roof, ceiling, walls and windows), we also define the percentage of glazing area of the buildings based on this typology. All these parameters are given as input variables to the quasi steady-state heat demand model.

The use of building typologies for the construction of either: (a) urban heat demand models working at a microlevel, e.g. by classifying the digital cadastre into building types; or (b) aggregated national models can be found throughout the literature [1,3,5,6,10,11,26]. This paper presents a method that combines these two approaches: a model working at a microlevel able to asses the impact of national policies relevant to the energy efficiency of the building stock.

The IWU typology defines each building type by construction epoch and building type. Table 1 lists the predefined typologies with the defined heat demand value of the building type. In our model we do not use this value but the underlying parameters used for the computation of the presented heat demand value of each building type. We need to make use of the underlying parameters, rather than the heat demand values in order to: (1) compute the heat demand at a higher temporal resolution; and (2) open the door for a projection of the building stock under different policies targeting the retrofitting of existing buildings.

Table 1. IWU-de building typology matrix for Germany

	<1859	1860–1918	1919–1948	1949–1957	1958–1968	1969–1978	1979–1983	1984–1994	1995–2001	2002–2009
EFH^a	183	180	164	181	146	155	118	132	110	88
RH		153	137	156	106	127	127	98	78	86
KMH	190	143	168	156	129	134	118	122	92	79
GMH		127	144	142	131	117				
HH					114	113				

source: [12] Specific Heat demand (spez. Wärmebedarfskennzahl) [kWh/m^2a] (EFH) Single family house "Einfamilienhaus"; (RH) Terrace house "Reihenhaus"; (KMH) Apartment house "Mehrfamilienhaus"; (GMH) Large apartment house "Groes Mehrfamilienhaus"; (HH) High-rise "Hochhaus";

The computation of heat demand is performed with a quasi steady-state model implemented in the R language [15]. This is an implementation of the German norm DIN 18599 [7]. This norm is used for the heat demand computation of energy performance certificates of new and existing buildings in Germany.

The computation of heat demand is a balancing procedure between *heat gains* Qg and *heat losses* Ql. The difference between them is the needed heat demand to maintain a predefined internal temperature set-point of the dwelling unit. The internal temperature set-point in this model is fixed, we use the defined internal temperature of the DIN norm. Because we use the microdata sample for the estimation of heat demand, we have a rich description not only of the building stock but also about their residents, this data can be used for the definition of user parameters like internal temperature set-point, see [14,20] for this type of implementations.

The monthly heat demand Qh is computed using the estimated monthly heat gains Qg and monthly heat losses Ql, see Eq. 1, where m is the month of the year. The heat demand is defined as the needed heat to maintain the operative temperature and cover the heat losses. A fraction of all the computed heat gains are subtracted from the heat losses, this fraction is the usable share of the total heat gains. The fraction is computed with help of the *eta* (η) Factor.

$$Qh = Ql - \eta \times Qg \tag{1}$$

The monthly heat gains Qg are computed as the average monthly solar heat flow Ss plus the heat flow by internal heat sources Si, both measured in $[W]$, see Eq. 2. The monthly solar heat flow is computed based on: (a) the monthly solar radiation, defined by the climate zone; (b) the share of glazing surface, defined by the building typology; and (c) the building orientation, neglected on this model. The internal heat sources are fixed on this implementation. Similar to the internal temperature set point, this variable can be modeled as occupant behaviour.

$$Qg = 0.024 \times (Ss + Si) \times t \tag{2}$$

The computed heat losses Ql are computed as the specific total heat loss H measured in $[W/K]$ times the difference between the inside temperature (or temperature set point) Ti and the outside ambient temperature Te, measured in kelvin $[K]$, see Eq. 3. The internal temperature is set fix throughout the model while the monthly outside temperature varies between climate zones.

$$Ql = 0.024 \times H \times (Ti - Te) \times t \tag{3}$$

The most important factors of the specific total heat loss in our model are the transmission losses Ht. The transmission losses are computed as the sum of transmission losses of all building components encountered with ambient air. The individual transmission losses are computed as the heat transmission coefficient U of the building component (normally referred as the U-value, or R-value) measured in $[W/(m^2 K)]$ times the corresponding building component surface area A, measured in $[m^2]$. The heat transmission coefficients of the individual building components are defined through the building typology. The area of the components is taken out of the generated building geometry. The generated geometry is computed as function of the dwelling unit size. Equation 4 depicts this computation step. Other heat losses are thermal bridges and ventilation losses. In our model the ventilation losses are fixed throughout the model.

This variable, analog to internal temperature set-point and internal gains, could be modeled as occupant behaviour.

$$Ht = \sum_{i=1}^{n} \left(U_{(i)} \times A_{(i)} \right) \tag{4}$$

An example of this computation is depicted on Fig. 1 for a random building for all predefined climate zones. An example of the used code for the computation of heat demand for the example shown on Fig. 1 is listed below.

```
library(heat)
result <- heat(output_type='Month',_climate='Hamburg')
```

This method is normally used at a monthly resolution but can be used to simulate heat demand in a more granular temporal resolution. For now we limit the simulation to a monthly resolution because of the available climate data for the predefined climate regions in Germany, see next section for a description of this data.

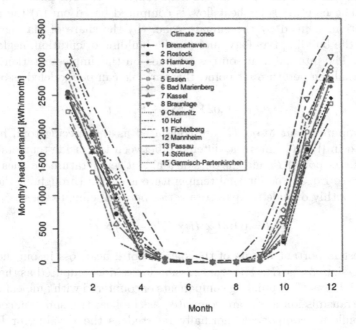

Fig. 1. Computed monthly heat demand for all climate zones

3   Defined Climate Regions in Germany

The simulation of heat demand for the entire country requires an explicit consideration of regional climatic conditions. In this paper we present the use of climate zones for the consideration of climate variation of different regions in Germany.

Figure 2 shows the 15 predefined climate zones in Germany. These climate zones are defined in the German DIN norm DIN 18599 [7]. The norm also provides the necessary climate-data for a monthly estimation of heat demand. For the computation of heat demand at a different temporal resolution implementing a quasi steady-state model we would require climate data with the same temporal resolution.

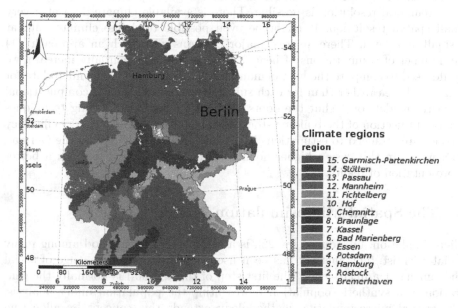

Fig. 2. Defined climate regions for the computation of heat demand

We modify the implemented quasi steady-state model used in this paper in order for it to be aware of the climate regions, making it possible for us to define the desired region simply by name. The implemented R library loads all the climate data on start-up and selects the needed data for the estimation of heat demand based on the user input.

We compute the heat demand of each individual on the survey sample previous to the re-weighting of the sample, see Sect. 4 for the re-weighting procedure. In order to incorporate the climate data, define by the climate zones, we could compute the monthly heat demand of each individual for each predefined climate zone. After the re-weighting procedure we would just have to select to climate zone corresponding to the NUTS–3 geographical area. This procedure is not very efficient. For the re-weighting procedure we do not use the entire sample survey, but select the records corresponding to the federal state (NUTS–1 level). This means that only climate zones overlapping a given federal states are relevant for all NUTS–3 geographical areas within that federal state. With this in mind we can define which climate zones to use for the computation of heat demand of each individual in the sample survey. A small example. The federal state of North Rhine-Westphalia (see Cologne on Fig. 2) overlaps with two climate zones: (5) Essen; and (6) Bad Marienberg. The re-weighting process for all NUTS–3 areas within this state will either select climate zone 5 or 6, but never use climate zone 7. For that reason, for individuals within the NUTS–1 region of North Rhine-Westphalia, we only need to compute the heat demand twice (with climate data from zone 5 and 6) instead of 15 times (for each climate zone).

The implementation of climate data at a higher spatial resolution at the same temporal resolution is possible. There is available climate data at a very small spatial resolution. It might be even possible to define climate data at a small area level. There are two major concerns with such an approach: (1) the number of computations of heat demand would exponentially increase, we would need to compute the heat demand of each individual of the microdata for each small area rather than for each sub sample, running such a computational intensive model could shut the doors to more interesting modeling techniques like the projection of the building stock into the future; and (2) energy efficiency policies are attached to estimations based on the data provided by the German DIN norm. In this case a higher fidelity of the model does not mean a better representation of reality.

4   The Spatial Microsimulation Model

Microsimulation, introduced by [22], is a commonly used method among many social scientist. This method has been used to simulate a large range of social phenomena at a micro-level. The first step of this method is normally the generation of a synthetic population representing the population under analysis. The spatial microsimulation methodology extends this concept by allocating estimated synthetic populations to geographical areas [4]. For overview of spatial microsimulation models, its applications and methods see [21,31]. For the presented model we use the Generalised Regression and Weighting of sample survey results, knows by its acronym GREGWT. We use the available GREGWT R library [19], this library is an implementation of the GREGWT algorithm. The GREGWT algorithm was originally developed by the Australian Bureau of Statistics (ABS) [2]. This algorithm is used by the National Center for Social and Economic Modeling (NATSEM) on their spatial microsimulation model spatialMSM [29,30].

The simulation process computes the weights for each area iteratively. Although the R simulation library GREGWT can internalize this process, we need to run the loop outside the library environment in order to store the data on disk efficiently. This type of simulation generates almost 8 Gb of data, this can be a problem if we try to store a large R data frame on RAM. The code below is a simplified representation of the simulation process.

```
library ( 'GREGWT' )
for ( area in small areas ){
      weights = GREGWT( simulation data , area code=area )
}
```

The lowest possible geographical identification on the microdata survey is the federal state (NUTS–1). For the re-weighting process at the small areas we only use the records of the corresponding federal state (e.g if a small area is within the federal state of Bavaria, we will only re-weight records from the microdata survey identified to the federal state of Bavaria).

For each simulation area we compute a new set of weights, this weights are stored on csv files. We use these weights to compute the total heat demand of each simulation area. The heat density is computed as the total heat demand divided by the area size expressed as $[Wh/ha * month]$.

4.1 Data

In order to define the synthetic building stock we re-weight the 2010 German microdata survey [27]. The re-weighting process is benchmarked to aggregated statistics from the 2011 German census [28] available at a NUTS-3 level. The used benchmarks are listed on Table 2.

Table 2. Used benchmarks from the 2011 Census and corresponding micro census attributes

MC Code[a] [27]	Census Code [28]	Unit[b]	Description
EF1	/	/	Federal State (NUTS–1)
EF952	/	Person	Weight
EF44	ALTER_KURZ	Person	Age (five classes of years)
EF49	FAMSTND_AUSF	Person	Marital status (in detail)
EF46	GESCHLECHT	Person	Sex
EF20	HHGROESS_KLASS	Person	Size of private household
EF492	WOHNFLAECHE_20S	Dwelling	Floor area of the dwelling (20 m^2 intervals)
EF494	BAUJAHR_MZ	Building	Year of construction (microcensus classes)
EF635	ZAHLWOHNGN_HHG	Building	Number of dwellings in a building

[a]Micro Census Code
[b]Refers only to Census

The census data is directly retrieved from the census web-page for each benchmark iteratively. The combined census data contains 11300 NUTZS-3 areas and 7 benchmarks described with a total of 44 categories. The microdata sample contains a total of 528 attributes and 489330 records. Out of the 528 attributes we only use the 7 attributes corresponding to the census benchmarks plus the original survey design weights and the federal state geographical identification number.

4.2 GREGWT

GREGWT is an implementation of method number 5 of Sigh & Mohl [25]. Tanton [32] makes a detailed description of the algorithm and its applications.

The mathematical description of the GREGWT algorithm presented below is taken from [24] and the algorithm description from [18].

Aim of the GREGWT algorithm is to find a set of new weights w that can be used to match the microdata survey X to a set of given benchmarks T (in this case NUTS–3 small area statistics) so that $T = \sum w_j X_j$ while minimizing the weight difference between the new weights w and the sample design weights d from the microdata survey. Note that T is given at a higher resolution (aggregated to the predefined geographical areas, NUTS–3 in this case) than the microdata sample. Thus, the re-weighting procedure computes a new set of weights for the microdata records so that the properties of T are generated, with the additional property that the new weights should be close to the old weights. For the distance D between design and estimated weights the GREGWT algorithm makes use of the truncated Chi-Squared distance function, represented in Eq. 5.

$$D = \frac{1}{2} \sum_j \frac{(w_j - d_j)^2}{d_j} \tag{5}$$

This is a constrained optimization problem where D is minimized subject to the constraints $T = \sum w_j X_j$.

Now given the new survey weights w_j for a NUTS–3 geographical area i, we compute the overall heat demand H of the geographical area as:

$$H_i = \sum_i \sum_j w_{i,j} * Qh_{i,j} \tag{6}$$

Where $Qh_{i,j}$ is the computed heat demand for individual i of the sample microdata and climate zone of geographical area j. Qh is given by Eq. 1.

For a spatial microsimulation model we need a last step. The algorithm needs a weight restriction in order to avoid negative weights, in such case the algorithm implements an iterative process to maintain a low weight distance within the weight constraints. The R GREGWT implementation defines boundaries constraints as a user input. The user can define an upper and lower bound. If the algorithm computes weights outside these bounds, the weights will be truncated to the predefined bounds. In this case the algorithm will iterate with the new computed weights until a predefined convergence parameter is met or there is no improvement in the iteration.

4.3   Benchmarking to Different Aggregation Units

The used census benchmarks of the small areas count different aggregation units: (1) Individuals/People, (2) Families/Dwelling units, and (3) Buildings (see Table 2). Our R library used for the re-weighting of survey data is able to perform an integrated re-weight. This can be useful for a re-weighting of the microdata survey for which maintaining the original family structure of the data set is important. An integrated re-weight does not give us the possibility to benchmark the survey to more than two aggregation units. The aim of this paper is to create a synthetic building stock with its occupants living on it. In order to create a representative data set we need to benchmark the micro-data survey to both the building stock characteristics and characteristics of its occupants. Available benchmarks at the NUTS–3 level count three aggregation units, as described above. We benchmark the microdata survey to these three aggregation units counting buildings, dwelling units and individuals (building occupants). In the literature there are alternatives listed for the re-weighting of survey at different aggregations units by either fitting the survey to the aggrega-tion units via an integerization of the weights [9,23] or through the computation of fitted values or the different aggregation units [13].

Because we do not need integer values on the re-weighted microdata survey, we implement a simpler method for the benchmarking to different aggregation units. The GREGWT library internally transforms the microdata survey into a binary array of one and zeros. Nonetheless, the computation does not require it to be a binary array, therefore we manipulate this array in order to represent aggregation units. This process has been internalized into the R library. For a more detailed description of this process see [17,19].

5   Results

This section describes the performance of the model and the simulation results. The performance of the model is tested as an internal validation. We compare: (1) microdata survey X times the computed weights w aggregated to each small area i, as $\hat{T}_i = X \times w_i$; with (2) the aggregated small area benchmarks T_i. The model presents a very good internal validation performance. An external validation of the model is not possible at the moment because of missing data on heat demand. The simulation model could be validated at a microlevel with high resolution heat consumption data or at an aggregated level. Data at low level of aggregation is hard to obtain and what is available is also aggregated by use type. Our model only computes domestic heat demand making it impossible to validate the model at an aggregated level. In order to make an external validation possible, we aim to include the non residential sector in our model.

5.1   Performance of the Model

The internal validation of the spatial microsimulation model is performed with help of the Total Absolute Error TAE and the Percentage Absolute Error $PTAE$. The TAE is the absolute difference between the simulated $\hat{T}$ and observed T benchmarks, the $PTAE$ is an extension of the TAE measure. The $PTAE$ divides the computed TAE by the total population pop of the geograph-ical area i. The mathematical expression of both measures are indicated below.

$$TAE_i = \sum_j \left| T_{i,j} - \hat{T}_{i,j} \right| \tag{7}$$

$$PTAE_i = TAE_i \div pop_i \times 100 \tag{8}$$

The performance of the simulation model is very good. Figure 3 compares the simulated benchmarks $\hat{T}_i$ and the observed benchmarks T_i for all simulation areas. The figure shows a very good fit between them. In this plot we can see the simulation areas with a large population at the top of the plot, these are the small areas with a large population (Berlin, Hamburg, etc.).

The mean TAE for the model is 25 with a standard deviation of 95.95, this means that on average the model has 25 persons that do not correspond to the reported statistics of the simulation areas. The maximum TAE value is 4675.58. There are 3 areas with a TAE bigger than 2000 and 1134 areas with a TAE value bigger than 50. These results are hard to interpret because the relevance of the number of misplaced people depends on the total population of the simulation area. 2000 misplaced individuals for a simulation area like Hamburg with a total population of almost two millions habitants would represent a 0.1 % error. In order to account for this difference we also used the $PTAE$ error measure in order to analyze the internal performance of the model.

The mean $PTAE$ value is 0.9 %. Only 516 areas have a $PTAE$ value higher or equal to 1 %. If we exclude these 516 areas from the simulation, we achieve a $PTAE$ value of 0.46 %. Figure 4 shows the $PTAE$ distribution for all areas with

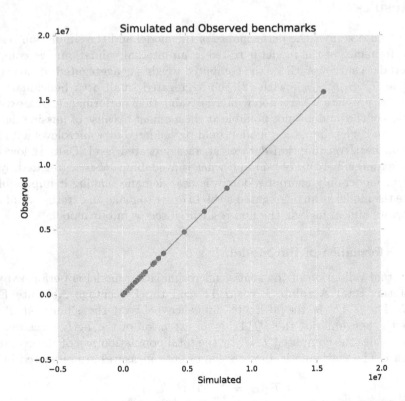

Fig. 3. Total Absolute Error (TAE) of all simulation areas plotted as simulated vs. observed values

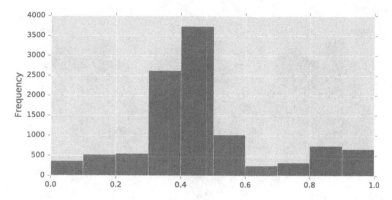

Fig. 4. Error distribution of simulation areas measured as the percentage total absolute error ($PSAE$)

a $PTAE$ value lower that 1 %. We set the 1 % barrier to define areas on which the re-weighting was effective. This boundary might still be too high. Setting the $PTAE$ limit at 3 % reduces the number of excluded areas to 10, this would represent 0.09 % of all simulation areas.

The performance of the model is very good. This internal validation of the model only validates the GREGWT re-weighting algorithm. The used library for the computation of heat demand relies on the German DIN norm which is a well established method. We still need to keep investigating the process used for the definition of a synthetic building stock. In this model we have neglected completely the building geometry, orientation and other energy relevant attributes.

5.2   Distribution of Heat Density in Germany

For the representation of heat demand in space we compute the heat density for each simulation area as monthly watt-hour per hectare [$Wh/ha \times month$]. Figure 5 shows the heat demand for each month on a color scale. We normalize the color scale for each month. The monthly variation on absolute heat density cannot be appreciated on this figure because of this normalization. The aim of the monthly normalization is to identify a variation on the spatial distribution of heat density rather than the monthly absolute heat density. In terms of heat density we do not observe much change in the pattern through the year. It is clear that the climate data used as input for the estimation of heat demand has a strong influence on the result. On the months of July and August the climate zone 12-Mannheim (see Fig. 2) is clearly outlined. We also appreciate a small decline of heat density during the month of April in the mid-west part of the country. The pink spot on the north west part of Germany is the largest urban agglomeration of the country. The two largest cities can also be spotted on the map, Hamburg on the north and Berlin on the north-east. The region surrounding Berlin has a decline on heat density during the month of July.

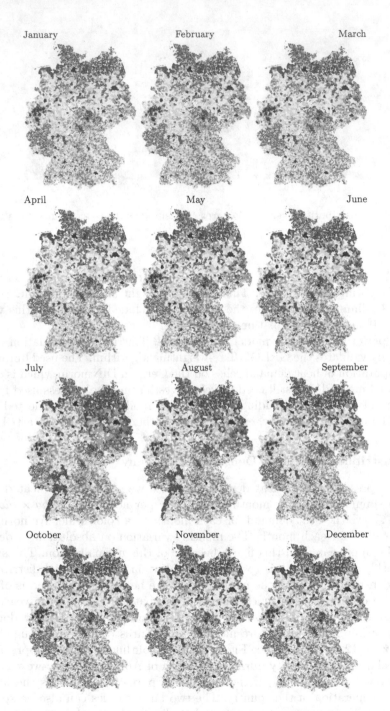

Fig. 5. Estimated heat density for all the simulated areas through the year using a color scale normalized for each month

The estimated yearly heat demand density for Germany is simply computed as the sum of the monthly heat densities. Figure 6 shows the results for the entire country. On this figure we can clearly identify the large urban agglomerations in Germany. The important issue to keep in mind is that the simulation process is occurring at a microlevel. The advantages of this type of models working at such a low level of aggregation is the ability to simulate the impact of new national energy policies. A simulation of this type would allow us to asses and predict the impact of energy relevant policies at the microlevel. We can identify sections of the population that are particularly affected by a certain policy and the impact on specific geographical areas.

The presented result show only the developed method for the estimation of heat demand at a low level of aggregation. The applications of this method for an energy policy assessment still need to be developed.

We apply this method at a national level because of the data available at this level. With more data at a lower aggregation level we can apply the exact same model at a city level. For certain applications the distribution of heat demand is more attractive at a lower aggregation level. Applications like the planning of district heat networks need an estimation of heat densities at a lower aggregation level. Another advantage of a simulation at a city level can be the use of the city digital cadastre or other datasets describing the building stock at a micro level. The use of the digital cadastre for the estimation of heat demand allows

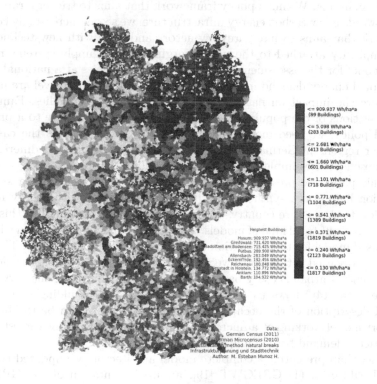

Fig. 6. Estimated heat density $[Wh/ha * a]$ for Germany

us to take further energy relevant parameters of the building stock into account. See Muñoz H. [16] for a detailed description of the geometry extraction of a digital cadastre for the simulation of heat demand. The disadvantage of models based on a digital cadastre is its transferability, many rural areas of Germany still do not have a digital cadastre. If the aim of this model is the assessment of national energy policies, we need to take the entire national building stock into account. Many rural areas might be particularly affected by a certain policy, not including them because of data availability would be a systematic error in the model design.

Another advantage of having a completely synthetic building stock– without a link to the digital cadastre– is the ability to project the building stock into the future under predefined growth scenarios. These type of models can be used for the assessment of national policies targeting a reduction of carbon emissions on the building stock. See Muñoz H. [20] for an application of a synthetic building stock projected into the future.

6   Conclusions and Further Implementations of Spatial Microsimulation Models for the Analysis of Energy Policy

The energy policy of a country has always been an essential part of the national economic planning. Within a policy framework that aims to trigger a rapid transition towards a low carbon energy infrastructure, we see an increasingly complex framework that aims to integrate new actors and cope with new technologies. The complexity attached to the new emerging energy supply systems needs a better model for the assessment of energy relevant policies at a national level.

National energy demand models working at an aggregated level are not able to capture the impact on national policies on individual families. Families of specific sections of the population might be specially susceptible to a proposed national policy, we need model able to capture this. Similar is the case with particular regions in Germany. Different regions will be affected differently by the proposed policies implemented at a national or European level.

In this paper we present a robust and quick way to generate a synthetic population living on a synthetic building stock, enriched with energy relevant properties, for the entire country. The underlying data generated in this model can serve as input to all kind of models. The generated data can be used within an agent based model for the simulation of all type of urban phenomena. Thanks to the rich survey used in this model we will be able to expand it for the development of more general urban activity based models. An enrichment of the survey with time-use data [14] allows us to represent not only the building stock, but a detailed description of the occupant activities. This data can be the base of a transport model working at a micro level or a detailed model for the estimation of electricity demand based on appliances use.

Rather than presenting a complete model architecture we updated two open source R libraries: (1) GREGWT [19], an implementation of the GREGWT algorithm, used for the re-weighting of the microdata survey; and (2) HEAT [15], an implementation of the German DIN 18599 [7], used for the estimation of heat demand. The described model is a combination of both libraries. We aim to develop further small libraries that can be either used individually or in combination with the above mentioned libraries. We see this development strategy more sustainable than the development of a complete software architecture.

The challenge ahead is to translate the energy policies in place into machine readable code in order to establish a basis for the assessment of new energy policies at a national level.

References

1. Balaras, C.A., Gaglia, A.G., Georgopoulou, E., Mirasgedis, S., Sarafidis, Y., Lalas, D.P.: European residential buildings and empirical assessment of the hellenic building stock, energy consumption, emissions and potential energy savings. Build. Environ. **42**(3), 1298–1314 (2007)
2. Bell, P.: GREGWT and TABLE Macros – User Guide. Australian Bureau of Statistics (ABS), Canberra (2000)
3. Caputo, P., Costa, G., Ferrari, S.: A supporting method for defining energy strategies in the building sector at urban scale. Energy Policy **55**, 261–270 (2013)
4. Clarke, M., Holm, E.: Microsimulation methods in spatial analysis and planning. Geogr. Ann. Ser. B Hum. Geogr. **69**(2), 145–164 (1987)
5. Dall'O', G., Galante, A., Torri, M.: A methodology for the energy performance classification of residential building stock on an urban scale. Energy Build. **48**, 211–219 (2012)
6. Dascalaki, E.G., Droutsa, K.G., Balaras, C.A., Kontoyiannidis, S.: Building typologies as a tool for assessing the energy performance of residential buildings - a case study for the hellenic building stock. Energy Build. **43**(12), 3400–3409 (2011)
7. Deutsches Institut für Normung e. V. Din V 18599: Energetische Bewertung von Gebäuden – Berechnung des Nutz-, End- und Primärenergiebedarfs für Heizung, Kühlung, Lüftung, Trinkwarmwasser und Beleuchtung: Berechnung des Nutz-, End- und Primärenergiebedarfs für Heizung, Kühlung, Lüftung, Trinkwarmwasser und Beleuchtung Sonderdruck 2012 (2011)
8. Diefenbach, N., Cischinsky, H., Rodenfels, M., Clausnitzer, K.-D., Gebäudebestand, D.: Datenerhebung zur energetischen Qualität und zu den Modernisierungstrends im deutschen Wohngebäudebestand, 1st edn. Institut Wohnen und Umwelt (IWU) and Bremer Energie Institut (BEI), Darmstadt (2010)
9. Guo, J., Bhat, C.: Population synthesis for microsimulating travel behavior. Transp. Res. Rec. J. Transp. Res. Board **2014**, 92–101 (2007)
10. Hrabovszky-Horváth, S., Pálvölgyi, T., Csoknyai, T., Talamon, A.: Generalized residential building typology for urban climate change mitigation and adaptation strategies: the case of Hungary. Energy Build. **62**, 475–485 (2013)
11. Kragh, J., Wittchen, K.B.: Development of two danish building typologies for residential buildings. Energy Build. **68**(Part A), 79–86 (2013)
12. Loga, T., Diefenbach, N., Born, R.: Deutsche Gebäudetypologie: Beispielhafte Maßnahmen zur Verbesserung der Energieeffizienz von typischen Wohngebäuden (2011)
13. Ma, L., Srinivasan, S.: Synthetic population generation with multilevel controls: a fitness-based synthesis approach and validations. Comput. Aided Civ. Infrastruct. Eng. **30**(2), 135–150 (2015)

14. Esteban Muñoz Hidalgo, M.: A microsimulation approach to generate occupancy rates of small urban areas. In: 2nd Asia Conference on International Building Performance Simulation Association, IBPSA Japan, Nagoya University, Japan (2014)
15. Esteban Muñoz Hidalgo, M.: heat: R package to estimate heat demand of residential buildings (2015). github.com/emunozh/heat
16. Esteban Muñoz Hidalgo, M.: Construction of building typologies from a regional material catalog: assessment of urban heat demand and the environmental impact of retrofit policies. Manag. Environ. Qual. Int. J. (2016, in Press)
17. Esteban Muñoz Hidalgo, M., Dochev, I., Seller, H., Peters, I.: Constructing a synthetic city for estimating spatially disaggregated heat demand. Int. J. Microsimul. (2016, in Press)
18. Esteban Muñoz Hidalgo, M., Tanton, R., Vidattama, Y.: A comparison of the GREGWT and IPF methods for the re-weighting of surveys. In: 5th World Congress of the International Microsimulation Association (IMA) (2015)
19. Esteban Muñoz Hidalgo, M., Vidyattama, Y., Tanton, R.: GREGWT: an implementation of the GREGWT algorithm in R (2015). github.com/emunozh/gregwt
20. Esteban Muñoz Hidalgo, M., Vidyattama, Y., Tanton, R.: The influence of an ageing population and an efficient building stock on heat consumption patterns. In: 14th International Conference of the International Building Performance Simulation Association (IBPSA) (2015)
21. O'Donoghue, C., Morrissey, K., Lennon, J.: Spatial microsimulation modelling: a review of applications and methodological choices. Int. J. Microsimul. 7(1), 26–75 (2014)
22. Orcutt, G.H.: A new type of socio-economic system. Rev. Econ. Stat. 39(2), 116–123 (1957)
23. Pritchard, D.R., Miller, E.J.: Advances in population synthesis: fitting many attributes per agent and fitting to household and person margins simultaneously. Transportation 39(3), 685–704 (2012)
24. Rahman, A., Harding, A., Tanton, R., Shuangzhe, L.: Methodological issues in spatial microsimulation modelling for small area estimation. Int. J. Microsimul. 3(2), 3–22 (2010)
25. Singh, A., Mohl, C.: Understanding calibration estimators in survey sampling. Surv. Methodol. 22, 107–115 (1996)
26. Singh, M.K., Mahapatra, S., Teller, J.: An analysis on energy efficiency initiatives in the building stock of Liege, Belgium. Energy Policy 62, 729–741 (2013)
27. Statistische Ämter des Bundes und der Länder. Forschungsdatenzentren der statistischen Ämter des bundes und der länder – Mikrozensus (EVAS 12211) – 2010 Scientific-Use-File (2010)
28. Statistische Ämter des Bundes und der Länder. Statistisches bundesamt – Zensus 2011 – Zensusdatenbank (2011)
29. Tanton, R.: SPATIALMSM: the Australian spatial microsimulation model. In: The 1st General Conference of the International Microsimulation Association (2007)
30. Tanton, R., Williamson, P., Harding, A.: Comparing two methods of reweighting a survey file to small area data: generalised regression and combinatorial optimisation. Int. J. Microsimul. 7(1), 76–99 (2014)
31. Tanton, R.: A review of spatial microsimulation methods. Int. J. Microsimul. 7(1), 4–25 (2014)
32. Tanton, R., Vidyattama, Y., Nepal, B., McNamara, J.: Small area estimation using a reweighting algorithm. J. Roy. Stat. Soc. Ser. A (Stat. Soc.) 174(4), 931–951 (2011)

How Smart is the Smart City? Assessing the Impact of ICT on Cities

Michal Gath-Morad(✉), Davide Schaumann, Einat Zinger, Pnina O. Plaut, and Yehuda E. Kalay

Technion, Israel Institute of Technology, 32000 Haifa, Israel
{michalm,deiv,einatm,arpnina,kalay}@campus.technion.ac.il

Abstract. The notion of "smart cities" has gained much popularity over the past few years, fueled by emerging needs and opportunities, and accompanied by considerable political and commercial hype. But in fact, throughout their long history cities have always strived to become "smarter", in order to mitigate existential challenges such as defending their citizens, providing them with water, disposing of waste, facilitating access, and more. They did so by making use of available (often new) technologies, such as new fortification methods, water supply, sewers, and transportation systems. The reciprocal relationship between cities and technology has, in turn, shaped urban form, function and use patterns. Cities, in the twenty-first century, are confronted by unprecedented social, economic and environmental challenges. In response, they are attempting to enlist Information and Communication Technologies (ICT) —the current "new" technology —as one of the leading strategies to mitigate urban problems, increase efficiency, reduce costs and enhance the quality of city life. It is the use of this particular technology which is viewed as making cities "smart." History teaches us that every such new technology, while advantageous in some ways, also has unforeseen side- and after-effects. Due to the highly ubiquitous and distributed nature of ICT, it affects individuals directly and in highly personalized ways in terms of spatial use patterns, consumption habits, and social interactions. The large number of variables and interactions affected by ICT makes it difficult to predict its explicit and implicit effects on the spatial and social use patterns of people in cities. What will be the effects, side- and after-effects of integrating ICT in cities, as it becomes ubiquitous and more accessible to both city governments and citizens? How will it transform people's interactions and behavioral patterns? How will it affect the form, function and —especially —the use of cities? In short —what will be ICT's impact on cities, and how can we assess it? Current tools used by city planners fail to account for these new types of interactions and transformative behavioral patterns. New tools, capable of forecasting dynamically and at high resolution the behavior of many individual people in a city, are needed. This paper aims to provide a framework to assess the impact of ICT on the form and function of cities, through its effect on people's spatial behavior patterns.

Keywords: Smart cities · Architectural design · Urban design · Human behavior simulation · Agent based simulation · Form · Function · Use

© Springer International Publishing AG 2017
M.-R. Namazi-Rad et al. (Eds.): ABMUS 2016, LNAI 10051, pp. 189–207, 2017.
DOI: 10.1007/978-3-319-51957-9_11

1   The Effects of Technology on Urban *Form*, *Function* and *Use*

Urban form is a derivative of technological, social, economic, and other factors, intended to serve a multitude of needs and constituencies [30], while coping with various existential challenges. The range of technologies that have shaped urban form is large and diverse, ranging from defense systems (fortifications), urban water supply, sewage and waste disposal, to transportation and power systems. We argue that such technological developments have always been intended to make cities "smarter", in the sense of improving their functioning and the services cities provide to their citizens. This quest for "smartness" shaped cities time after time, directly and indirectly, as the integration of technologies in cities caused a chain reaction of side-and after-effects, many of which were not foreseen in advance [33].

A case in point have been the coincidental inventions of the safety elevator by Elisha G. Otis (1853), Henry Bessemer's mass produced steel (1855), and Werner von Siemens' (1880) electric elevator [20]. While initially intended to afford easy vertical transport between floors of a building, they eventually facilitated the design and construction of skyscrapers, and ushered the rise of modern cities [20]. Cities like New York, which up to that time consisted mostly of four or five story buildings and expanded horizontally, started to grow vertically in what was called "the tall building revolution." These new technologies fostered new growth patterns and had far-reaching implications on cities skyline (*form*), zoning regulations (*function*), economy, culture and everyday life of cities (*use*) [20].

Technologies, however, differ from one another, and so do their impacts on the form, function, and use of cities. A major characteristic that differentiates technologies is their degree of centrality/distribution. The rigid and costly nature of centralized technologies such as a railway station or a street car line, require planners to predict —with high degree of certainty —their future urban implications in terms of infrastructure, schedules, safety regulations and human-technology interfaces. In contrast, the effects of more distributed technologies, such as the automobile, which is owned and operated by individuals, are far more difficult to predict: people may use their cars in ways not foreseen by planners, resulting in congestion, accidents and air pollution [41].

Contemporary Information and Communication Technologies (ICT), increasingly integrated in everyday objects and urban spaces, are arguably the most distributed technologies ever: they are ubiquitous and affect each citizen directly and personally [13, 16, 18, 26, 46, 47]. As such, the ability to predict ICT's impact on citizen's spatial use patterns, and as a result the changes in urban form and function, is a difficult task. For example, using a Global Positioning navigation System (GPS), an automobile driver may take routes considered by city planners to be residential, rather than throughways, thereby disturbing well-planned quiet neighborhoods [45]. Hence, despite the inherent difficulty, the ability to predict how technology impacts people's behavior is prerequisite to designing livable cities that meet their citizens' needs.

The difficulty of predicting human behavior in built environments is well known in both architecture and urban design. Environmental psychologists like Lynch, Canter, Barker and others have researched it for the past 50 years [3,9,29]. Scientific methods, such as Space Syntax [24], have been developed to cope with it, and professional organizations, such as EDRA (Environmental Design Research Association), have been established to provide forums for discussing it. Still, the large number of variables which characterize human behavior, coupled with the unique and complex nature of cities themselves, makes prediction of human behavior in built environments a central challenge in the process of designing buildings and cities [5,26].

The integration of ICT in cities further amplifies the complexity of this task, because it affects each one of the three main characteristics of cities: their form, their function, and their use (Fig. 1). For example, networking the city with surveillance cameras that feed continues data to a traffic and emergency services command center (Fig. 2), can provide city authorities with up-to-date information on various conditions in the city (traffic, fire, crime, etc.), which allows them to intervene appropriately when necessary and thus effect the function and use of the city. This would be considered a "centralized" intervention, when the system as a whole, its function and use are commissioned, intended for, and used by the city government.

In contrast, ICT is a distributed technology. It is owned by individuals and puts the technology literally in their pockets, and affects their behavior directly and in highly personalized ways [13,18]. ICT's impacts on urban form, function, or use cannot, therefore, be centrally planned. Rather, they emerge bottom-up, through the use of ICT's technology by the citizens themselves [16,46,47]. The ubiquitous presence of smart-phones, with their data-collecting, processing, and communication abilities, puts up-to-date urban information at the individual citizens' fingertips, who make their own decisions on how to act on this data, based on their own goals and abilities. Their decisions may coincide with planners' and city mangers' objectives, conflict with them, or be totally un-related to them.

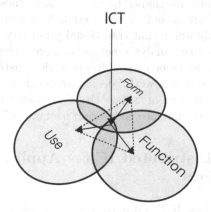

Fig. 1. Contemporary information and Communication technologies effect the *form*, *function* and *use* of cities.

For instance, citizen's accessibility to air pollution data and other types of environmental information makes citizens more environmentally aware of health hazards. In turn, they may act upon that knowledge by avoiding highly polluted areas. Such individualized use patterns could conflict with planned occupancy of places as intended by city planners.

Researchers like, Canter, Hillier, Lynch and Whyte showed how urban form affects —even directs —people's behavior in urban settings by influencing their spatial cognition abilities [9, 24, 29, 50]. ICT, on the other hand, has the unique ability to expand the range and quality of people's spatial cognition, by availing to them information not directly perceived by their senses, such as the level of air pollution and the congestion of roads not directly visible to them. Such expanded spatial awareness can inform and impact individuals' decision making processes in ways that planners have not accounted for. Augmenting the received spatial and environmental data by means of "smart" algorithms, which process the data before it is presented to the end users, enables individuals to make more informed decisions about their future actions. GPS systems, for example, allow drivers to choose less congested routes, even if the congestion is not visible from their current location on the road. Additional processing of the data allows drivers to avoid toll roads, or choose shortest time routes over shortest distance routes.

How should planners cope with such scenarios, over which they have little or no control? Will they make different design decisions? At the moment, in the absence of adequate prediction and evaluation tools, planners mostly rely on their own experience, past case studies, norms and regulations or statistical information, all of which fail to account for this new variable (ICT) which transforms the way people behave in cities.

The aim of this paper is not to provide answers to this question. Rather, its aim is to raise awareness to this new phenomena, and argue for tools that can help planners better understand the effects of ICT —or more broadly, the new "smart" environments —on people's decision making processes which re-shape their use patterns in cities. We claim that by availing to city planners tools that will help them foresee behavior patterns shaped by placing "smartness" in the hands of citizens, they will be able to make better informed decisions concerning the form and the function of cities. We argue that traditional predictive tools, such as norms, regulations, POE and spatial analysis methods among others, fail to account for the effect of this new phenomenon on people's behavior. Instead, we propose to use Agent Based Simulations as a powerful design and evaluation tool. To customize this approach to the evaluation of "smart cities" we develop a simulation model, and elucidate its ability to simulate pedestrian navigation in cities.

2   Centric and Distributed ICT - Applications and Implications

The wide discourse on how ICT can make cities "smart", "wired", "intelligent", or "networked", involves two main paradigms: a "centric" one, and more recently —a "distributed" one [4, 5, 10, 13, 14, 18, 19, 46, 47]. The first paradigm is intended

Fig. 2. The smart-city operations center of Rio De Janeiro: a "centric" model command and control center. IBM website (press release).

to optimize a building's or city's function through a centralized command center (Fig. 2), where information from various sources is received, processed, and coordinated. Its physical manifestation is typically a large command center that controls fixed assets such as surveillance cameras and traffic lights, as well as mobile assets like police, fire and medical units, which can be directed to respond in real time to ongoing events. The data processed is varied, but consists mostly of fixed sensing entities such as cameras. Relying on the sensed data, a team of experts analyzes the city's performance remotely, and acts upon such analysis, for instance by coordinating first responders' arrival to crime or disaster scenes. Such centralized control has proven highly reliable and effective for coordinating systems involving large numbers of assets with similar and relatively simple goals. It is, therefore, implemented in military, industry and corporate settings where collective actions rely on relatively simple behavioral rules [2].

Yet, in the context of urban settings, such centralized models are often criticized for their reliance on limited sensor data both in terms of quality and type; their simplistic hierarchical structure, which is not suitable for dealing with complex, heterogenic systems such as cities; their inability to leverage vast communication and distributed decision making abilities now possible through ubiquitous wireless sensor networks supporting mobile devices owned by citizens; their emphasis on global system optimization at the expense of its individual parts; and at times for invasive monitoring of citizens' activities, resulting in a "big brother" syndrome [46, 47].

The second paradigm, which could be regarded as a natural evolution of the use of ICT, relies on a distributed model where "smartness" is literally in the hands (or pockets) of the citizens: in lieu of a centralized command authority, according to this paradigm, data flows in networked form from one individual to another, each one of whom becomes a data-collector, processor, and actor on its own [13, 18, 46, 47]. This type of "smartness" collects data from tens of thousands of sources in real time, and can generate multiple coordinated or un-coordinated actions. It confronts planners with a far less predictable and far more complex challenge in terms of predicting citizens spatial use patterns. In this case, which has become a reality for most cities around the globe, "smartness" emerges via the personal smart-phone of connected citizens. It provides citizens with real time access to the city, and makes them aware at once of changes in the city's physical or virtual spaces. A multitude of application at citizens' disposal help them process information in real time and empowers them with new decision-making capabilities, which enable them to act according to their individual goals as they gain what we term "artificial spatial intelligence."

The sources of the information received by the citizens vary: at times information comes from the municipality, and can be regarded as "authoritative." At other times it may come from other citizens, who have sensed it directly and processed and distributed it via the network [13]. In such cases, the authority of the information may be questionable: it may be more accurate than the centrally provided information, due to time lag and limited sensing resources, or it may be erroneous, deliberately or not. In the context of this paper the source of information so provided is secondary to the effects such information has on citizens' behavior. Thus, the following examples aim to highlight a shift in behavioral patterns as a result of ICT used by citizens, and their wider implications at the city scale.

The term app (abbreviation of "application"), is defined by Cambridge dictionary as "a computer program or piece of software designed for a particular purpose that one can download onto a mobile phone or other mobile device." The number and variety of "apps" at citizens' disposal is constantly growing, as do the types of urban problems they aim to solve [13,16,18,47].

Everyday activities, such as finding a child-friendly park or restaurant in a city, are being optimized by a network of parents sharing experiences and rating the child friendliness of urban places ("MomMaps") [13]. Other apps, such as "BrezzoMeter" (Fig. 3), aim to mitigate health related challenges faced by urban dwellers. By visualizing air pollution levels in cities followed by a recommendation whether or not to go outside and for how long, citizens change their conceptions about their cities or neighborhoods and in turn avoid specific places in order to protect their health.

The first example is typical of "social" awareness apps, whereas the second is typical of "environmental" awareness apps. A third typology, often referred to as "navigational" or "route planning" apps, bypasses awareness altogether, and explicitly and directly affects individual's spatial decision making. Such apps rely on LBS (Location Based Services) supported by smartphones' built in GPS (Global Positioning Systems), augmented with high resolution, real time spatial, social and environmental information. Citizens often use such apps to search for and plan available and/or personalized routes from an origin to a destination. These apps are available for a multitude of travel modes, and their effects should therefore be studied separately [13].

Fig. 3. On the left: "BrezzoMeter" app, provides citizens with air quality information and recommendations. "BreezoMeter" website.

Fig. 4. On the right: The use of route optimization app Waze® conflicts with neighborhood design objective, Sherman Oaks, California. Los Angeles Times web addition [45].

A good example for such app is Waze®, a route planning app that helps drivers navigate through the least congested route. The app uses crowdsourced information from other drivers to assess real time congestion loads, and help drivers optimize their travel routes, saving time, energy and fuel. However, using the app also has side-effects: as can be seen in a recent article from Los Angeles Times (Fig. 4). The use of Waze by drivers in the Sherman Oakes neighborhood, in California, caused an influx of vehicles traveling through residential streets, not designed for through traffic, to avoid congestion in main roads [45]. In this case, ICT causes a conflict between the planners' functional objectives, manifested in the form of designing a residential neighborhood, and the citizens' use pattern of the city, acting on their own goals of avoiding congestion.

The effects of these amplified decision-making abilities directly affect citizens use patterns, often in ways that were not predicted by city planners. In fact, the broad implications of citizens being made "smarter" via ICT do not necessarily make the entire city "smart". On the contrary, the fact that citizens change their actions to optimize their own goals may contradict planning norms used in determining urban form and function, which are meant to serve collective goals.

We believe that the ability of citizens to make informed spatial decisions augmented by ICT, due to the fast pace of proliferation of smart devices and applications, is the essence of "smartness" of "smart cities". We argue that such abilities must be taken into account as planners make their design decisions about the form and function of a city. The aim of this paper is not to predict how ICT-based empowerment of citizens' decision making abilities will affect city planning —that topic deserves to be researched separately. Rather, in this paper we argue that the arsenal of tools used by city planners to help them make informed decisions must include tools that can account for the independent, yet coordinated, decisions made by ICT-empowered citizens. We claim that such tools will enhance planners' ability to integrate the numerous variables and interactions in a manner that will show the effects, side- and after-effects of spatial decisions made by both planners and citizens. In essence, we argue that this means computationally augmenting the use component of the Form-Function-Use triad, by means of agent-based simulations that can help predict human behavior in complex environments, including ones such as "smart" cities.

3   Predicting *Use* Patterns in Built Environments

Cities are often regarded as complex systems made of numerous and diverse elements that interact with each other in non-linear ways [36]. Accordingly, the emergence of meaningful use patterns in cities is often the product of a collection of actions and interactions between people and their environment. The ability to predict the impact of a physical setting (Form and Function) on people's behavior (Use), manifested in their actions and interactions, has fascinated many researchers in fields such as psychology, sociology, ergonomics, philosophy, and cognitive science, among others [1,22,28,32,34,48]. It is also a central task in urban and architectural design process [5,12,26,27].

Predicting human behavior in built environments is considered highly complex. A building's or a city's impact on its occupants' behavior is a composite of many factors: the functionality of the spaces it is comprised of, the spatial relationships among them, how well it supports the living and working habits of its users, the social and cultural comfort it affords them, and many more. Following, determining a city's impact on its citizens involves not only the form of the city itself, but also its intended function, and the manner in which it will be used by its citizens. It is further complicated by the dynamic nature of use patterns: the same people are likely to use the same building and city differently, at different times.

Current methods used by planners to evaluate how people behave and interact with built environments, are varied. The most basic and immediate one is Post Occupancy Evaluation (POE), a method that enables planners to interrogate the performance of built environments that have been built and occupied [26]. The results of such interrogations form precedents which findings can be referred to and used in other, similar design situations, often encoded in the form of norms and regulations.

However, the uniqueness of design problems and their solutions makes inference from past experiences inherently unreliable, because every design situation is different from every other one, in terms of site conditions, demographic/cultural conditions, and more. A different method, involving direct-experience behavior tests, enables planners to observe the responses of actual intended users to some proposed design solutions, in physical or virtual settings. This method is, of course, expensive both in terms of cost and expertise, and is therefore difficult to implement, especially in large scale projects such as cities which involve large and often heterogeneous populations [26].

In contrast to these largely qualitative methods, quantitative methods like Space Syntax have been developed. Such methods use spatial analysis to asses and explain the impact of the built environment's form on people's perceptual and cognitive abilities [24]. They can be used to test the proposed design solution against certain functionalities, such as way-finding capabilities and visual connectivity. Despite their ability to explain some patterns of human behavior, such approaches lack both the functional definition of space (not only how it looks, but also what can be done in it) and an explicit representation of users' motivations and individual behaviors [35]. The absence of both function and users makes it difficult to understand why people behave as they do, and in the context of this paper such methods exclude the possibility of testing how ICT-augmented spatial decision making will affect city use, let alone urban form and function.

A more accurate way to predict human behavior involves simulation —a technique that allows abstracting a complex real system into a relatively simple model, and conducting experiments on it to test the behavior of the system under predefined circumstances [26,38,43]. This is particularly useful for architectural and planning problems, considered "wicked" problems [37], where a solution that will meet the stated needs depends on the formulation of those needs themselves at the same time as developing solutions that meet them. That is why design problems do not have "optimal" solutions, only "satisficing" ones [43]. Trade-offs need to be made to find a satisficing solution, due to the many and often-conflicting needs that must be met. In the context of "smart cities," planners equipped with such simulation tools could be made aware of future conflicts emerging between new, ICT-empowered use patterns, and existing or proposed urban form and function.

Simulating human behavior, however, is not a simple task, due to the dynamic, stochastic and context dependent nature of human behavior. Different models have been proposed to simulate human behavior at different levels of abstraction and with different degrees of complexity [11,15,17,26,42,44]. The depth and breadth of human behavior simulation research and methods is far too large to be included in the scope of this paper. However, it is important to note that different simulation paradigms model human behavior differently, as they rely on different levels of abstraction. Methods range from process —or system-based simulations, to discrete-event simulations, and agent-based simulations [21]. Among existing simulation methods, Agent-Based Models (ABM) have been proved useful in testing people-environment interactions. In particular, ABM allows representing a system's behavior as an emergent phenomenon that originates from situated interactions between goal-oriented agents with their physical surroundings [6,7].

In ABM, autonomous agents dynamically inhabit spatial environments, and sense, plan and act autonomously within these environments to achieve their specific goals [25,31,52]. Agents' behavior is triggered by local spatial condition, and the behavior of other agents in the same environment. Each agent pursues its individual goal (e.g., exit the building, in case of a fire egress simulation), while reacting to the environment it perceives (e.g., fire, smoke), as well as to the actions and behaviors of other agents (e.g., crowding). Complex behaviors emerge from the unfolding of low-level behaviors and interactions among agents [6,7,17].

We argue that the use of ABM to asses the effect of ICT on cities is a worthwhile research direction that can help planners make better informed design decisions. The model that underlies human agents' behaviors and drives agents' actions and interactions could be augmented to include information feeds from a "smart" environment, resulting in behavioral patterns that reflect current shifts in spatial decision making driven by ICT. Furthermore, the ability to simulate the individual actions of many diverse agents, operating in a smart environment, and measure the resulting system behavior and outcomes over time, could be especially useful to evaluate the effects of ICT across spatial and time scales.

4   A *Form*, *Function* and *Use* Model to Simulate Smart Cities

To develop a time-based simulation of a "smart" (ICT integrated) city in use, three separate inputs —a city's form, function and use(r), are streamed into a simulation engine, responsible of converging and "activating" information derived from each database (Fig. 5) [39].

Form describes the physical properties of an environment, including its size, shape, position in space, and the materials it is made of. It can answer such questions as "what does it look like?", "What is it made of?"

Function indicates the semantic properties of an entity. It adds meaning to the entity, in relation to a specific context. It can answer such questions as "What does it mean?", "What do we call it?", "What can we do with it or in it?"

Use is a property that adds time-based, socio-cultural information to the represented object. It answers such questions as "Who uses it?", "How is it used?"

The Form and Function properties are indexed in spatial zones which often represent parcels or activity areas, assigned to a plan of a building or a city by

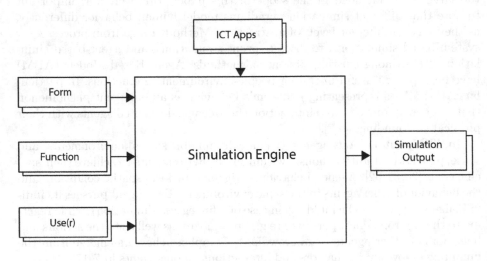

Fig. 5. Simulation system architecture

Table 1. *Form* and *Function* model database

Static attributes			Dynamic attributes				
Name	Type	Function	Current use	Occupancy	Objects	Noise	Density
SW_1	*Side walk*	*Passage*	*Cycling*	*Agents list*	*Object list*	*value*	*value*

architects or planners. Information stored in zones is either static or dynamic. The function, or land use data is the very basic property of each zone (e.g. sidewalk, crossing, main road, public building, housing, etc.). Function properties as well as materiality (e.g. paved/not paved) are considered static properties which are encoded in zones prior to the simulation activation (e.g. size, materials). Dynamic properties, such as noise, crowdedness and location of obstacles, are calculated and stored in spatial zones during the simulation itself (Table 1, Fig. 6).

To support and integrate the proposed model in the design process, form properties are modeled in 3D modeling software such as CAAD or BIM [26], generating a three dimensional representation of a city or a building, with which agents interact during the simulation (Fig. 6).

Unlike the form and function databases which relate to the environment, the use database includes the description of potential use(rs). This database is indexed into human-like agents and similarly to the form and function databases, it consists of both static and dynamic properties. Static properties include type, age, gender and experience. Dynamic properties affected by the environment and the activities agents perform include tiredness, stress, exposure to stimuli

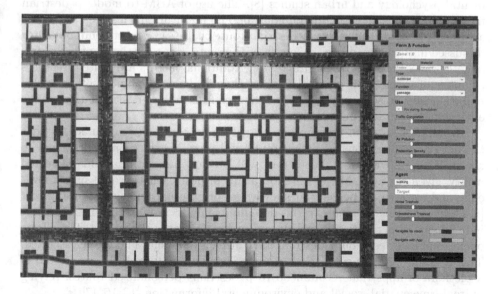

Fig. 6. A model of the selected case study area. The model was generated using procedural modeling in ESRI CityEngine®.

(e.g. noise, crowd, scenery). Also encoded are group affiliations and social connections, perceptual abilities, and knowledge about the surrounding world. Each human agent has an individual threshold of tolerance for environmental and social parameters —essential to calculate agent's behavioral choices.

To be able to evaluate the effects of ICT on urban form, function and use patterns, a fourth database —ICT based apps —is also streamed into the simulation engine. These apps, very much like in the real world, interact with users once the simulation starts. The rules of interaction are encoded in each app-like entity. Each app aims to optimize a certain type of user activity. To do so, it can "pull" information from all three databases (form, function and use).

The simulation engine combines all four inputs and activates the model. It updates, at specific time frames, and according to preset rules, the status of the world and all the entities in it. The simulation output takes the form of visual and quantitative representation of human movement patterns, hot spots and social interactions. In The next section we shell demonstrate the model's ability to simulate pedestrian navigation, in cities with and without ICT support.

5   Case Study - The Effects of ICT on Pedestrians *Use* Patterns

To illustrate the capabilities of the proposed model, we simulate a fundamental type of human behavior, essential to the understanding and design of cities: pedestrian route choice [6,8,26,50,51]. This topic has been studied extensively in a range of disciplines from mathematics to physics, transportation, environmental psychology and urban studies [8]. The use of ABM to model pedestrian navigation is considered highly popular [6], and literature in this area highlights a variety of factors that affect pedestrian route choice. The most common factor discussed in the literature is the length of the route, as pedestrians appear to frequently choose the shortest route, [8,40]. Additional factors are route directness (number of turns) [23], pleasantness, habit, crowdedness, number of crossings, pollution and noise levels, safety and shelter from weather, stimulation of the environment and trip purpose [8].

In addition, a main assumption in pedestrian route choice studies, is that the act of walking along a certain route will provide utility or incur a cost to the walking individual. A pedestrian will predict and optimize this expected utility, given the available information at his disposal, whether it is past knowledge and experience, perceptual knowledge, or external knowledge of any sort [8,23,49]. Existing literature in this domain mainly focuses on the effect of internal and spatial perception knowledge on pedestrian route choice [51]. The effects of external knowledge on pedestrian navigation are therefore under-investigated. This is despite, and in conflict with, the growing ubiquity of ICT, manifested in a plethora of apps that recommend to pedestrians personalized routes, relying on real-time spatial, social and environmental information [13,16,47].

The simulation aims to highlight potential differences in pedestrian navigation under two distinct settings. The first setting is navigation in an unaided manner [51], where agents rely on local perception to plan and follow a walking route that best matches their preferences, from origin A to destination B (Table 2). The second setting is a "smart" environment, where agents are required to perform the same task and have the same preferences, but this time an "app"-like entity provides agents with external knowledge in the form of spatial awareness (beyond their immediate perception) about specific spatial attributes (in our case, noise levels and crowdedness). In both settings, agents have no prior knowledge of the navigational environment.

The simulation utilizes an abstract representation of a city, modeled using procedural rules in ESRI CityEngine®. The area of the city chosen for the purposes of this demonstration has a very clear hierarchy of main, secondary and tertiary streets, as well as a distinction between public and private functions, evident in the buildings typology. Public building along main streets have almost no side setback, whereas residential buildings have a distinct side and back setbacks to afford semi private outdoor spaces (Fig. 6).

Each human-like agent is programmed with individual route preferences, in this case noise and crowdedness thresholds (Table 2). Both noise and crowdedness levels are indexed in spatial zones overlaying the model. High or low levels of each, or both of these factors, could act to either attract or repulse pedestrians from traversing specific zones, depending on their individual thresholds. For instance, an agent with a low noise threshold (high sensitivity) will avoid zones that have high noise values. In our case, both agents in the smart and unaided settings have low thresholds for noise and crowdedness (with some random variations between them), meaning that they prefer the least noisy and least crowded routes. In this sense, agents at both settings plan and follow the least-cost path from origin A to destination B. The major difference is that whereas in the unaided setting, agents plan in a tactical manner, constrained by their limited vision —agents in the smart setting are supplied with the route data for the least-cost path that matches their preferences (searched on the entire search space, regardless of agent's vision).

In order to find the least-cost path, four steps at each time-frame are executed:

1. Noise and crowdedness levels are mapped (Fig. 7). In our case both maps have an identical range of values (1–5), where five (darkest areas) signifies high levels of either noise or crowdedness, and one stands for low levels (lightest areas). Areas that are impossible or illegal to cross receive a "null value" —basically acting as obstacles.

Table 2. Agent's description in use database

Static attributes						Dynamic attributes		
Name	Age	Gender	Stimuli thresholds (1=low, 5=high)			Stimuli exposure		
			Noise	Crowd	Distance	Noise	Crowd	Distance
Ped_1	25	Male	value	value	value	value	value	value

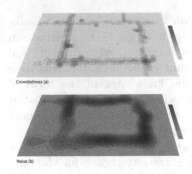
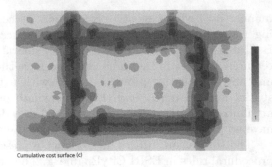

Fig. 7. A spatial weighted overlay between a noise mapping (a) and crowdedness mapping (b) results in a cumulative cost surface (c) where the darker the zone is the more costly it is to traverse and vice verse.

2. Each map is assigned weights that represent agents' preferences. For instance, an agent with higher noise sensitivity will have a higher weight for noise and a lower weight for crowdedness. In our case most agents have an equal weight for both. It is important to note that such multi criteria weighting could account for many more than the two factors demonstrated in this case. They could account for air pollution, slope, ground cover, safety, obstacles friends' location, etc.

3. Upon assigning weights, a spatial overlay calculation is made to combine the two maps into a single "cumulative cost surface" which reflects the cost of traversing each zone at each time frame (Fig. 7). This cumulative cost surface is then used to find the least-cost path for a specific agent. When there are several alternative paths, the shortest one is chosen. Whereas in the smart setting the app identifies the least cost path as the minimal continuous series of zones from an origin to a destination, in the unaided setting agents vision acts as a mask that lets them choose only the next best step, without the ability to plan the entire path to the destination. In this case, the horizon effect (being unable to tell what is behind a turn, a building or a wall) plays an important factor in agent's route selection.

Simulation results show that agents who navigate in the un-aided case traversed main streets to get to the assigned destination (Fig. 8). The logical explanation to this is that since they relied on limited vision and no prior knowledge, they were incapable of assessing the cost of zones that were not visually accessible to them. In this sense, the street visual connectivity plays an important role in their route choice. In our model, the street network was less connected to the internal secondary and tertiary streets (characterized by low noise and crowdedness levels). In the absence of information on significantly lower-cost alternatives, agents remained on the main streets which were more continuous and visually connected.

In the aided setting, where pedestrians' decision making processes were augmented with fore-knowledge about the noise and crowdedness level at each

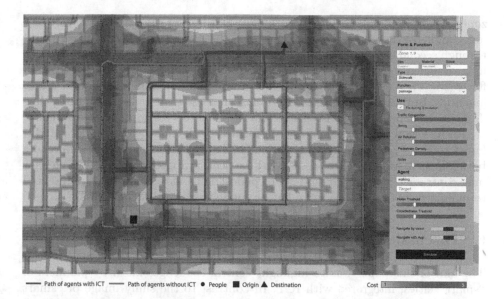

Path of agents with ICT ——— Path of agents without ICT ● People ■ Origin ▲ Destination   Cost

Fig. 8. Simulation results: traversed paths by two types of agents (with and without ICT abilities)

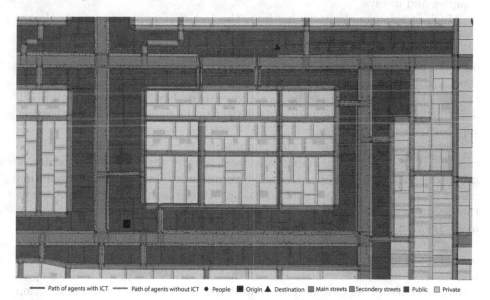

Path of agents with ICT ——— Path of agents without ICT ● People ■ Origin ▲ Destination ■ Main streets ■ Secondary streets ■ Public □ Private

Fig. 9. Analysis of simulation results: The shift in use patterns conflicts with expected form and function. Agents without ICT abilities traversed main streets (in orange) vs. agents who navigated with ICT abilities traversed less noisy and crowded streets, crossing through a residential neighborhood (in yellow). (Color figure online)

zone, agents were able to plan accordingly and thus traversed significantly less noisy and crowded routes (Fig. 8). However, the majority of their routes crossed through secondary and tertiary streets, which consist of mainly residential buildings, designed to serve local residents rather than accommodate large pedestrian flows (Fig. 9). As such, they lack adequate sidewalks, crossings, and other street amenities. In this case, although individuals increase their walking comfort, they do so at the expense of other citizens who reside in this residential neighborhood.

Results show how the same task, performed by the same agents under two different settings, one with and one without ICT, resulted in significant differences between their walking patterns. As can be seen in Fig. 9, the shift in behavior may contradict planners' intentions of pedestrian's movement —to be directed to main streets designed to serve higher capacities of pedestrian flows.

6   Discussion

The aim of this paper was to highlight central challenges faced by planners of "smart" cities, integrated with ICT. In contrast to the shiny image of "smart cities" promoted by large ICT firms, where cities are made smart from "above," we argue that the generation of smart, livable and sustainable cities is far more complex and messy.

Much of this complexity stems from the fact that unlike past technologies used by cities as part of a strategic plan, carefully devised by planners and experts, today's most powerful technology —ICT —is used and owned by everyone: planners and citizens alike. In such reality, planners' strategic actions in the short and long term may conflict with citizens' spatial use patterns, driven by the use of ICT. The ability to predict and evaluate how the application of ICT affect people's use patterns in cities is critical to the design of livable cities that support their citizens' needs.

The lack of evaluation tools that can address this problem, coupled with the complexity of cities and planning processes, situates this task at the center of urban design practice and research. The computational agent-based simulation model outlined in this paper aims to strengthen the human-centric approach to the design of smart cities and thus empower planners with innovative tools to assist them in their design process.

As demonstrated, the ability to simulate individual agents' behavior and how it is affected by enhanced spatial awareness facilitated by ICT, could result in new understanding of how a city is used, making visible less predictable use patterns and contributing to a more accountable design of urban form and function by planners.

To conclude, the question of how "Smart" a city is, should be evaluated in a complex, multi-criteria manner against the pre-set goals of different stakeholders. Using such a simulation engine, design stakeholders, such as architects, city planners and administrators, can test the impact of proposed ICT solutions, which affect the behavior of individual citizens, on the overall performance of the city. Instead of extrapolating from past experience or outdated norms and regulations, planners will have at their disposal data provided by the simulation (such as travel time, distance, circulation paths, activity duration, trends, and space utilization), and the ability to observe the simulation itself while looking for expected and unexpected patterns of behavior to support their design decisions, and ultimately find a satisficing match between the planned *form*, *function* and *use* of cities.

Acknowledgments. This research is supported by a European Research Council grant (FP-7 ADG 340753).

References

1. Alexander, C.: The Timeless Way of Building. Oxford University Press, New York (1979)
2. Bar-yam, Y.: Complexity Rising: From Human Beings to Human Civilization, A Complexity Profile 1. In: Encyclopedia of Life Support Systems, pp. 1–33, 01 December 1997
3. Barker, R.G.: Habitats, Environments, and Human Behavior. Jossey-Bass Incorporated Pub., San Francisco (1978)
4. Batten, D.F.: Network cities: creative urban agglomerations for the 21st century. Urban Stud. **32**(2), 313–327 (1995)
5. Batty, M.: Big data, smart cities and city planning. Dialogues Hum. Geogr. **3**(3), 274–279 (2013)
6. Batty, M.: Agent-based pedestrian modelling. In: Advanced Spatial Analysis, pp. 81–106 (2003)
7. Bonabeau, E.: Agent-based modeling: methods and techniques for simulating human systems. Proc. Nat. Acad. Sci. **99**(suppl. 3), 7280–7287 (2002)
8. Bovy, E.S.: Route choice: wayfinding in transport networks. Ann. Assoc. Am. Geogr. **82**(2), 320–342 (1990)
9. Canter, D.: The Psychology of Place (1977)
10. Castells, M.: The Rise of the Network Society, vol. I. Blackwell Publishing, Massachusetts (2010)
11. Chu, M.L., Pan, X., Law, K.H.: Incorporating social behaviours in egress simulation. J. Comput. Civ. Eng. **650**, 544–551 (2011)
12. Cranz, G.: Ethnography for Designers. Routledge, London (2016)
13. Desouza, K.C., Bhagwatwar, A.: Citizen apps to solve complex urban problems. J. Urban Technol. **19**(3), 1–30 (2012). 0732, May 2015
14. Dirks, S., Gurdgiev, C., Keeling, M. Smarter cities for smarter growth. IBM Global Business Services, 24 (2010)
15. Ekholm, A.: Activity objects in CAD-programs for building design - A prototype program implementation. In: de Vries, B., van Leeuwen, J., Achten, H. (eds.) Proceedings of the Computer Aided Architectural Design Futures 2001, pp. 61–74. Springer, Netherlands (2001)
16. Evans-cowley, J.: Planning in the real-time city: the future of mobile technology. J. Plan. Lit. **25**(2), 136–149 (2015)
17. Goldstone, R.L., Janssen, M.A.: Computational models of collective behavior. Trends Cogn. Sci. **9**(9), 424–430 (2005)
18. Goodchild, M.F.: Citizens as sensors: the world of volunteered geography. Geo-Journal **69**, 211–221 (2007)

19. Goodspeed, R.: Smart cities: moving beyond urban cybernetics to tackle wicked problems. Camb. J. Reg. Econ. Soc. **8**(1), 79–92 (2015)
20. Gottmann, J.: Why the Skyscraper? Geogr. Rev. **56**(2), 190–212 (1966)
21. Heath, S.K., Brailsford, S.C., Buss, A., Macal, C.M.: Cross-paradigm simulation modeling: challenges and successes. In: Proceedings of the 2011 Winter Simulation Conference, vol. 1 (2011)
22. Heidegger, M.: Being and time. In: Media, vol. 6 (1962)
23. Hill, M.R.: Spatial structure and decision-making of pedestrian route selection through an urban environment. University Microfilms International (1982)
24. Hillier, B.: The Social Logic of Space. Cambridge University Press, Cambridge (1984)
25. Huhns, M.N., Singh, M.P.: Cognitive agents. IEEE Internet Comput. **2**(6), 87–89 (1998)
26. Kalay, Y.E.: Architectures New Media: Principles, Theories, and Methods of Computer-Aided Design. MIT, Cambridge (2004)
27. Kalay, Y.E.: The impact of information technology on design methods, products and practices. Des. Stud. **27**(3), 357–380 (2006)
28. Lefebvre, H.: The Production of Space. Urban Studies **29** (1974)
29. Lynch, K. The Image of the City, pp. 1–103. The M.I.T Press, Cambridge (1960)
30. Maeng, D., Nedovi, Z., City, G., Garnier, T., Lloyd, F., City, B.: Urban form and planning in the information age: lessons from literature. Spatium **17–18**, 1–12 (2008)
31. Maes, P.: Modeling adaptive autonomous agents. Artif. Life **1**(1–2), 1–37 (1993)
32. Merleau-Ponty, M.: Phenomenology of perception Dispositvo de entrada. Cogn. Sci. **4** (1962)
33. Moss, M.: Technology and cities. Cityscape **3**(3), 107–127 (1998). http://doi.org/10.2139/ssrn.156913
34. Noë, A.: Action in Perception (2004)
35. Penn, A.: Space syntax and spatial cognition. In: Proceedings of the 3rd International Space Syntax Symposium, Atlanta, pp. 11.1–11.17 (2001)
36. Portugali, J.: Self-organization, cities, cognitive maps and information systems. In: Spatial Information Theory A Theoretical Basis for GIS, pp. 329–346 (1997)
37. Rittel, H.W.J., Webber, M.M.: Dilemmas in a general theory of planning. Policy Sci. **4**(2), 155–169 (1973)
38. Robert, S.: Introduction to the art and science of simulation. In: Proceedings of the 1998 Winter Simulation Conference, pp. 7–14 (1998)
39. Schaumann, D., Morad, M.G., Zinger, E., Pilosof, N.P. Sopher, H., Brodeschi, M., Date, K., Kalay, Y.E.: A computational framework to simulate human spatial behavior in built environments. In: SimAUD 2016 Symposium on Simulation for Architecture and Urban Design (2016)
40. Senevarante, P.N., Morall, J.F.: Analysis of factors affecting the choice of route of pedestrians. Transp. Plan. Technol. **10**, 147–159 (1986)
41. Sheller, M.B., Urry, J.: The city and the car. Int. J. Urban Reg. Res. **24**, 737–757 (2000)
42. Simeone, D., Kalay, Y. E., Achten, H., Pavlicek, J., Hulin, J., Matejovska, D.: An event-based model to simulate human behavior in built environments. In: Ecaade 2012, vol. 1, pp. 525–532 (2012)
43. Simon, H.A.: The Sciences of the Artificial. Computers and Mathematics with Applications, 3rd edn., vol. 33 (1997)
44. Tabak, V., de Vriesh, B., Dijkstra, J.: Simulation and validation of human movement in building spaces. Environ. Plan. B: Plan. Des. **37**(4), 592–609 (2010)

45. Thornton, P.R.: Readers React: How an app destroyed their streets: Readers count the Waze? http://www.latimes.com/opinion/opinion-la/la-ol-waze-traffic-app-neighborhoods-readers-20150506-story.html. Accessed 4 Aug 2016
46. Townsend, A.: Smart Cities Big Data, Civic Hackers and the Quest for a New Utopia. Norton and Company, New York (2013)
47. Townsend, A.M.: Life in the real-time citiy: mobile telephones and Urban metabolism. J. Urban Technol. **7**(2), 85–104 (2000)
48. Tuan, Y.-F.: The perspective of experience. Contemp. Sociol. **7** (1978)
49. Van Berkum, E.C., Van Der Mede, P.H.J.: The Impact of Traffic Information: Dynamics in Route and Departure Time Choice. Delft University of Technology, TU Delft (1993)
50. Whyte, W.H.: The social life of small urban spaces. Common Ground (1980)
51. Wiener, J.M., Bchner, S.J., Hölscher, C.: Taxonomy of human wayfinding tasks: a knowledge-based approach. Spat. Cogn. Comput. **9**(2), 152–165 (2009)
52. Wooldridge, M., Jennings, N.R.: Intelligent agents: theory and practice. Knowl. Eng. Rev. **10**(2), 115–152 (1995)

Author Index

Printed in the United States
By Bookmasters

Printed in the United States
By Bookmasters